MEMORY, MINING A
VOICES FROM AYRSHIRE COMMUNITIES

The 'Lost Villages' project is grateful to the following organisations for their support:

MEMORY, MINING AND HERITAGE
VOICES FROM AYRSHIRE COMMUNITIES

Yvonne McFadden and Arthur McIvor

© Yvonne McFadden and Arthur McIvor, 2024.

First Published in Great Britain, 2024.

ISBN - 978 1 911043 20 1

Published by Carn Publishing Ltd.,
Lochnoran House,
Auchinleck, Ayrshire, KA18 3JW.

Printed by Bell & Bain Ltd.
Glasgow, G46 7UQ.

CONTENTS

LIST OF FIGURES

CHAPTER 5

CHAPTER 6

CHAPTER 7

LIST OF ABBREVIATIONS

BAFT	Barony A Frame Trust
COSA	Colliery Officials and Staffs Area
EEC	European Economic Community
FES	Friends of the Earth Scotland
IOM	Institute of Occupational Medicine
NACODS	National Association of Colliery Overmen, Deputies and Shotfirers
NCB	National Coal Board
NHS	National Health Service
NMMS	National Mining Museum of Scotland
NUM	National Union of Mineworkers
PTSD	Post Traumatic Stress Disorder
RCOAG	Rankinston Community Opencast Action Group
RSPB	Royal Society for the Protection of Birds
SCEBTA	Scottish Colliery Enginemen, Boilermen and Tradesmen's Association
SNP	Scottish National Party
SOCA	Scottish Opencast Communities Alliance
SSEB	South of Scotland Electricity Board
TB	Tuberculosis

ACKNOWLEDGEMENTS

We owe an enormous debt to many people who have assisted with the genesis and production of this book. Our most deepest thanks and appreciation go to all those who have given their time to be interviewed by the project team (they are named and listed in the bibliography at the end of the book) and share their memories. This oral history book is based on these personal accounts, and without this sharing of stories and outpouring of memories it could not have been written. In this respect a special thanks goes to Glenbuckian Sam Purdie, our first 'pilot' interviewee. Sam has been enormously generous providing leads, access to unpublished writings, and with his advice and guidance over the course of the project. Dr Kate Wilson acted for spells in 2022 and 2023 as a part-time research assistant on the 'Lost Villages' project on which this book is based and we are immensely grateful for her contribution, including several wonderful interviews. The project was commissioned by the Coalfield Communities Landscape Partnership (CCLP) as one of ten or so 'work packages', and we are very grateful to CCLP lead Colin MacDonald for his unstinting support throughout the project, the research and writing process over almost three years. Other CCLP staff that have assisted include Cynthia Bahi, Carolann McPhillimy and Kate Dickens.

We have also enjoyed very welcome support from within Ayrshire communities. Our thanks here go to Councillor Drew Filson and Councillor Donald Reid who both helped in innumerable ways, to Rae Smith and Sharon Rowan at the Dalmellington Community Centre and to Marion Wylie and Isabel Campbell at the Lugar Heritage Centre and to Kay McMeekin of the Cumnock History Group. Thanks also to Barbara Alexander, Sam Purdie, Drew Filson and Nanette McKee who assisted with site visits to the 'lost villages' of Glenbuck, Commondyke, Lethanhill and Benwhat. NUM President Nicky Wilson, Ayrshire and Scots poet and writer Rab Wilson, and singer-songwriter Seán Gray have also been very supportive, Rab and Sean speaking and singing at several of our community events. We have also benefitted from the work of project volunteers Nanette McKee and Bob Gray, Rab McMurdo, Debbi Hannah, Haley Hughes and work placement students from our History Work Placement programme at the University

The Lost Villages of East Ayrshire

1: 'Lost Villages' project logo, designed by volunteer Nanette McKee

of Strathclyde: Billy Cassidy, Andrew Pohler, Olivia Ross, Kaysha Watson, Lucy Smith, and Rosanna Brown. Volunteer Nanette McKee designed the 'Lost Villages' project logo which adorns the project website: https://www. thelostvillages.co.uk/

Local archivists have also provided invaluable support locating documents and files, enabling copying of materials, and in finding and making accessible many of the photographs that illustrate this book. They are Jo Dunlop and Claire Gilmour of the East Ayrshire Leisure Trust, and Lyndsey Jess at the Dick Institute, Kilmarnock, Heather Dunlop at the Burns Monument Centre and the team at South Ayrshire archives. Thanks too to the staff at the Moving Images archive at National Library of Scotland for their help with archive film footage and the complex world of licences. David Bell of the National Mining Museum, Scotland, also assisted with locating materials, including a series of photographs, as did Donald Reid.

And we'd like to thank Victoria Peters and Rachael Jones at the University of Strathclyde Archives for their help and support across many years.

We would also like to express our thanks to those who provided funding for the 'Lost Villages' project on which this book is based. The core funders are the National Lottery Heritage Fund and Historic Environment Scotland, with funding coming through East Ayrshire Council and coordinated by the CCLP. The University of Strathclyde provided direct support through matching a proportion of the external funding, limiting University overhead costs and providing research facilities and a supportive environment in which to work. Funding was also won from the Scottish Museums Year of Stories 2022 to allow us to run events within the community including a film screening. A small supplementary grant was awarded via the University Humanities Arts and Social Sciences Faculty Research and Knowledge Exchange scheme to run a number of storytelling workshops in Ayrshire. We are enormously grateful to Ayrshire storyteller Allison Galbraith for contributing to these in 2023.

Colleagues at the Scottish Oral History Centre (SOHC) and the School of Humanities at the University of Strathclyde where we both work have been hugely supportive. And the University has provided a really supportive research environment over the years we've worked there, including major investment in the oral history work of the SOHC. Amongst the colleagues who we'd like to highlight for thanks in this respect over the duration of this project are David Murphy, Kirstie Blair, Emma Newlands, Laura Kelly, Angela Turner, Fearghus Roulston and Aaron Sheridon. David Walker stands out as someone Arthur has especially benefitted from working with closely over many years. David is one of the UK's most experienced oral history interviewers and shares a deep interest in Scottish social and labour history. Alison Chand – our senior oral history trainer at the SOHC – covered for us at times, allowing us the time and space to devote to research and writing. We are also immensely grateful to those who conducted previous interviews with Ayrshire coal miners on which we have drawn in this book, including the doyen of Scottish oral history interviewing, Ian MacDougall, and Ronald Johnston. We've also drawn inspiration from a number of oral historians and oral-labour historians over the years who we would like to thank, particularly Lynn Abrams, Callum Brown, Steven High, Andy Perchard, Jim Phillips and many others. The University IT specialists provided expert support for the project website (and continue to do so) and we are indebted to Robyn and Richard of the Humanities IT film crew for travelling out to film some of our interviews and activities in Ayrshire. The oral history project was subject to the usual rigorous process of ethical approval within the University, and we are grateful to the School Ethics Committee for their feedback on this.

We have benefitted enormously from the conversations with DePOT colleagues in the Deindustrialization and the Politics of our Time (DePOT, 2020-2027) research network, including with the gender initiative lead Jackie Clarke. We also owe a great debt to all the undergraduate and postgraduate students we have supervised who have explored aspects of oral-labour history, and those who have endured our Scottish and oral history classes at the University of Strathclyde and Arthur and Kirstie Blair's 'Mining Lives' MOOC class.

The authors and publisher wish to thank the following for permission to reproduce copyright material:

East Ayrshire Leisure / East Ayrshire Council
The National Mining Museum Scotland
Donald Reid
Cox Family
David Young
Neil Family
Bill Mathie Collection

Note: Where there is no attribution for figures in the book these are photographs taken by the authors. Every effort has been made to trace rights holders, but if any have been inadvertently overlooked the publishers would be pleased to make the necessary arrangements at the first opportunity.

We also want to thank our publisher, Dane Love, for all his support, advice and guidance through the publication process from typescript to finished book.

Most important of all we want to thank our families for all their support and encouragement over the years. Arthur's civil partner Margot took some photographs used in the book, and she and sons Kieran and Tom have provided inspiration and distraction, and enduring and unstinting love and support, whilst the growing brood of grandchildren have been brilliant stress busters! Much of this book is about families, communities and informal support networks that sustain people in their everyday lives. Yvonne wouldn't have been able to gallivant all over Ayrshire collecting stories and visiting the 'lost villages' without the enduring love and support of her parents, Catherine and William, and in-laws, Irene and David, over the years, especially for grandparent daycare. Yvonne's husband Steven deserves special mention not only for his support and love but for roaming the hills of Ayrshire, making tea at events and providing tech support and her children Andrew and Isobel have provided distractions and fun breaks throughout.

INTRODUCTION

When asked if there was anything else to say about the village of Glenbuck in Ayrshire, Scotland, Stewart Burns who moved there when he was seven years old replied: 'Naw really, just like an ordinary village as I say with no electric, nae streetlights or nothing.' This book is about living and working in these 'ordinary' miners' row villages throughout the Ayrshire coalfields and shows that there was something rather extraordinary about them, from their unique remote locations and living conditions to the enduring sense of community and identity that stayed with the men and women who lived there and was passed down to their families.

Our book is a social and cultural history of coal mining in Ayrshire as recalled and narrated by women and men from these mining communities. It is the result of a two and a half year research project (2021-23) at the Scottish Oral History Centre (University of Strathclyde) conducted under the auspices of the Coalfield Communities Landscape Partnership (CCLP) and funded by the National Heritage Lottery Fund and Historic Environment Scotland. We have drawn extensively upon people's own voices and memories from within the region, privileging the ways they witnessed the past and remembered their lived experiences and told their stories of life and work in the 'lost' mining villages of Ayrshire. Our sources include a set of 44 newly conducted co-created oral history interviews and several recorded storytelling focus groups for this project: in total collecting stories from 56 people. We also drew upon 32 existing, archived oral history interviews, together with a cluster of personal memoirs and autobiographical materials. All are listed in the bibliography at the end of the book.

The catalyst was an early 'pilot' interview we conducted with the redoubtable ex-Glenbuck resident (and mining engineer) Sam Purdie (born in 1936) in 2019. This conversation provided insights into what living in these mining villages meant to residents, the way in which mining village depopulation and rehousing happened, and how people felt about this – their emotional journey from past to present.

Our process thereafter was to search widely for existing archived oral history interviews conducted in the past, as we were aware these memories

2: The University of Strathclyde film crew (Robin and Richard) with Ayrshire storyteller Allison Galbraith at the Dalmellington Community Centre, June 2023.

would stretch back further in time. We discovered tranches of interviews conducted with Ayrshire miners and their families in the 1980s, 1990s and 2000s. One of these, conducted in 1982, was with a former resident of Benwhat (Mrs Currie) born in 1897 and who started her employment as a domestic servant, aged 14, in 1911, three years before the First World War started. The memories we draw upon therefore stretch over more than a century of turmoil and change in Ayrshire. We also initiated our own new oral history project, not least because we had a different set of questions we wanted to ask of our respondents. Our project interviewee recruitment, under the auspices of the Coalfield Communities Landscape Partnership, included a number of local community events at which we talked history and sometimes showed archive film of the 'lost villages', followed by some individual and focus group interviews. People we spoke to knew others, so 'snowballing' provided other interviewees. We also recruited, trained and supervised several local volunteers and work placement students for the project (as already noted) and they also conducted some interviews. Storytelling workshops, led by Allison Galbraith, also drew us to a group

3: Sam Purdie, ex-Glenbuck resident and project advisor (2021)

of new interviewees, including members of Dalmellington Addiction Recovery Group. Interviewees for the project ranged from Cheryl Hynd and Nicola Higgins born in the late 1970s and 1980s to Tam Hazel and Jean McMurdo born in the 1920s. As mentioned, these are all listed at the end of the book in the bibliography. These primary sources form the bedrock of this book, and they have been supplemented with some archival and web-based research, as well as a review of existing published material to contextualise and elucidate some areas. The bibliography lists our sources and provides a guide to additional reading.

Why another book on the social history of coal mining you might ask? Well, we would argue that the social history of coal mining communities in Ayrshire is particularly neglected and merits more attention. There are many really insightful studies of Scottish miners – such as those by Jim Phillips, Alan Campbell and Rob Duncan - and a wonderful recent book by Ewan Gibbs (predominantly focussing on Lanarkshire miners), whilst Ian MacDougall's seminal work on miners has focused on Fife and the Lothians. We have been inspired by and are indebted to this body of research and aim to add to it with this book.

Memory, Mining and Heritage explores a century of turmoil and change, and how this was remembered and negotiated by miners and their

4: Conducting an oral history interview for the project at Logan Church Hall in 2021

families, taking the story from the early twentieth century when deep coal mining in Ayrshire and across the country was at its peak in terms of production and numbers employed, and the mining villages were thriving. We bring this story of the social and cultural life of mining communities up to the present day, traversing the deep mine closures, the open cast era and deindustrialisation. Whilst we draw upon a wide range of mining community history and lived experience across the county of Ayrshire, we explore our subject area particularly through the lens of six mining villages: Glenbuck, Benwhat (sometimes spelt Benquhat – we have opted to use the spelling Benwhat throughout this book), Commondyke, Darnconner, Lethanhill and Burnfoothill (the latter sometimes referred to collectively as the 'Hill). These were all long-established mining settlements, some

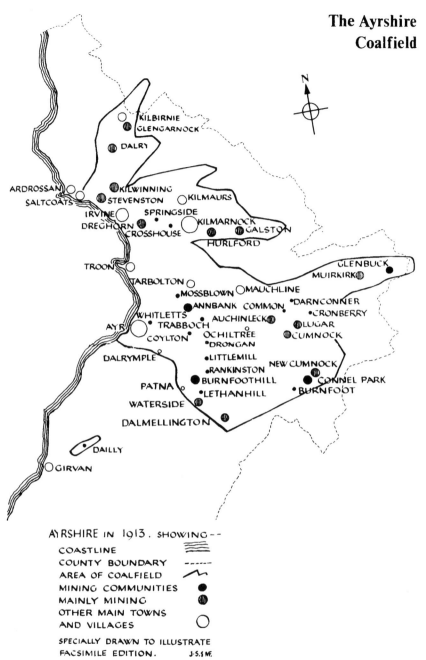

The Ayrshire Coalfield

N

KILBIRNIE
GLENGARNOCK
DALRY
ARDROSSAN
SALTCOATS
KILWINNING
STEVENSTON
KILMAURS
IRVINE
SPRINGSIDE
DREGHORN
CROSSHOUSE
KILMARNOCK
GALSTON
HURLFORD
TROON
TARBOLTON
MAUCHLINE
GLENBUCK
MUIRKIRK
MOSSBLOWN
DARNCONNER
ANNBANK COMMON
CRONBERRY
WHITLETTS
AUCHINLECK
LUGAR
AYR
TRABBOCH
CUMNOCK
COYLTON
OCHILTREE
DRONGAN
DALRYMPLE
LITTLEMILL
RANKINSTON
NEW CUMNOCK
BURNFOOTHILL
CONNEL PARK
PATNA
LETHANHILL
BURNFOOT
WATERSIDE
DALMELLINGTON
DAILLY
GIRVAN

AYRSHIRE IN 1913. SHOWING --
COASTLINE
COUNTY BOUNDARY
AREA OF COALFIELD
MINING COMMUNITIES
MAINLY MINING
OTHER MAIN TOWNS
AND VILLAGES
SPECIALLY DRAWN TO ILLUSTRATE
FACSIMILE EDITION.   J·S·S·M·

*5: The Ayrshire Coalfield in 1913, drawn to illustrate the facsimile edition of the
Miners Rows report to the Housing Commission.
Courtesy of Ayrshire Archaeological & Natural History Society*

going back to the days of ironstone mining, which was superseded by coal mining. Bigger and wider historical developments were refracted through the lived experience of these villages and their impact is discussed here, including transitions in housing provision and policy from private coalowner landlordism to state-owned housing, the two world wars and interwar Depression, the nationalisation of coal in 1947, the Welfare State and the 'Golden Age' for worker rights and empowerment from the 1940s to the 1970s, and Thatcherism and accelerated mine closures, mine mechanisation, modernisation and deindustrialisation from the 1980s. Mining communities lived through these developments in the wider world – and in their memories people shared how they personally felt and reacted. But they also forged and shaped their own history and destinies, mobilising their resources in strong, resilient, mutually supportive communities, and engendering positive and progressive change, not least through the collective actions of miners' powerful and enduring trade unions, the most important of which was the Ayrshire Miners' Union and the National Union of Mineworkers. More contextual information can be obtained on these now lost mining villages in Ayrshire from our research project website https://www.thelostvillages.co.uk/ and in the important local histories authored by Donald Reid and Dane Love (see the bibliography) – and we recommend these for those wanting to read more widely. We are very much in debt to these Ayrshire researchers and writers, as well as the academic researchers that have preceded us. This book adds to their conversations and analyses with a more systematic oral history project exploring the history of Ayrshire mining communities.

Despite these contributions, gaps in our knowledge and understanding about mining communities remain, many of which this project aimed to remedy. Relatively neglected, we feel, is the social and cultural history of the miners' rows in the first half of the twentieth century, the complexities of women's lives and changing gender relations, and the sensory, embodied experience of paid and unpaid work. Also, the multi-faceted impact of pit closures, village depopulation and deindustrialisation, the era of open cast mining, and the ways that Ayrshire's mining past have been erased, preserved, contested, commemorated and memorialised. We have also made a conscious effort here to locate the experience of miners and their families within the landscape they were embedded in and reflect on the ways the industry – deep mining and surface (or open cast) mining – affected the landscape.

The stories of the mining communities are retold through narratives of resilience, solidarity and camaraderie. The harsh living conditions were to some degree countered by gala days, cantatas, bands, school sports days

6: *One of our interviewees, Alice Wallace, with her published memoir and painting of the Benwhat miners' rows at a project 'Open Day' at Dalmellington Community Centre in 2021. Note. Covid-19 protection is evident.*

and Ne'er parties, as well as the wide range of other pastimes and competitive sports, including football, that miners engaged in. As one narrator put it: 'not a penny to our name but happy all the same'. Personal memories are not produced in a vacuum but intertwined with the memories of family, friends, communities or even national events.[1] The years of failing of industry, the trauma of closure and loss is present in the memories of the mining villages and contributes to a collective narrative and a nostalgia for a time when people were culturally rich but materially poor. Barbara Alexander, who lived in Glenbuck in the 1940s and again in the 1970s commented: 'An', er, *doing* fer one another, you know, if somebody did nae have something an' you had – *although* there was no' a lot of anything that you had but if you had something an' they needed it, you would give them it an' vice versa. *That's* how it worked!' The move from a remote village where almost

1 Lynn Abrams, *Oral History Theory* (London: Routledge, 2010), p.95-96.

everyone worked for the same company and in the same poor housing was contrasted with new lifestyles (usually in council housing schemes) with bedrooms, electricity and televisions, but also with not knowing your neighbours and now locking your doors at night. When remembering the past in the present, we often compare our past selves and lives to how we live now. One of our interviewees commented:

> Oh, it's, when you think back tae it, it's, but [Pause] I would say it was a better life than what it is noo! Definitely!!
> *YM: In what, in what way?*
> Now, fer a start, you've no' got drugs! It's, what everybody says, that's when a neighbour was a neighbour. If you need't help, your neighbour was there! T' help yer! Fer anything! If something happened, you hed an emergency, it would be [bangs] the first person t' step in an' say, "I'll take the weans! Go, you go and I'll see tae the weans!"

Marion Wylie, community organiser and one of the driving forces behind the Lugar Heritage Centre reflected on the differences between community in Lugar and Logan then and now:

> The main thing is that everybody kent everybody else an' we all, kinda, mucked in an' we just [Pause], if somebody was needing help, well, somebody was there t' help them. It was fine. It's a wee bit different now. Folk are no' wantin' tae be so [Pause] friendly, if you like! However!

Some younger participants with no direct experiences of the rows felt that in some villages there was still a sense of community (though admittedly less so today). Older villagers conveyed a sense of a lost community and the rupture of being forced to rebuild or reconstruct their lives within the new housing schemes. Many of the stories are positive and there was the frequent use of 'happy' when reminiscing about past lives. However, the poor living conditions were undeniable and for women created a heavy burden upon their shoulders. Some cast these challenges as character building compared to how 'easy' subsequent generations have had it (and still do today). The daily toil of fetching water, sleeping with your siblings, wearing handmade clothes, having no toys and visiting the outside dry closet were not necessarily portrayed as enjoyable, but there was a pride in taking these things in your stride and getting on with the business of living. Some referred to themselves and their peers as 'hardier' than their contemporary counterparts, despite the stories of loss and ill health within the miner's

7: Recording memories over a cuppa and biscuits at the Logan Church Hall, 2022

rows. One woman described life in the miner's rows as a 'different world'. Throughout the book, we aim to explore this world, unimaginable to many of us in the twenty-first century. As we hear about the unity and cohesion of the villages, there are also stories of isolation and incomers, people with internal water taps and new clothes, and some who were glad to move away, to a new house with hot water and new neighbours. Here the complexity of individual lives is evident and a reminder against presumptions of the universality of experience. An interviewee reflected:

But we were very, very poor, like, in they days. It's hard tae talk about.

[Pause] I mean, you, I went…t' school wi' a patch on ma trousers, ken! Ma short trousers. I hope that's [Laughing] wha' you're looking for! But I'm being honest with ye!!

This man felt the need to assure us of his 'honesty'. Everyone in our book was 'being honest' with us. Some might dispute the stories here; perhaps a date was incorrect or the neighbour was misnamed. The reliability of oral history was once challenged and dismissed as anecdotal additions to the writing of histories. Today, historians accept oral testimonies as important sources which can be used to uncover marginalised histories. Since the late twentieth century, oral history has been pivotal in the development of labour history and women's history. It privileges the voices of the working people – women and men - who are often omitted from the official archives. Reading the Ayr County Housing Minutes for this project highlighted this omission. While reports from central government or the county architect were always attached as an appendix, when the people of Lethanhill and Burnfoothill wrote their complaints about the rehousing process, their letter was not attached or transcribed. Their voices were interpreted by the committee with occasional quotes. Capturing people's experiences creates a new history of childhood, community life, and in particular, women's work to name a few. Sadly, many of the older villagers are no longer with us to tell their story but their descendants continue the oral traditions of passing on family stories about their heritage. We have had the pleasure and privilege to hear and record them for this project and for the archives.

In our book we have chosen to focus on seven themes, weaving together third person narrative and analysis around extensive deployment of people's memories. In Chapter 1 we explore what it meant to live in the miners' rows in the 'lost' mining villages, investigating housing conditions, living standards and health, and ending with village depopulation and residents' perceptions of what it meant to transition to the new council housing estates in nearby towns like Muirkirk, Patna, Dalmellington and Cumnock. Chapter 2 focuses on leisure and recreation in the isolated mining communities of East Ayrshire. Miners and their families enjoyed a wide range of recreational activities, sports and hobbies. In this chapter a key theme is how 'enjoying life' was very much gendered, with women having very prescribed 'private' lives in comparison to men who accessed a much wider range of activities and sports more in the 'public' domain. Chapter 3 investigates the unpaid and paid work of women in these communities, exploring how women perceived their roles as housewives and carers, and how things changed over time, drawing upon their own recollections and memoirs. Chapter 4 turns to the menfolk, focussing on how ex-miners recalled the work that they did, the joys and the perils, with sections on danger and ill-health, the embodied experience of mining work, and how work and relationships at work changed over time, with mechanisation and modernisation. The role of the miners' unions, strikes and worker activism feature here, not least because narrators place importance in their accounts on collective action and solidarity, and on the key milestones associated with pit disasters, the war, nationalisation (in 1947), and strikes, including the pivotal 1984-5 miner's strike.

The final chapters of the book focus more on the recent past and the legacies of the past in the present. Chapter 5 examines the end of deep mining in Ayrshire and the devastating impact of mine closures on individuals, families and communities as Ayrshire underwent transformation with deindustrialisation, economic transition and the shift to a post-industrial economy and society. This was a long, drawn-out process of 'ruination' which left deep scars in the psyche of these communities, as recounted by those who directly witnessed and experienced being thrown on the 'scrap heap'. Deindustrialisation has also left enduring legacies of deprivation and ill-health, evident in levels of disability, drug-related deaths and premature death with stagnating standardised mortality rates. In navigating through this identity and health crisis, narrators in their testimonies show a sharp awareness of their diminished status and self-image, and who and what were responsible for the destruction of their living standards and their treasured, much-loved communities. In Chapter 6 we focus on the final stage of coal production – the open cast era – discussing how this was remembered, drawing upon the oral testimonies of ex-miners and open cast workers. Here conflict between the two groups gave way to a degree of acceptance and assimilation. And we reflect on issues around job creation versus environmental degradation. Finally, in Chapter 7 we reflect on the past in the present – what has survived in the landscape, such as the blight of open cast craters and pit bings (waste tips) – and examine the heritage and memorialisation of coal mining in Ayrshire, discussing the importance of preserving people's memories. Much of the material heritage of mining – the collieries, the miners' rows and the villages – has been destroyed, bulldozed or left to the ravages of nature. We reflect on efforts to reverse this process of erasure, particularly the agency and activism of community groups and committed individuals and local politicians involved in memorials, commemorations, reunions and efforts to protect or create grass-roots heritage initiatives. This chapter ends with some reflections on the vital importance of oral history – the recording and preserving of memories of participant eye-witnesses – as intangible heritage. In their rich and evocative stories, Ayrshire people provide a lens through which we can better understand the culture of miners and their communities – and how they felt about the harsh living conditions but vibrant communal spirit in these now lost mining villages of Ayrshire.

1
LIVING IN THE MINERS' ROWS

In the nineteenth and much of the twentieth century miners and their families were housed in what became known as 'miners' rows'. The miners' rows were basic. Built in the 1840-50s by mining companies throughout Britain, they were single storey terraced houses usually formed of one or two rooms and scullery/kitchen. They had no running water or decent sanitation. External dry closets (toilets), often lacking a door, were shared by multiple households. The Ayrshire Miners' Union submitted a detailed report on the Ayrshire miners' rows in 1913 to the Royal Commission on Housing, which published its findings in 1917. The evidence compiled by Thomas McKerrell and James Brown (who later became Labour MP for Ayr South) made a compelling read, describing the living conditions of the miners and their families in strong and illuminating language. Here is their description of Burnfoothill in the Doon Valley:

> Many families have absolutely *no washing house, no coalhouse, no ashpit,* NO CLOSET! What do the people do? That is a question which should not be asked too loudly! From time to time one hears rumours that fever is rife here. We have only these rumours to go by, but there is certainly plenty of fever breeding ground. [emphasis original][1]

The report was effective and contributed to the transformation of Scottish housing during the interwar period and into the mid-twentieth century. Housing throughout Scotland was not fit for purpose and contributed to infant mortality, childhood diseases, outbreaks of illness (including tuberculosis or TB) and chest complaints from the damp and cold homes where many working Scots resided. The Royal Commission recommended state intervention in the housing market to relieve the living conditions of the working population by constructing new public housing schemes to

1 Thomas McKerrell and James Brown, Ayrshire Miners' Rows Report 1913: evidence submitted to the Royal Commission on Housing (Scotland) by Thomas McKerrell and James Brown for the Ayrshire Miners' Union (Ayrshire Archaeological and Natural History Society: 1979), p.52. Accessed at: http://www.ayrshirehistory.org.uk/Bibliography/monos/amr.pdf.

8: Polnessan Row, Burnfoothill
By kind permission of East Ayrshire Leisure Trust/East Ayrshire Council

'decant' communities. This process was lengthy and disrupted by war. Here we have the entry for Darnconner in the 1913 Miners' Rows Report:

> For these 48 houses [Railway Rows] there are two closets without doors and two open compartments, and one closet in ruins, but surrounded by a sea of human excrement. The population of these houses is 137. The houses are very damp. The floors are brick tiles with a very uneven surface, and in one case where a tenant had attempted to improve the amenities by putting in a wooden floor, the damp was so destructive that the floor rotted, and we saw a floor with half of the wood relifted and the other half of the floor with the original brick tiles. The unpaved roadways in front of the houses are in a horrible mess. Pools of water several inches deep lay at the very doors, and all the pathways were quagmires … The population of Darnconner is approximately 400, and there is not a closet, for the whole of the population, with a door on it. There is not a washing house, and the whole place reeks of human dirt and "glaur."[2]

Time and time again, the story of housing in Scotland centres on the poor living conditions for working Scots in the early twentieth century. Overcrowding ran at more than double the rate of English working-class dwellings at this time. While statistics and reports by official observers make

---

2 McKerrell and Brown, Miners' Rows Report, pp.12-13.

14

for vivid and stark reading, personal testimonies illuminate what it was like to live in a village with no water, to leave the house in the pitch black to visit the toilet or to stay in one room with the rest of your family. Moving into the interwar period, the 1920s and 1930s, we can see that living conditions in the mining villages had not improved much from the 1913 report. Eddie Smith's grandparents lived in Darnconner. His grandfather would walk around five miles to the Barony Pit and back:

> They [mines around Darnconner] were starting to close down so they were. They weren't all just coalmines they were shale and different things in the mines up there and I think more money and to go to the Barony there'd be a chance of a house in Dalsalloch that was the kind of maybe idea so it was. But he took me as a boy to show me where he walked to go to his work. Just think of that coming off the backshifts and it's snowing, aye, no washed, walking that distance.

As he walked with his grandfather, Eddie was told stories of living in Darnconner in the 1930s and 1940s:

> He said it was ... I know there were, I think there were only two toilets for the full row but my grandpa built a kind of shack doon the back which was the Dipple Burn over that and he used that as the toilet.
> YM: *Because there was only two for the whole row that he lived in?*
> Aye, hmm mm ...
> There were no doors in them neither there were, but there you are.
> [...]
> YM: *Did he ever talk about his house or the village?*
> He said it was rough, just a stone floor so it was, cold, the fire had to be on all the time to keep you warm.

Eddie's grandfather moved to the Dalsalloch Rows in Auchinleck, where Eddie was born in 1944. Eddie remembered the house where he lived with extended family:

> We had one gas mantle in the living room, there were no lights in the rooms it was a coal fire in all the rooms there was 12 of us stayed in the house so they were. Two recesses in the living room with a bed in each of them so they were.
> YM: *And how big was the house then if you had 12 of you?*
> It wasnae that big neither it was. No the living room wasnae that big it was, for all it was in it was a table, a couch, 2 chairs and a wireless

15

that worked with a battery so it was.
YM: And then was there just a wee kitchen at the back like a scullery?
It was just like a cupboard, a closet it wasnae big, just a sink in it cold water.
YM: Did you have a tap then, did you have...
Just one tap in the kitchen so it was, we must've cooked in the fire so it was.
YM: And did you have a toilet inside?
No, no outside toilet outside and the door, there was 6-inch space at the bottom and the top. You went out with a candle and a windy night it would blow out and that was you, aye it was that.

As the communities waited to be rehoused in the new social housing schemes, families lived in deteriorating houses. Sam Purdie born in Glenbuck in 1936, describes the living conditions of the village as 'primitive':

Glenbuck itself was, being so small, it was a complete community. *Everybody* knew everybody else! First of all, Glenbuck was primitive – there was no electricity, there was no gas, so all cooking was done on the fire and this huge grate formed the mains hub of the living room because miners lived in rows, comprising two apartments and sometimes ten of a family in these two rooms. The Shanklys, for instance, er, there were ten of them and they were in one of, one of these houses, which was two apartments. Eventually, they managed to acquire the house next door, so they annexed another two rooms but you can imagine the living conditions. The other thing that was not, er, water wasn't piped into any of these houses. These houses were built in the mid-nineteenth century by the coal owners. There was no sanitation, there was no water. Sanitation was all outside. There were no flush toilets, toilets that were built were built over open middens and that was the sewage system, which existed until 1954 when we left.

The privately-owned mining companies were ultimately responsible for the poor living conditions of the miners until rehousing initiatives funded by the central government. Thomas McQuillan's final words in his book *The 'Hill and its People* were reserved for the mining companies stating:

[T]he harsh discipline the company imposed on their workers and families offset much of the good they had accomplished [in creating the villages and jobs]. Even worse was their abject failure to deal with the appalling sanitary conditions in most of their houses which, despite constant campaigning, remained materially unaltered until demolition.[3]

The mining companies exerted considerable control over the mining families' lives. The villagers were dependent on the companies for work, housing, and supplies. Tom Wilson, born in Benwhat in 1926, described life under the company in the 1920s and early 1930s:

> And in the old days we were so captive to Dalmellington Iron Company as it was, before Bairds and Dalmellington, before they amalgamated, that they actually barred private vans from coming up to the village, because you were paid by the company and all your pay went back to the company in rent or food, clothing. So they had a captive population.

Margaret Sim, born in 1922 in Lethanhill, estimated the amounts 'taken off' wages by the company: 'We used to pay, erm, well, you didn't pay, it was taken off the wages and you had a shilling for rent, a shilling for light and … a shilling for coal, I think.' The miners' housing was tied to their work. If the miner lost his job or died then the family were evicted, or in some cases, a miner's son would start work in the pit to keep the family house. Eddie McGhee commented on the control the companies had over the miners' lives:

> They were guaranteed a job as long as they didn't, erm [pause], you know, if you started missing your work because you were drinking too much and that would happen [pause], erm, you were kicked out but you also lost your house. You lost everything! Erm, so there was, there was huge social control by, erm, the mining companies who provided the housing.

If a miner was unable to continue due to ill health or perhaps suffered a trauma underground, often a new role above ground was found for them. Jean Wilson's (nee Mathieson) father and his gang were involved in a serious accident at Pennyvenie mine that resulted in hospitalisation, he was unable to return to the pit. He was given a job winding the lift for the men and later driving the engines. It was essential that men were redeployed, otherwise both their main income and house would be lost.

---

3 Thomas McQuillan, The 'Hill: its People and its Pits: a history of the Village of Lethanhill/ Burnfoothill (Ayrshire: Cumnock and Doon Valley District Council, 1988), pp.93-94.

9: Lethanhill, no date.
By kind permission of East Ayrshire Leisure Trust/East Ayrshire Council

Jean Burns' dad had a bad accident before she was born in 1931 which left him unable to go back down the pit, so he worked above ground sorting with the 'skree' (picking the dirt from the coal). Similarly, Alex Kirk's father in Burnfoothill was unable to work due to lung disease. The family were given the gatekeepers house at the old road up to Lethanhill:

> My father, he'd to come out the pits for ill health and we got moved down to Doon Bank an' we got moved into a house, the Gatehouse, they called it and it was that original, old road I told you about that was the original road to Lethanhill. We kept the keys for they gates, where it crossed the railway. If the farmer wanted t' move cattle, who had the fields at the side o' the river up into the fields up the 'Hill, we'd the keys to open the gates to let them through.
> *YM: So, was that, like, was that still a new house or was it...?*
> Oh, well, it was newer than the one that the 'Hill was. It was a nice, wee hoose. In fact, I tried to buy it. After my father died, we, the Coal Board, they said they were going t' put somebody else into it and we had t' move and we got a council hoose at Doon Bank then.

For families like the Kirks, housing was still tied to their fathers' job even once the National Coal Board took over when the industry nationalised in 1947. This later changed when the mines were closed, with the mining industry public housing stock reclassified as 'general needs' housing.

18

When asked to describe the village shops in Lethanhill Agnes Auld, known as Nan, who lived there from 1932 onwards replied:

> Well, there was just the usual thing but the Store actually belonged to the Coal Company so onything you bought in the Store went back to them, if you ken what I mean? The pub was, the pub was owned by the Store, er, the Company. The Store was owned by the Company so, I mean, it was just all one thing.

Until 1926, access to the 'Hill was controlled by the Dalmellington Iron Company using a gate across the road which was locked at night and all-day Sunday. Before this the company made it difficult for other services to reach the hill. Thomas McQuillan, a former resident of the 'Hill who collected stories from the villagers in the 1980s, notes that eventually the road became worn down and unusable. The company refused to fix it. Alex Kirk continued his story about the road:

> There's a track that comes frae where the schoolmaster's hoose is and straight doon the hill – that was the original road to Lethanhill. An' then, on the, Lethanhill was full a ... wi' all the folk livin' up there. All the people paid a pound each into something and, er, that money

10: Monkey Row (or Auchinstilloch Cottages), Glenbuck. Barbara Alexander identified this as the Shankly family pictured here on their doorstep. Courtesy of Sam Purdie

was used t' make the road that's there to Lethanhill now.

The fact that the miners, who did not have much, contributed towards a new road indicates the importance of creating a new access route that was not controlled by the company. Tom Wilson from Benwhat described the chains across the road to stop unsanctioned suppliers accessing the villages in the 1920s. Eventually, buses and other services, like mobile shops and Co-operative vans, regularly visited the villages, reducing their dependence upon the mining companies.

Sanitation in the villages often continued to be rudimentary. Alex Kirk lived in Polnessan Row, Burnfoothill, and recalled the sanitation conditions in the 1940s:

> It was a great place to stay. Lethanhill and Burnfoothill. Everybody helped one another and, er, I mean, the, the houses, I mean, there was no running water in them or anything like that. You had to go out to a spout. There was these big, metal *spoots* [spouts] with, a kinda lion's head on them every so often up, in every row an' you went to whatever spout was nearest your house, you ken, and filled pails wi' water and water was all, you hed t' take it in in pails. The toilet situation, well, it was a different story! It was a wee, brick house at the top o' the garden wi' a wooden seat in it an' a pail an' that was where the toilet was. An' the pail had t' be emptied about every second day, taken up into the moor. Further up, behind the houses. You dug a hole an' buried it an' washed out the pail an' then put it back in the toilet.
>
> YM: *Did you have to dig the hole or did there, was there like a [laughing] whole community hole?!*
>
> No, no, everybody dug a hole just, er, up behind, behind where their own toilet was. It was quite a thing, especially on a cold night up at the 'Hill, wi' the wind blowing! [both laugh]
>
> YM: *I can imagine! An' did you, er, like, did you always go out to the toilet through the night or did you have something in the house?*
>
> Oh, you had something in the house just in case.

When researcher Yvonne McFadden described the pails (pictured) lying about on a site visit to Lethanhill, former resident Nan Auld kept her right on what these would have been used for: 'That'd be the toilets!'

Sam Purdie recalls a village story about when Secretary of State for Scotland Arthur Woodburn visited Glenbuck. The visit was reported in the Housing Committee Minutes in January 1948 by the chairperson.

11: Remains of pails, Lethanhill, September 2021

The Secretary of State assured the community that the housing problems in Ayr County would have his 'sympathetic consideration' and he would 'favourably' respond to the County's building plans. What the records do not show is the surprise expressed by Woodburn at the living conditions of the residents of Glenbuck:

> We had an instance where Arthur Woodburn, Secretary of State for Scotland, the first Labour Government, '45 [1945], must have been about '46 [1946], he started to think about the conditions of the miners' rows and it was his vision that we could do away with miners' rows, so he came to Glenbuck to visit. And he was visiting around the houses. Now, if you can imagine the configuration of these houses – there was a front door, then there was a tiny lobby where, usually, the drinking water was kept. And a couple o' pails of coal. Then, there was the, the inside door that led into the living room. So, Arthur was going round an', er, he was in this house, visiting, and, almost as an afterthought on his way out, he said to the, the wife, "Where's your

12: Remains of a dry toilet, Lethanhill, September 2021

toilet, dear?" She points to the pail in the lobby! [laughs]
AM: [laughing] there you go.
Ex, ex, ex, exit Arthur Woodburn in a hurry! [laughing]

The villages had very basic sanitation systems, if any. The 1913 Miners' Rows Report described the Grasshill Row, Glenbuck. Comprised of thirty-three houses with around 123 inhabitants the ashpit, coal store and dry toilets were housed in one building, shared by four households but there were no washhouses. There were no pavements and 'dirty, sluggish, open syvors' pass by the residents' doors. The sewage ran in an open drain until it reached the main road and according to the villagers smelt bad in summer. In Benwhat, Jean Wilson, nee Mathieson, born in 1932 remembered the streets outside her row house and a very unfortunate experience after school:

> We went to number 18 and that was next to the smiddy where the man that emptied the ashes and shughs. Do you ken what a shugh is?
> *YM: No tell me*
> Aye well. Everybody used to go out and empty their poes [pots] in the shugh they peed in a poe and it went down the wee sheuch at the doors.
> *YM: Is that like the wee thing that ran down the street?*
> That's it.
> *YM: So you would empty your pots or buckets?*
> Your poes or your buckets.
> *YM: Right okay and so you would do that and then it would wash down*
> Even the jobbys [excrement] went down that.
> *YM: Oh did it*
> No oor yins we had the toilet. We had a wooden outhouse with toilet oh I came hame from the school one day and I was so bursting I went in, opened the door and sat myself doon and landed right inside the pail.
> *YM: Awww no*
> My mother had been in and scrubbed the toilet scrubbed the seat and left it up to dry I was so desperate I sat doon and sat in the … well that was a greet, aw you think it's bad noo in my clothes all that. Aww I was and she had scrubbed the woodwork but the pail wasn't empty so there was dirt in the pail and I went among this with my school clothes and everything on. That was some day that was. Anyway, we did have a toilet. I was always well aff as a wean. We had, there was only two of us and we always seemed to be well aff.

From Jean's story, it was not common to have a toilet in Benwhat and that having one was a marker of being 'well aff'. The Mathieson family only had two children compared to many of the other mining families. Jean felt this put her family in a better position than others in the village. In Lethanhill,

Andrew and Margaret Sim's father was employed by the mining company, Baird and Dalmellington, to maintain the houses. On the side (outside of his official duties), he built toilets for people in the villages. This equated to a wooden hut at the back, similar to the one described by Jean.

Margaret Sim, who lived in Lethanhill as a girl, was interviewed by her daughter, Sorrel Weaver, in the late 1990s and remembered the sanitation conditions:

> It was, it wasn't, originally, there was no sewage at the 'Hill. There was no sewage as such. I mean, there was, um, er, the soil … people would empty their buckets, er, over, what was it called? The midden. And that was their [unclear] and tin cans and bottles and there was always one of these [unclear] but there was no, and those that had … er, water closets, er, I think there was only three and in the school, in the school we had [new ones?], I think, sort of cess pits. So, there was no drainage and really, till water was put in. My father put in water to the house when we first went to the 'Hill. I was about a year old. He got a friend to come and put water.
>
> That was from the, that was from the main tap on the, there was three … in each row. There were rows of houses and I think, was there two for each row, something like that. They collected it at the, what was it called?

13: Miners' row at Pennyvenie
By kind permission of East Ayrshire Leisure Trust/East Ayrshire Council

SW: It was called the…

The spoot! As opposed to the spout! You know, it was the spoot! And it was a metal thing that you turned the handle and water came out of the spout and people collected their, they were filling their buckets with water. All that was just added work. No washing machines in those days!

SW: Were you one of those

We were one, I don't know how many houses Lethanhill had … two hundred and fifty? And there was only three houses that had water. And I think they all put it in themselves – before we had finished, er, for Dad knew the plumber. Was at school with him. And, er, he put in one and said it was just as easy to put in five basically once the main, sort of, water has been fed in. The water came straight from the hills. It didn't, it wasn't collected [??unclear]. Cold, spring water. Like that, you know when you went up to, that, erm, the little pipe that was coming out the ground. Where D___ lived.

SW: Yes, I understand. [unclear]

That's right, up at the top. […] Yes. Yes, that was as though, that was where the waters came from. Yes. And when it was very wet, it used to be brown. Peaty.

14: Remains of a washhouse at Commondyke, May 2022

25

15: Postcard of Commondyke from the Bing, Shows the communal washhouses.
Courtesy of Rab McMurdo whose uncle took the photograph.

The most common and probably, most well used facility of the mining village was the water pump. There was usually one per row, on a longer row maybe two. Known as the 'spoot' or 'spicket', the pumps often had a lion's head on them and were usually from a natural source on the hillside, as described by Margaret Sim above.

In Glenbuck, Sam Purdie recalled the etiquette for the washhouse:

> Now, the procedure for the washhouse is, there's a huge cast bowl and the housewife whose turn it is to do the washing, goes round

16: Miners row at Pennyvenie. Note the proximity of the colliery.
By kind permission of East Ayrshire Leisure Trust/East Ayrshire Council

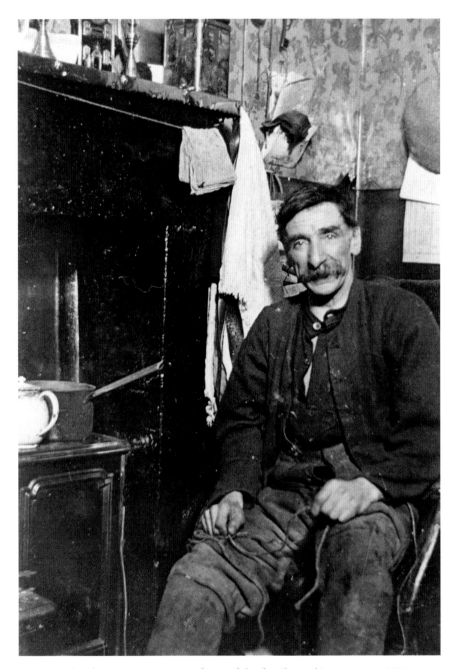

17: Ayrshire miner sitting in front of the family cooking stove, c. 1900.
By kind permission of East Ayrshire Leisure Trust/East Ayrshire Council

about four o' clock in the morning and light the fire so the water in this cast iron tub is going to be hot enough to do her washing. It doesn't matter what the weather's like, if it's your turn for the washing you've got to do it this week or you can't do it until next week!

Eddie Smith remembered the washhouse at Dalsalloch Rows:

There was a washhouse outside and it was shared with about 12 people. Maybe somebody would be washed in the morning then somebody in the afternoon. There was a coal fire in below the big kind of brick boiler where the water was.

INSIDE THE HOUSE

Inside the houses many families lived in cramped and overcrowded conditions which were sparsely furnished. The company-built houses were either one- or two-apartments with a scullery at the back. In Lethanhill, a two-apartment house was described in the 1913 Miners' Rows Report:

That which we called the first row has 21 two apartment houses built of brick. The kitchen is about 17 feet by 11 1/2 feet, the room about 9 feet by 9 feet, the scullery 8 feet by 7 feet or thereby. The rent is 2s 3d a week.[4]

The villagers we talked to were largely remembering their homes in the 1940s and 1950s. The 'kitchen' referred to in the report was also the living room. In one-apartment houses families slept in beds recessed into the wall. Alice Wallace recalled her house in Benwhat:

It was one room and a kitchen. And that room was the living room, the bedroom, the dining room, everything! So, you had your three-piece suite set round the fire and there was a table and chairs an' one wall was actually taken up wi' two recess beds. Now, if you know what that is, Yvonne, they're built into the wall, right. A partition up between them, quite a strong one. I mean, I suppose it would maybe be a brick partition, to separate these two beds. Now, the beds were actually built in. They were quite high. The framework was built in. And my Mum and Dad were in one bed and [my two brothers] and myself were in the other and in below these beds, as I say, they were high, there was storage down below [chuckles] and there was what they called hurly beds down below! And these were hurled out and

4 McKerrell and Brown, Miners' Rows Report, p.49.

18: Early twentieth century miners' row interior. Note the gas mantle lights.
Summerlee Industrial Museum.

hurled back in as they were used. Well, we didnae have a need for the beds really but there was loads of storage for everything else – all the toys and everything that was lying about was just thrown in there and out of sight. And there was curtains that shut these recesses off through the day and the place looked lovely and tidy but in there, there would probably be quite a lot of clutter but it was out of sight! Aye!

Alex Kirk lived with his parents and brother in a one apartment in Burnfoothill:

Just a living room with built-in beds in it. An' that was it. Everybody, we, we just all slept in the one area kind of style. The beds were built into the walls.
YM: And was there anything separating the beds from the room?
Aye, you just put a curtain up.

David Murray gave a detailed description of the kitchen stove, which was located in the main living room:

Aye, it had a big coal range in the kitchen with the oven and that was a terrible big black thing you know. And a smoke board at the front. A big wide open place for your grate sat in but it sometimes smoked. So there was a board at the top, a metal, wasn't a board but we called it a board but it was a metal shutter thing. You could bring it down a bit and if it was smoking you'd bring this down so it could get more draft to get the smoke away [laughs]. They cried it the smoke board. But then there was a big arm that come swinging out from the top of the fire. You could hang your pots and things cooking so that when you brought it out you could tend to them, more salt or something, you ken, then swing it back in above the fire. That's what they called the swee [laughs]. Hanging your pots and kettle on.

Furnishings were often simple in the miners' houses. Jim McVey born in Lethanhill in 1935 reflected in his unpublished memoir that 'The furnishings of most houses were very sparse, it was usually the basics, if you even had that. A table, some chairs a bed and little or no floor covering.' Barbara Alexander's story about the pub in Glenbuck in the 1940s and 1950s emphasises the lack of goods the miners had. The pub had to take quite extreme measures to counter theft:

An' the pub … *on* the bar *in* the pub, *everybody* was stealing the glasses! You've got to understand, Yvonne, everybody was *poor! So poor!* Nobody had anything more than the other person, *so* they got glasses wi' rounded bottom an' they dug wee *holes* in the *bar* so that they're sitting in it, so, if you took this glass home, if you did nae have a hole t' sit it in, it was nae worth taking it home!

A common joke about the mining communities is that they never had to lock their doors because they had nothing worth stealing. There was a solidarity in a shared experience of hard living and poverty due to the working and living conditions of the row villages.

Alice and Alex's families were small compared to other stories we heard. Sisters Frances McNulty and Margaret McQue lived in the village of Lugar and they told us about their family living arrangements to allow for the care of a large family:

MMcQ: Well, erm, when ma grandmother died, ma mother an' ma Auntie Rosie, had tae, well, they left school an' had tae keep the house. An' they were…
FMcN: Aye, but they were fourteen years old at that age.

> MMcQ: … They knocked … two houses, they knocked two houses into one t' keep the family. An' so, it was cousins and her brothers and sisters. How many is it? Twenty-three or something like that in the house?
> FMcN: Well, sometimes about twenty-two in the house.

Knocking together houses to accommodate large families was remarked upon in the 1913 Report and this was still going on in the 1940s. The large Shankly family in Glenbuck knocked through to enlarge their living space for the twelve of them. David Murray's gran in Lugar lived in one and half houses:

> Aye, I was born there [pointing at image of Lugar's front rows] and they were two doors down there was my grannies and then, her house was actually one and a half houses. They made three houses into two for some reason. One house got the kitchen, another house got the room. So one house was like that, and the other was like that. And because of the extra room there, after my grandpa died, we moved in with my granny to look after her too.
> [...]
> *BC: Was that quite common, people joining up the houses together?*
> Aye, I think that because they had two of sons and a daughter. So I think that's maybe how they got that house. Mrs Aitken who was in the other house, the neighbour, she had sons and daughters – a mixture of family too. So I think she got into that wee house just for the same reason and they took the extra.

The suggestion being that families with children of mixed genders were given larger houses to allow for separate sleeping arrangements. An Ayrshire miner recalled being rehoused for that reason: 'So, you'd your mum and dad here an' … my brother, this side. An' then, ma sister happened along! An' in they days, the Cooncil would nae allow a mixed family in one room so, therefore, we moved [pause] to another Row.' Even with combining houses, the number of people in some of the houses led to overcrowding. Jean Wilson and Jean Burns both counted themselves as better off than most due to their smaller family size.

FOOD

With a limited budget the women were skilled at making their food supplies last. Tom Wilson born in Benwhat in 1926 was asked whether he felt he had enough to eat growing up. 'We werenae deprived.' He continued, 'No, ma mother … There were always … Ah think the women were clever at utilisin' everythin'." Janis Chamber's mum, Margaret Neil (nee McBride), known as Pearl was born in 1927 at Lethanhill and she told Janis about how they cooked in the rows:

> She *did* mention something about the … *big pot* just sat on the … the hearth *thing*, you know, with whatever was getting cooked, erm … in it an' it was just the *soup* or whatever an' just put *more* stuff in it, just keep it going for [Chuckling] a *good few* days!!

Margaret Sim living in Lethanhill during the interwar period remembers a conversation with her sister about what her neighbours used to eat:

> And she said, "Do you remember what they used to have to eat?" And I said, "No!" She said, "They had a great big pan of potatoes. Mashed potatoes with margarine. And they all had a spoon and they ate it out of the pan!" And I said, "I don't remember that!" "Oh, yes!" She said, "We really didn't know how other people lived." Every now and again you would learn something and you would be absolutely goggle-eyed at this! We didn't think that they were necessarily deprived – we just thought it was a different way of life! [pause] So, it was potatoes. And I think there was, there was quite a bit of soup made. You could get a marrowbone for very little money and the marrow gave the fat and there was, you know, pulses that went in, you know, beans and lentils. Erm, I know about that one because the, um, one of our neighbours once … she was a … [unclear], she was a bit, sort of, harem scarem and, um, she'd make soup and she just lifted a bag of, of, um, barley, and she just tipped so much into the soup. She never washed it! So, all the flour from the barley was in this and when [laughing], when the soup came out, it was solid!! [Interviewer laughing] And she gave it to Mrs B____ for her hens [Interviewer laughing] and we watched the hens scraping away at this barley for days afterwards!! [Both laughing]

Nan Auld's family who also lived in Lethanhill remembered eating tattie (potato) soup when she was younger. Also, sheep's heid (head), rice pudding and stovies; 'Or onthing she [her mother] could get her hands on!' For breakfast, Tom Wilson usually had a roll in butter with tea before school and for lunch some toast and tea. The main meal was when his father came back from the mine. He remembered having mince and tatties or soups with the occasional semolina pudding. The Glenbuck villagers used to supplement their diets with the local rabbit population. Sisters Isabel Hendry and Ella Reynolds remember eating rabbits caught by her father:

> ER: My dad used t' go out and he'd bring in a dead rabbit – oh, my God!! [KW chuckles] I says, "Is that what we're havin' fer wur tea?!!" [laughs]
> IH: Oh, I remember it!!
> ER: A dead rabbit, dear! We used t' watch ma mum cleaning 'em!
> KW: Ugh!
> ER: I used t' watch her cl, yes, I did!! [KW laughs] I watched her! I watched her cleaning them all! Skinnin'. Taking all the skin off an' cuttin' anything that needs tae be cut away an' thrown away. Not just thrown away, she'd a special bin she wanted it in just in case, in case … a dog or a cat got a ho'd o' it, mebbe.
> IH: Or a fer, or a ferret! [chuckles]
> ER: But once you, you started eatin' the, the rabbit, it did nae taste any different from anything else!! [laughing] It did nae!! It was meat!!!

In Glenbuck, Tam Hazel had a gun and shot rabbits, grouse and other game for the pot. He remembers on his last day playing football some ducks landed in the burn; '"Well, boys! I'll be back in ten minutes!" Up to the hoose – gun – doon – the ducks were, bang! Bang! Twa ducks!' Owning a gun was not common but Tam said the villagers setting snares for rabbits was. Boys and men also fished for trout and perch which was welcomed back home on the family table.

The miners would take their 'piece' with them into the mine, as James Whiteford recalled:

> An' your, your, your, eh … your piece, come piece, [chuckles] it was shaped like a plain breid, it was shaped like a Scottish loaf! An' you hed a tin, an' your mum fillt, your mother filled it wi' tea, an' your sugar an' put a soak [sock], put it in a [laughing] soak [sock] tae keep the water off! [laughing] An' it would ay end up cauld! [laughing]

John Neil and his sister Janis Chamber's family came from in Lethanhill. Their grandfather, Samuel McBride, born in 1897, was a miner and every morning their gran, Margaret, known as Daisy, would get up early to make an unusual pit piece:

> I think my gran was just … busy … looking after the house! I know she got up in the morning and made … scones for my grandpa to

33

take for his … piece, as they called it, erm, because he did nae like bread!! [JC and YM laughing] So, he would have scone and jam, and cre, and cheese, he used to like that! Soda scone and jam and cheese on it!

Families were resourceful. Most villagers grew vegetables to supplement the family diet. Hugh Hainey in Lethanhill recalled he 'planted the garden with vegetables to supplement the food supply.' Alex Kirk when asked about the gardens in Burnfoothill in the 1940s replied: 'Everybody used their gardens. Most people grew their own potatoes an' turnips an' leeks an' all they kind of things.' Eddie McGhee who came from mining family recalled the role of home-grown foods in his community:

> They grew stuff, generally stuff to feed the family, you know, so they'd, they'd plant a few tatties, a few leeks, a few carrots, cabbages – I'm just trying to think of all the things that ma Dad grew! Eventually, ma Dad got two greenhouses but initially, I mean, all the stuff that ma Dad put in the ground was to feed us!

Gardening was a common pastime for men, with women often taking responsibility for the cooking. The testimonies show that for the miners it was a significant addition to the family diet, with men growing soft fruits or foraging for wild berries which were then made into jams by women. Eddie McGhee's granny could make jam from anything:

> Ma Granny McGhee was a legendary jam maker! [pause] Erm, she would [pause] erm, well, the boys would pick brambles at the back end, but when the strawberry season was in, you know, lots, lots o' the miners would grow strawberries and stuff like that, all of which became part of their diet but ma Granny McGhee made jam with just aboot everything! Gooseberries, blackberries, apples, strawberries, raspberries, everything, you know? The great hunt was always for jam jars because, again, you couldn't go into Wilco or any of these places and just buy a dozen jam jars! You had t', there was a great example of recycling. [pause] So, they had all, I mean, the women had all of these skills, erm, and I think all of them. Some families kept chickens in their gardens. All gardens had to be well fenced In to keep the other local population out: the sheep.

Sam Purdie reflected that these practices were a bonus during wartime rationing:

Glenbuck because we were in the village we kept hens. One or two people kept hens. We had eggs, we had rabbit, we had trout, we had our own vegetables. It wasn't so bad for us during the war as it was for people in a city, for instance.

MODERN CONVENIENCES?

As the century progressed, there were some improvements to the mining villages. The main change for some was the introduction of electricity. In the 1920s and 1930s electricity was becoming more common place in many homes throughout Scotland. In the mining villages of Ayrshire, homes were fitted out with electric lighting, usually one socket in each room. Alice Wallace remembers having electricity in her house in 1940s Benwhat:

> No' for a long time but Benquhat got it through an error from another place. Now, Loch Doon, which is a few miles away from us and it's quite scenic, it's a lovely area. Er, there were prisoners of war and different groups had made a, kind of, railway up there. There were various things going on but to feed the electricity up to Loch Doon, it was, sort of, it started off at Waterside an' then it fell through, the whole thing up at the loch. So, this electricity power station was working and it had this electricity ready for use so they fed it up to Benquhat but there was only enough to give everybody a ceiling light in the house – that was all! They had no sockets, you could nae plug anything in. They didnae have electrical stuff anyway but, there you go, aye. It was a ceiling light and that was all. And I remember once, my brother had come running into the house to say that Mrs so-and-so (I can nae remember who it was) had, er, got a hoover and the hoover was connected in some way into this ceiling light fitting an' she was trying to hoover the floor wi' this but it was nae strong enough and it had exploded! [laughs] An' he had come running in to tell ma Mum and all these folk were looking into this woman to see if she was OK! Aye! [laughs] So, it would nae work any hoover or anything at all! Aye, just a ceiling light and that was the only electricity. An' that was only because Waterside could nae use it for anything else so it was fed up the hill t' us!

A single socket in each room for one light seemed to be the standard throughout the villages before the Second World War. In 1933, the Dalmellington Iron Company installed one socket in each house in Lethanhill and Burnfoothill. Intended only for radios, this quickly became used for other modern appliances.[5] Andrew Sim, born in Lethanhill during the General Strike of 1926, stated in his autobiography that the electricity supply was enough to power an iron. The people of the 'Hill gradually incorporated electricity into their lives:

> Electricity was new to the 'Hill at this time generated from Dalmellington Iron Co Power Station at Waterside. It was very cheap. You could burn all the lights in the house for 24 hours a day at no extra charge. Sometimes when I see our electricity bill nowadays, I am sorry they ever closed that place down. You'll realise, the people were not allowed to have any electrical appliances other than a wireless. The electric wireless was just beginning to oust the old battery sets. The joke was, 90% of the people couldn't afford them.
>
> As time went by all the new innovations began to appear, electric irons, kettles and the master of them all, the electric oven. Every year, coming round to Christmas and the New Year all the folk with electric ovens were busy baking shortbread and currant buns, the electric irons were on full bore. Down in the Power Station the tell-tale needle was creeping up towards maximum output and all of a sudden off went the power and you were in the dark for about two hours, everything in the ovens was ruined. The story goes, that a woman in the 'Hill who had one of the first electric ovens, decided that her first attempt would be to roast a chicken for the Sunday dinner. Now there was no such things as those oven ready birds. However, the chicken was prepared and put into the oven. When the family sat down for their dinner, some time passed and her man says "That chicken has a funny taste". Whereupon the lady replied "Aye ah Ken, it got a wee bit burned, so a rubbed it wi' a bit o' Vaseline."

Andrew's sister, Margaret (in a recording with her daughter Sorrel Weaver) remembered that the family had extended their lights into the kitchen and their mother had an iron she plugged into the light socket, but nothing else. She estimates it was 1929 when the 'Hill got electricity.

David Murray, born in 1930, described how people in Lugar tried to circumvent their limited electricity supply:

> No, you couldn't run a cooker or nothing. Lots of people got cookers and got people to plug … wire them in. But the wiring went up into the lofts [laughs] and went from one house to another through the

---

5 McQuillan, *The 'Hill*, p.42

lofts. That had started to overheat and they used to get problems with them [laughs]. Because it was overloaded and wasn't for cookers or anything like that. So going up to Logan no, they had all these new hot water and bedrooms and all the rest of it. It was big difference to us, quite good to get a newer house you know.

While the row villages had electricity, clearly the mining companies thought one lamp was adequate for the miner's and their families. In villages such as Glenbuck, gas lamps were still used until residents were rehoused in the 1940s and 1950s.

Nan Auld grew up in Lethanhill in 1932 in a two-room house with no water, no indoor toilet and paraffin lamps. When she was twelve the family moved to the new council houses in Patna. These new houses had hot water, indoor toilets, electricity and bedrooms. When she married a miner in 1956, the National Coal Board assigned the couple a house in the rows at Pennyvenie. The conditions were better than her family house in Lethanhill, as both her marital homes had an internal cold water supply and flushing external toilet. There were still challenges for Nan as a modern housewife in the 1950s and 1960s. Here she talks about the women attempting use twin tub washing machines in Pennyvenie:

Well, the thing was, you were nae supposed to have washing machines or och like that. But we all had them, if you ken what I mean? But if the ones at the bottom o' the row had their washing on in the morning, you did nae get any water. We had t' wait until they were feenished afore we got water!

YM: Ah, right. OK. [YM and NA laugh] So what…

And then they come, they came an' complaint, the young uns at the bottom were all complaining, "I've no' got water at night!" Well, they come oot to investigate this an' tellt them straight, they'll have t' put their washing machines off in the mornin', they would get water at night! We can nae get it in the morning!

Well, it was a case o' next door run the water, you got nane. [laughs] So, if you fell oot wi' your neighbour, they just turned the water off!! [laughing]

YM: [laughing] So, what did youse do, like?! How did you get your washing done? Did everybody just do it anyway?!

Well, we had t' wait till the bottom o' the row wasn't using their washing machines! An' then we…

YM: You had to stop?!

Aye, well, we'd nae option! Er [pause] then they decided they would put in … they'd sort the pipes an' the [?unclear] so the pipes were that all the burst an' we were left wi'out water for three days an' we had t' go doon t' the burn! [chuckles] There was a burn runnin' doon at the bottom an' we had t' go t' the burn for water.

YM: Because the pipes weren't working?!

Aye because the pipes all burst when they went to sort 'em! [laughs]

YM: An' did they fix it then so youse could use your washing machines?!

Aye, well, they'd some, they used their washing machines … But, eh, they'd problems with the electricity tae. I mean, it was a box, a box in the living room. An' when, if you put the kettle on an' put something else on along wi' it, it was like Blackpool Illuminations up an' goin'! [AA and YM laugh] Guid fun!

From Nan's story, the electricity supply in the later rows in the 1950s and 1960s remained unsuitable for the new modern lifestyle and its consumer trappings.

HEALTH

The oral testimonies show that ill-health was a serious issue before the Second World War in the isolated mining villages of Ayrshire (and elsewhere). At the same time, self-help and local remedies played a much greater role in healthcare than post-war following the creation of the NHS, when health was much better resourced. Two sets of attitudes or beliefs were also apparent in the stories people told us: firstly, that people were expected to sort themselves out and fix their own problems; and secondly, that people were inherently hardier and more resilient.

The Ayrshire Mining Villages report of 1913 had clearly linked housing conditions and overcrowding in the rows to poor health, identifying the spread of infectious childhood diseases and deadly tuberculosis to the ease of contagion in the confined space of miners' accommodation. Indeed, the authors, McKerrell and Brown, deployed evidence on infectious disease rates from the County Medical Officer of Health Report for 1912, which they correlated to particularly over-crowded and insanitary mining communities, to demonstrate the clear link between ill-health and living environment in 'miserable miners' rows.'[6] Diptheria and scarlet fever were amongst the most prevalent of infectious diseases at this time. In its conclusion and summary of findings the 1913 Report indicted the coalowner-landlords and claimed collusion by the local authorities:

---

6 McKerrell and Brown, Miners' Rows Report, pp.29-30, p.51.

19: Miners' row (unknown) in winter.
By kind permission of East Ayrshire Leisure Trust/East Ayrshire Council

The Public Health Acts, so far as the Ayrshire mining rows are concerned, are practically dead letters. Had there been no Public Health Acts at all some of the rows we have seen could not possibly have been in a worse condition. The only conclusion we can come to is that the Public Health Acts have not been put into operation because, in many cases, the owners of these houses are the representatives on the County Council, and that the Sanitary Inspectors do not desire to offend the men whom they regard as their employers by compelling them to conform to the Public Health Acts.[7]

Infectious disease remained a major killer in the mining villages between the wars as the fundamental problem of overcrowding persisted. Nan Auld recalled: 'Oh, there was quite a bit o' TB at that time in the village … An' then just the usual children's diseases. Er, mumps an' all that kind a thing. But TB was one o' the things'. And infant mortality rates remained persistently high. In an interview with Kate Wilson, Glenbuck resident Isabel Hendry recalled she had five surviving siblings: 'But ma mother lost three boys an' they were nae even a year old!' The deaths were put down to febrile convulsions. Bob Gray recalled:

---

7 McKerrell and Brown, *Miners' Rows Report*, p.69.

There was, I think it was 15 kids altogether, born in Darnconner to my great great grandparents and of course only five of them survived to adulthood the rest all passed away. But that was probably the way of things then … And I've managed to trace them all too and a lot oh them died in infancy. And some were … dreadful diseases they ah died of I don't think there was anyone who died ..actually in child birth, but they were all at some months old, some a few years.

Between the wars health care was much more rudimentary in the mining villages, and calling out the doctor was discouraged by the cost, especially during the Depression years. Jean Burns recalled: 'You didn't call a doctor out. We didn't have the money to pay.' And when asked, 'Was there a doctor or somebody that came up?', Nan Auld replied: 'No … no' on the 'Hill there was nae, there was a doctor at Waterside but he did nae come oot, you had tae go to him.' Children got some benefit from health monitoring and treatment at school, including vaccinations and some dental treatment. Benwhat resident Alice Wallace recalled:

> I can just remember the school dentist. I can nae remember being at a dentist's before that. And the school dentists were always, I was dreading that because he was quite a gruff man. It was always the same one that came, especially to Bellsbank, an' he was quite gruff and, er, he was just there to do his job, he was nae going to mollycoddle children in any way! It was, "Right, open your mouth wide! Wide as you can!" and you're opening it wide and "Hold still! Don't try and swallow!" Och, just, just shouting orders at us. And er, I mean, you got a jag and a drill going in an', I mean, no' a kind word. "Hold still!" [laughs] … So we always cleaned wor teeth t' make it that it would last an' yer didnae have t' go t' the dentist or see the dentist often! [laughing] Och aye! Everybody hated the dentist then! It was hard.

Glenbuck resident Barbara Alexander commented that families coped with the support of neighbours and local untrained assistance:

> All I can say is, if anybody was ill and a next-door neighbour knew anything or, I suppose there would always be ladies that would be, em, you know, that you would go to … who could deal with these things. I don't remember doctors. Don't ever remember, well, in, mebbe, mebbe when I was a teenager, there were surgeries in Muirkirk. Dr Weir and Dr Munn. An' doctors there. But, you would nae [pause]

never knew ambulances or anything! … I think everybody would mebbe have been healthier in these days … an' less likely t' send fer medical help unless it was a matter of life an' death.

Barbara added: 'There was never anything wrong wi' me!'

Pointing out her granny in a family photograph Jean Burns recalled:

I never knew her. But my dad used to tell me stories about her. Anyway, she was, she was a kind of, not a trained midwife. Not a trained mid wife but somebody who didn't mind doing it and could do it and she went after the doctor to deliver the baby … And see to the dead. That was her job.

Alice Wallace remembered in Benwhat:

There was a lot o' babies always born up there an' you had the nurse an' it was just one o' the women that acted as the midwife. Two or three o' them were able to do that an' there was always one of them available to help the nurse.

Hugh Gunning, who lived in Lugar, recalled a tragedy:

I also had another sister born in Lugar an' my mother was gonna call her Isobel, I've been told, but [pause] she never got the chance to name the child because that child was stillborn in the cottage when I was about four years old an' I seen the … the baby was born … feet first. A breach birth … And it was strangled by the cord an' I remember as a kid, er, hearing my mother screaming an' that an' I was trying t' battle with the midwives an' that – "What are you doing to ma mother?!!" And all this time, she was having this terrible birth with the feet first! … An' then, the baby died an' I remember seeing, seeing the midwife holding the perfectly formed child in the corner. It was dead.

Stillbirths and the deaths of young children were much more common before Second World War and the NHS, and the trauma of this could leave deep scars seared into the memories of parents and siblings.

Faced with ill-health, families had their own medical cures, potions and remedies, from poultices for boils, to castor oil and aspirin for headaches, and cold baths to bring down a high temperature. Jean Burns:

You, you had … *iodine. Germolene. Dettol* and [chuckles] er, Germolene is because of germs, iodine, it was, iodine, it was for bleeding and then nips! It nips! Nips like – I was going to swear! [RB and JB chuckle] Er, and I didn't like it because, oh dear! That means, er, it was a bit sore. *Dettol* if you, the wound … was, er, dirty and mum will wash it with Dettol. But that was the kind of remedies and the big folk, *they* used Askit *powders.*

Nan Auld commented: 'We used oor ain remedies' and recalled of her mother:

'Oh, aye! Syrup of figs was one o' her favourites! A big dose of syrup o' figs an' you'll be fine! That was, that was the kind of attitude they had … 'an' there was nae pampering'.

Alice Wallace was fortunate to be from a strong and relatively healthy family. She recalled:

No, I can nae remember my Dad ever really being ill an' off his work. He'd maybe have an odd day off wi' a bad cold or something but no. And ma Mum was strong and healthy. Ah, she was nae a big woman and she was very thin, like, wiry and strong. And we were all quite strong and healthy. Do you know what she gave us? Cod liver oil every day. Now, you get it at the clinic. So, you get your cod liver oil and yer concentrated orange juice and the orange juice was lovely and that was the only fruity drink we got and loved it! So, she made us take the cod liver oil first. "You'll take this first and then you'll get your orange juice!" So, we had to swallow this spoonful of cod liver oil first before we got anything else an' then we got wor drink of juice, you see. I hated that cod liver oil! It was oily, fishy stuff, ugh! But we took it every day, gladly, just to get this drink o' orange juice. [laughs]

In Lethanhill, Jim McVey ran about in his bare feet, as many children did then to preserve their shoes, and suffered from 'stone bruises':

Coming from school at night your shoes or boots had to be taken off and very seldom did you have anything to replace them with therefore most children ran around in bare feet, in fact during the summer months this was the norm. Many a time I and many others, remember only too well suffering from "stone bruises". I should explain these were due to a particle of dirt getting under your skin causing the foot to poison and form small ulcers which were very sore.

I can always remember one woman who lived in our row. "Maggie Knox" was her name and she was an expert in bursting these ulcers and cleaning the wound.

In more serious cases the doctor or nurse would be called when this could be afforded. In many families the miners subscribed to a local healthcare service through deductions from their salaries. Alice Wallace recalled that the nurse was seen more frequently than the doctor:

> But the nurse was the one you would see oftenest an' there was sixpence a week deducted from every miner's pay to cover the cost o' the nurse because the National Health Service didnae come in until, what was it, 1948 so they had to pay for treatment before that in that way. An' the nurse could deal wi' the most of it and that's what it was, sixpence a week from every man! Every miner. An' that was for the nurse.

The scourge of TB continued to stalk the overcrowded miners' rows, as it did the urban tenements. Lethanhill resident Hugh Hainey and his future wife both contracted TB and had spells in Glenafton Sanatorium, near New Cumnock. Hugh spent a year there aged nineteen to twenty recuperating. He described the experience in his written (unpublished) memoirs:

> The men's quarters were constructed of wood, a tunnel of corrugated iron linked it with the dining hall, to the left there were the women's quarters. The hospital accommodated about 32 men and about 30 women, one doctor only in attendance. The rooms were mostly individual roughly 10 feet by 12 feet with windows occupying the 10 feet end away from the door and mostly kept open. Each room had a large volume radiator. This was where I reported to on the 14th of January 1941, and was allocated room 5 in the duty room corridor. After a bath and examination I was pronounced bed C. This meant I was allowed up to wash and toilet. My first visitor was Willie Hainey. He was just back from a raid in Norway and was home on seven days leave. He discovered there were two men of his regiment in the sanatorium and after he left one of them, Ken Hannah, came to my room regularly with regimental photos and tales of their time in Egypt, Palestine, India and China. The other fellow William Lawson

was bedfast but I was allowed up. I visited him. In February I was transferred to the X-ray room corridor and had frequent visitors from Archie Connor who had been an electrician at Barony. He looked very well with a shock of very dark hair and we had a few good talks together before he went for an operation at Hairmyres hospital. When he returned six weeks later I was shocked with his appearance, his head had been shaved and all his ribs on one side had been broken to permit the removal of two lobes of his lung. He did not survive long, like Ken Hannah and William Lawson and all of those I knew who did not survive.

I was fortunate being a medical case. I escaped surgery or other treatments like gold, tuberculin injections, having the phrenic nerve cut, having the lung collapsed with compressed air or having a suction extraction from the lung. All the treatments did not have a high rate of success and few people survived. Towards the end of my stay Dr Murray the resident doctor gave a lecture in the hall to explain that it had been discovered that tuberculosis was a highly infectious disease and not hereditary as had been thought, due to the number of people in a family who had developed the disease.

The coming of the NHS in 1947 was remembered as a great boon – an enormous relief to families, and especially for mothers who traditionally carried the burden of responsibility for the health and well-being of the family. Almost simultaneously the antibiotic streptomycin became widely available post-war. Deployed together with detection via x-ray, the blight of TB was finally conquered by the 1950s.

MOVING TO THE NEW HOUSE

Gradually, the miners and their families were moved into the new social housing schemes being built under the Housing Acts and under the auspices of the Scottish Special Housing Association. From the 1930s onward, row after row was served with closing orders and eventually demolished as the people were decanted. This process went on until the mid-1950s, by which time most of the miners' row villages in East Ayrshire were gone. During this time Scotland's housing stock profoundly moved from private to public hands, and stories of communities displaced and ripped apart have often been the focus of the historiography of this period. Unlike the transitions from tenements to peripheral schemes around the urban centres, the movement of whole villages to county housing schemes meant that many villagers remained relatively close neighbours as they moved into their new modern homes.

Due to the sheer numbers of people who needed rehoused and the impact of the war and subsequent material shortages on the building industry, households were moved in stages. The result was that some were left to live in effectively derelict ghost villages. In a film of Darnconner in the 1930s, *The Missionaries*, the camera pans along from piles of rubble and half demolished rows to the people living in the next row: out on their doorsteps, children playing, their washing hanging out to dry. The contrast is stark.

The priorities for moving the villagers were decided by the central government and implemented at local level. According to Thomas McQuillan, the last man to leave the 'Hill was widower James Stevenson at 18 Burnfoothill who had left almost three months after the last family in August 1954.[8] Diane Cox was James Stevenson's niece and she remembers going up to see him in his lonely house on the 'Hill. As she entered, a sheep ran out the back door; these were her uncle's only neighbours for those three months up the 'Hill. As with most new developments in the post-war period, wider amenities for the rehoused families were not immediately put in place. As a result, the children of the 'Hill were bussed back up each day until the new school in Patna was built in 1959.

The Reynolds family were the last to leave the Highhouse Rows in Auchinleck. Here Mary Baird and her sister Margaret Fleming describe their mother's story of living in the empty row:

> MB: But at that time, oor family, an' another family, were two o' the last t' move out of the Rows. […]
> She used to say that, er, ma dad was constant nightshift at the Barony Pit at that time and he would nae be due in till about seven in the mornin' but she was up around four o' clock [pause] an' away t' … set the fire underneath the boiler when it was her washday. And she says, "I was scared stiff!!" Goin' out! Because they were the only two families, I think one family was at opposite ends so the place was really quiet and really dark! Er, must have been a hard life for them!
> MF: Oh aye, they talk about "the good, old days"! I don't think they were!

In an interview with Mary and her mum, Isabel Hendry, Isabel was asked if she sad to leave Highhouse; she unsurprisingly replied, 'Never gave it a thought! [pause] I was glad t' get oot it!!' In another interview, when asked about moving to Patna from Lethanhill, one man's reply reflected the lack of agency the villagers had about where they lived:

---

8 McQuillan, *The 'Hill*, p.54.

> We moved doon to Patna [pause] when we moved doon '49 [pauses] Ehhh [pauses] just had to take in yer stride and that's what was happening, the village was getting emptied, and the houses were coming down and we moved intae a new house [pauses] ehh which was different, and it had four bedrooms, so it was all different so ye just had, aye, cause aye.

The village of Glenbuck strongly opposed being 'decanted' to Muirkirk. A report in May 1937 concluded that of the one hundred and eight houses in Glenbuck only forty-two were habitable and even these were in 'poor condition'. The water supply and drainage were inadequate and estimated to cost £5,000 (around £430,000 in today's terms) to bring up to date. The report finished by noting 'We are informed not only is there no work in the Village, but that the majority of men, who are employed, are working at Muirkirk.'[9] This assessment is echoed in Sam Purdie's reflections on the demise of the village of Glenbuck:

> So, so, the, killing the pit killed the village really an', you know, the village population just steadily declined an', you know, row after row of houses got demolished as people moved away; and the hardcore were left, er, to be moved in 1954. And they moved us all to one street … in Muirkirk

In 1937, the villagers send a deputation to 'protest' being moved from Glenbuck. The committee did seem to take their protest seriously, with the Sanitary Inspector surveying the residents' views and finding that of the sixty-nine tenants, sixty-two expressed the wish to remain in Glenbuck. In February 1947, the Earl of Glasgow raised the depopulation of the rural villages in Parliament citing Glenbuck specifically:

> Glenbuck—your Lordships have never heard of it, I suppose—is an Ayrshire mining village on the borders of Lanarkshire. Against the wishes of the people, the health authorities at Edinburgh propose that the new housing scheme should be sited in Muirkirk, a town four miles away, on the ground that it is not worth while spending money on the enlarging of the Glenbuck water supply and bringing electricity to the village. They have a case, but these indefatigable planners have entirely overlooked the human aspect—namely, that the village dwellers have an affection for the place inwhich they were

---

9 County Clerk report signed by Medical Officer of Health, County Engineer and Chief Sanitary Inspector, 28th May 1937, in Housing Committee Minutes (Ayrshire Archives), June 1937, p.20.

born and brought up. The people of Glenbuck have no wish to be uprooted and moved into a town. An argument which the noble Lord who replies will no doubt put forward is that the coal seams are worked out and that there is no future for the village. That may be true with regard to the coal seams which exist in the proximity of Glenbuck, but unproved seams of coal exist between Glenbuck and Muirkirk, and although the larger portion of those lies nearer Muirkirk, a distance of three or four miles will not precludethe miners of Glenbuck from working in any new pits which, dependent on the Coal Board, may be opened.

Most of the Glenbuck men work in or near Muirkirk but they have not the slightest wish to live there. A few work at the Douglas coal pits in Lanarkshire, and if they were moved to Muirkirk they would have further to go to their work. There is a great community spirit in Glenbuck. If the people are moved into a town, that will be lost, and surely it is the community spirit of the villages of the countryside which we want to preserve. It is quite true that the enlarging of the water supply and the installation of a new drainage system would cost money, but it would be money well spent. Providing that the Government will give the usual grant, I am quite sure that the ratepayers of Ayrshire will not grudge their share so that these people may live where they have always lived. I ask that this matter may be reconsidered and that the provision of whatever services are required for the village may be approved.[10]

It was many years before the villagers of Glenbuck were moved. In 1952, the Department of Health wrote to Ayr County enquiring why the County was not doing more to rehouse the people of Glenbuck. The County noted sharply that their protests had delayed the process by at least two years and that they were constantly moving people now. Margaret Hynd married a man whose family came from Glenbuck – the 'Shanklys' of footballing fame – and later lived in Glenbuck herself from the late 1970s to the mid-1990s:

> Oh they didnae like it oh they didnae want to come here [Muirkirk]. Aw my mother-in-law just didn't like Muirkirk folk they just didnae click they did not want to come here it was a shame, it was a shame, it was. And they never, ever I mean they mix now because their families are married into one another over the years but they never wanted to come here.

10 Earl of Glasgow, Scottish Housing Schemes, Hansard, Volume 145, Columns 404-405, 5 February, 1947.

In contrast, on 4th July 1950, the Ayr County Housing Committee received a letter from Mr James McDowall of 56 Burnfoothill on behalf of one hundred and forty-five ratepayers residing in Burnfoothill and Lethanhill expressing 'complete dissatisfaction at the rate of progress being made to re-house the village'. It referred the committee to the 'disgusting sanitary conditions and deplorable state of the houses generally' complaining that the recent allocations in Patna did not consider the poor living conditions of the people left in the 'Hill. The response from the Chief Sanitary Inspector and County Factor to this complaint to the County Council was that the 'Hill people were being treated fairly by the guidelines and there are many 'black spots' throughout the whole County. In the meantime, they committed to continue to press the Central Government to obtain more houses for the County. The key criteria for rehousing were 'unfit', overcrowded' and those with 'sub-tenants'. This is consistent with people's memories. A man recalled that his neighbours were moved before him as they were classed as 'overcrowded' but when his family joined them in the new housing, they lived still only a few doors away.

Despite this, the 'Hill folk, like the Glenbuck villagers, were not all supportive of moving to Patna. Sheila Crosswaite's Aunt Meg, who lived in Lethanhill, told Sheila that the villagers were unhappy about being moved. Here she remembers the story about the village water supply:

> So anything I know really about Lethanhill it was from stories from Aunt Meg, because Aunt Meg was, she was, she became a Mrs Wiley, David Wiley was her husband. He was from Dalmellington, but when she married, she must've stayed up at Lethanhill and then they were rehoused down to Patna, which, oh that was really going down in the world, literally you know, they didn't fancy Patna at all. But she was rehoused in Patna and I was always told it was because of the water supply, that was why they cleared Lethanhill, it was the water supply, don't know whether that's true or not.

In his unpublished memoir, Jim McVey, born in Lethanhill in 1935, noted a generational difference in the villagers' response to their relocation to Patna:

> In the "Hill", in a good many cases, this move to another place was frowned upon and was received with a great deal of apprehension, mostly, I must state by the older generation (my mother being one). They had their own way of living and didn't take kindly to it being interrupted. One worthy was heard to say "He'd rather be at a wake

in the Hill than a wedding in Patna" it was more enjoyable and "the only good thing to come out of Patna was the road".

To the younger generation it was looked on as a great adventure. Firstly moving to a house with its mod cons, something that was completely alien to them on the "Hill". Also not having to climb the steep road after having to go to Patna to a shop or to Doonbank to the doctor nor the steep incline which many walked as it was the shortest route to Waterside from where the bus or train was cheaper if you were going to Dalmellington.

The villagers held a 'Farewell Reunion and Social' in the village hall at Lethanhill in April 1955 with regular annual reunions beginning in 1965 until the late 1980s.

When Jean Burns, born in 1936, moved from Trabboch to the new village of Drongan she likened it to a 'different world' with streets and light:

> Well, I was quite sad but excited to be going to a house where you had a proper toilet and a switch to put the light on because … you didn't have electric light either. It was all lamps. All lamps! And … you had to, you were given, you had to light the lamp, trim the wick, get the paraffin an', it was paraffin. Erm, and there was one person sold it in the village and coming up to Drongan, it was like a different world because I hadn't been used to streets. I didn't know electric lights. Er … and … lights in the, on the, er, street – that was funny because we didn't have that because with only the light from the windows and we were [?unclear] [chuckles], there was no light! And to come to a place where there were lights to take, er, to get you around – that was funny. Erm [pause], no. It was a different world!

The process of moving to Drongan was difficult for Jean as her mother had injured her foot and thirteen-year-old Jean had to organise the whole move:

> Well … well, it was quite traumatic … when I left the village. Two or three days, or two or three weeks before that, my mother had a very nasty burn on her foot and so she couldn't do anything and I had to prepare … what … I could do, to put all the things that you would do in a flitting. I hadn't a clue. I knew you had to get everything in boxes or, and get things but a good friend, came down and helped me to get things, get the things.

She continued:

So we had to get a trap ready to go and dad went with that. And mum and I got a taxi, would be…one of these from here and we got to the … house. My mum was a bag of nerves, I think. She was worried how she would cope with this new house.

The new prefab house in Drongan came with two bedrooms, electricity, running hot water, double sinks and a refrigerator. Reflecting on the move, Jean felt it was mostly positive:

Well, the positives were that my mum could, er, turn on a tap in her house and get water and get hot water from the fire!! And so, that was a real positive!! Er, lots of positives. Er, the negatives were the prefabs were cold. They were awful cold. Yeah. In winter. [pause] No, there wasn't many negatives. The only negative for me was having to go to a different school and I'm not keen on, er … maths and we didn't get Algebra … and they did at this school. A + B = C! [Both chuckling] [laughing] I still couldn't do it!! [both laugh] No, I didn't like it. So, when there was a, erm, once lots more houses came up here, we got a bus to take us back to Trabboch School and, er, that was fine.

20: New miners' housing at Drongan.
By kind permission of East Ayrshire Leisure Trust/East Ayrshire Council

Sam Purdie recalled the Glenbuck villagers' reactions to their new houses when they moved in 1954 to Muirkirk:

> One, they didn't all disappear but most of the miners' rows went and they built these houses on a greenfield site, to the west of the village and the last, almost the last houses to be built were, er, a street of timber houses that had been gifted by Norway. You remember Norway was gifting a lot of timber houses, to Britain at that time, in recognition of our contribution in the war. So, the Glenbuck people went into these timber houses in 1954 and it was called Hareshaw Crescent because the name of the hill in Glenbuck is Hareshaw.
> And, and, and the, it was quite, it was, it was, it was quite a transition for people to make first of all ... they'd water in the house! Baths! [pause] The other big thing was, there was an upstairs! Now, they'd always lived on the flat ... Hareshaw Crescent was built as far away to the left as the Muirkirk people could get it! Get them away there! And it was quite high up on the edge o' the moor. First day there was a high wind, here are these people, who'd been in the habit of living on the ground – this house was making noises! Shaking! And everybody's out in the street because they thought these houses were going to blow away! The other excitement was, because these houses had water, they had a back boiler, put behind the fire, to heat the water and this back boiler started to rumble and everybody thought the place was going to blow up! [both laughing]

The new housing schemes prioritised rehousing based on the poor living conditions with social provision lagging behind. It was common for the relocated village children to then send years being bussed back to their former village for school until the planners caught up. The children of Lethanhill and Burnfoothill were bussed back to Lethanhill School from Patna. One remembered:

> Ye see that's where they [pause] most people went there were few went to Dalmellington [pause] but all, but all the people that were in ma school class and all the rest of it we all came down went intae a school class in Patna and went in we done the school down there maybe for [pause] two year. Then we went back to Lethanhill. To the school [pause] up there tae [pause] tae we left the school the last three years.

Hugh Gunning's family of nine were moved from a small house in Lugar to the new housing estate of Logan. At six years old, Hugh had to walk back to Lugar to attend school until the new primary school opened in 1963 and he was in Primary Four.

Alice Wallace describes her family moving from the village of Benwhat to Bellsbank, one mile outside Dalmellington:

> Now, that's the kinda things they did an' they all got rehoused about the same time in Bellsbank, fairly near one another, as I said, and that's great. And we got this house in Park Crescent an', no, Craiglee Crescent and, er, I got a room to myself; there were three bedrooms – Mum and Dad in one, [my two brothers] in the other an' I got one to myself! I thought this was marvellous! It was great! It had a nice, big window an', oh, it was lovely an' I just loved this! I could bring ma pals in because in Benwhat, you hudnae room tae bring your pals into the house. Sometimes we stayed in and we'd hide underneath the table and if the adults saw youse, "Right! Out! Come on! Outside! You're no' staying in here listening to folk!" So, it was great t' have a room an' I could take ma pals in and I could go to theirs as well. Er, lovely to have a place of our own like that. Er, a nice toilet, flushing toilet. Running water, hot and cold – it was great! Because we got toilet paper! Up in Benwhat, it was just newspaper we used. It was cut into these squares, on a bit o' string on a hook in the outside toilet and that was your toilet paper. An' that's just how they lived up there.

21: New housing at Cronberry, near Lugar.
Courtesy of Kevin White collection

Aye. But here we were, up here, wi' running water an' toilet paper an' everything. Aye.

Moving to a house with separate bedrooms changed quite fundamentally how Scottish people experience home. In the case of the miners' rows, similar to experiences of tenements in Glasgow, this shift increased privacy between household members. Here we see that not only was having a flushing toilet a huge improvement from a pail and wooden bench, but also gave Alice, who was becoming a teenager in the later 1950s, space within the house to play and socialise with her friends.

The furniture needed to fill a one or two apartment house was hardly anything compared to three bedrooms, a living room, kitchen and bathroom where the miners now found themselves living. Alex Kirk described the furniture in his house in Burnfoothill and remarks on the move to Patna:

> Well, as I say, it was built-in beds an' that an' then you'd wardrobes and things of your own ken, but, I mean, when people started to move down into Patna an' that, they had to buy as much furniture because the houses were so much bigger than what they were at Lethanhill or Burnfoothill.

In the 1960s consumer expenditure in Scotland grew faster than in Great Britain as a whole due to greater stability of prices in Scotland. By the mid-1960s, there was a sharp increase in consumer spending on durable goods. This was largely due to more money being spent on furniture and floor coverings, while spending on electrical goods from radios and television to household appliances grew at a steadier rate by comparison. Mass production fuelled mass consumption as people across all social classes began to buy televisions, washing machines, refrigerators and furniture. By the mid-1970s, across all social classes, television ownership in Scotland was almost universal at 96 per cent.[11] This new consumer lifestyle was notable in all part of Britain, creating a dramatic shift in expected standards of living across all social classes.

The transition from a contained and often remote mining community where most people were in the same financial situation to a large council estate with people from different parts of the country arguably emphasised this new aspirational lifestyle. As Alice Wallace reflected: 'Well, when we lived in Benwhat, I don't think we ever went holidays at all. But Bellsbank was different because it was a different lifestyle. Modern houses

---

11 *General Household Survey, 1976* (London: HMSO, 1976), Table 5.36, p.148.

and bought clothes – no' everything was homemade any more. And, er, just a different lifestyle and at that time.' The modern houses encouraged occupants to fill them with the trappings of modern life. When asked how her mother felt about moving, Alice discussed the different community they had moved to in Bellsbank:

> She loved it! She wanted to go! All the women did, especially the young ones and, er, they looked forward to it and they loved getting a new house. Going to get new furniture an' stuff. Ma Dad would nae allow any tick, no hire purchase here – "There'll be nae shilling-a-week men chapping this door! You'll only get something if you can afford to buy it an' if you can nae afford it, you'll dae without!" And, er, ma Mum had to get some second-hand stuff at first and then save towards the next thing that she wanted. I mean, as I said, that house we got a television. It was holiday pay money when a lump sum came, things like that. Er, but, she loved it an' yet, it was different in Bellsbank because … people were coming from other areas, it was nae just the wee, local villages that were moving down to Bellsbank and Dalmellington […]
>
> An' some o' them were so showy, and, er, because they've got a brand new house, they wanted everything flashy and they were getting a lot o' tick, as they talked aboot, all this hire purchase. An' then, I mean they only had the miner's wage coming in, they could nae afford to pay all this and, at that time, there were warrant sales and these warrant sales were published in the local paper, the Ayrshire Post, when it came out on a Friday, an' a list o' names and addresses for warrant sales. An' there was one woman, she had got a lovely three piece suite an' bedroom furniture an' so on an' all this stuff was gonna be sold off in her house, so the public could go to that house that day and, er, some o' them were saying, "I think we'll go doon because that was a nice suite she had, we'll see how much that would go fer!" [laughs] An' my Mum, "Oh no, I would nae daw that! I feel sorry for the woman, I just could nae, that's embarrassing the folk, I would nae dae that!" So, she never ever went t' anywhere like that. But, er, she realised what my Dad said was right enough – it went to their heads, some folk, right, we've got a nice new house, brand new, I'm gonna get nice, new stuff an' have it all sittin' lovely! An' they just could nae afford it!

Nan Auld who lived in low Pennyvenie in the 1950s, was allocated a house in Dalmellington. When asked to describe her new house she listed the rooms but also the problem of furnishing a much larger house: 'Three bedrooms, living room, bathroom, big kitchen, big living room an' a big cloakroom. There was mair room that I had furniture than t' put in it!'. The new house was furnished using hire purchase.

Communities were often moved together which meant everyone was near their neighbours and friends. Sam Purdie noted that when the villagers were moved: 'they moved us all to one street […] in Muirkirk.' Similarly, Alice's old neighbours from Benwhat were either in the same street or round the corner. One man, now in his 70s had lived within a couple of doors of the same neighbour his whole life from the rows to the new social housing. The rows in Glenbuck were eventually demolished and the villagers moved to Muirkirk, albeit reluctantly. This was not the end of Glenbuck life as a village. Barbara Alexander's family bought a cottage in the village, one of two older properties and remained there with the nine council house tenants until she married in the mid-1970s. Her mum and dad remained until health problems made staying somewhere so remote impractical. Barbara's parents sold the house to another descendent of the Shankly family, the Hynds whose father's mother was Bill Shankly's sister. When asked: 'So, how did your mum and dad feel about having to move?', Barbara replied: 'Well, terrible. Awful. Awful. Because ma mum, that was, ma mum, she had been there all her life!'

Cheryl and her mum had a similar story of rupture and strong emotions about being forced to move, though under different circumstances. Cheryl Hynd was our youngest Glenbuck resident interviewed, born in 1978, Cheryl lived in the village, her parents eventually buying the house next door to create the family home. They remained there until the opencast mining expanded operations around the area and they moved to Muirkirk in the mid-1990s. The demolition of the Hynd's home was traumatic for Cheryl as a teenager. Similar to the mining families in the 1940s and 1950s, the move was forced upon the Hynds. Cheryl and her mum Margaret both talked about their 'love' for their life in Glenbuck, with Margaret saying, 'I would never had moved oot it because I just loved it.' Cheryl and her mum both loved living in Glenbuck but for Cheryl moving away was a formative experience that was still very raw for her. The rupture of moving away from 'your love', the small close knit community, to the larger village of Muirkirk took Cheryl some time to make her peace with. She still keeps in touch with the people she grew up with in Glenbuck and although many of them are spread all over, they often come back and go with Cheryl on occasion to visit the site.

The collective story of the miners' row villages is one of shared experiences, based in a common workplace and a shared standard of living.

Eddie McGhee compares the living conditions of poorer housing areas in Glasgow with the rural mining communities in Ayrshire astutely observing that while materially the living conditions were similar, the communities were different:

> Now, people from the Garngad [Glasgow] might look at these creatures living on the 'hills, you know, and in the mining communities in appalling housing and say, "Poor souls!" but qualitatively, I think it was a very, very different kind of experience. There was a great, erm, [pause] kind of mutuality about the people who lived in mining villages. A great equality.

Later he continued:

> I, I think the fact that, erm [pause], it meant, mining meant at least steady work, it might have meant horrendous conditions for the men, horrendous conditions for families to live in but it was survivable, you know?! Erm, and I think, unlike, you know, mass urban poverty in Glasgow, there was virtually no crime! [pause] Naebody had anything t' steal an' there were no rich people really roundabout [laughs], there was actually [pause] unless you used your feet or maybe occasionally a bicycle, you weren't going anywhere fast so they had, so they had to create an environment that somehow lifted them out of that [pause] kind of harshness and grinding poverty and that's where all of the things that happen, you know, the guys who grew the biggest cucumbers and the biggest leeks and the guys who had the best pigeons or the best canaries, erm, this was all, now, you'll erm, this was all, now, you'll notice that these are all men things, you know! And again, I think, sociologically there was a very different view of, I mean, women were the homemakers, and they had never any, I don't think they would ever have had any aspiration to go to work 'cause they couldn't have. If they were bringing up families in amazingly difficult conditions, erm, [pause] and yet there, there was still this strength about them!

Memories about the mining communities create a collective narrative that people were materially poor but culturally rich. The emphasis was on how safe the communities were, how no one needed to lock their doors, how they supported each other in time of difficulties. These intangible things that are not recorded in the archives, contribute to naming the sense of loss felt by the destruction of the villages. For the next generation, there is a sense of pride in their strong and resilient ancestors.

22: Hugh White and his cousin Helen White outside the door of 472 Brick Row Lugar looking away from the Kirk. They will be standing on what is the Par park now. c. 1945. Courtesy of Kevin White

2

ENJOYING LIFE:
LEISURE AND RECREATION

Life in the miners' rows and mining communities wasn't all about deprivation, ill-health and hard graft in the home and the pit. Miners and their families enjoyed their leisure time, which was shaped by age, gender and what the landscape had to offer. In interviews and their own personal reflections mining families usually recalled their recreation time in memories that were detailed and emotive, packed with much joy and fondness. These activities provided some relief, diversion and recuperation from hard working lives as housewives and miners. Leisure and recreation were experienced very differently, however, by men and women in the mining communities.

CHILDHOOD

Two recurring themes in remembering leisure and recreation in the Ayrshire miners' row villages were the freedom and the safety that were enjoyed by children. Mrs Currie was born in Benwhat in 1897 and lived there until being packed off to Glasgow to work as a housemaid aged 14 in 1911. She recalled in an interview in 1982 how there were no roads or buses before First World War, but the kids had the freedom to roam up and over the hills: 'We made our own merriment'. A generation later, Henry (Harry) Kennedy lived in Burnton for 21 years from 1932. He recalled:

> I was never aff they hills! An', er, as I said tae yer , we're up the glen, there's about four different glens up there an' we went up t' glen an', oh, we used t' get wur girds an' away up the hill! [note: girds were a round hoop or wheel like toy that was rolled, sometimes with the aid of a stick].

Sam Purdie, born in 1936 in Glenbuck, reflected:

> We had freedom to roam the hills. Absolute freedom in childhood

and, of course, in the seventeen hours of winter darkness (no street lights), we could do all kinds of things. But - we were never under any illusion that the adults knew what we were doing and who we were doing it with!

A Lethanhill resident, born in 1942, remembered:

Then there wis another bit they called jimmy's burn in the summer it was doon the bottom of the lake we all used to go doon what they called the canburn … and it was all great big ferns, some of the ferns were bigger than you and ye'd run through the ferns doon to a bit they called jimmy's burn … and that's where we swum …That would be quite fun actually, tae swim like.

There was also 'a kiting green' in Lethanhill for the kite enthusiasts on windy days.

Alice Wallace, born in 1945 in Benwhat where she lived for her first five years, reminisced at length about her childhood:

As soon as you could toddle and go out with the others, you were outside playing. An' you were told, "Right, stay oot there an' don't go too far away an' play oot there till I shout you in!" So, you'd t' stay outside an' then, she would come to the front door and shout our names and we would go in then. And you stayed out until you had to go in for your tea, which would be lunch kind of style, right, and, er, you got that an' then you were back out an' you were shouted in for yer dinner and then back out to play again! School days, I mean, you were at the school, er, but when you come back home from the school, you changed into your old clothes fer playing about with. The school clothes were laid aside again and, er, that was you. Same routine, out to play! "Don't disappear! Don't go too far!" Although we'd plenty of scope even just going round about the village because, er, the Rows, I mean they were all inline. They were, er, horizontal that way and you knew everybody and you were quite safe. And the bigger children looked after the wee'er ones – took them by the hand and led them about and watched them an', aye, it was good!

You'd plenty o' scope, plenty of freedom! You were nae scared of anybody an' there was no, paedophiles or anything like that in those days. I mean, that word did nae exist! People did nae know about these kind o' things! I mean, up there it was, you were safe. Aye. I think at one time, I remember my Mum saying there had been a man had a real kicking! He was battered by the men in the village because he had been doing it. He was suspected of doing it and that was giving him a warning and you would see him after that, he had black eyes and he was limping an' that was the result, so he never ever did it again! That's how they dealt with these kind of things in those days.

Aye. Aye. Quite strange, isn't it? I mean, we did nae know what that word [paedophile] meant! I mean, it was never spoken. It did nae exist! And you were free tae go and play wi' anybody, talk to anybody, all the adults, all the women in the village knew who you were. I remember once, I went away up the top road wi' the bigger girls and this woman was standing an' she says, "What's yer name, hen?" an' I said my name. "Oh, aye, you're yon o' they wee, redheaded ains frae doon the west raw!" [laughing] Because [my brothers] an' I all had red hair and, er, it was "red heided" [laughs] an' that's the way they talked about it! Aye!

Born a few years earlier than Alice in Benwhat, Flora Scobie recalled:

Along come Nettie McCrackan an' Jan Kennedy an' they had their

23: Lethanhill School class, 1921-22.
Courtesy of Cox family

24: Lethanhill School play 1921-22.
Courtesy of the Cox Family

children in go-chairs. [I] would say, "Can I come a walk with you?!"
"Aye! Nae bother, hen, come on!" [pause] Well, I could be away for
long enough! Ma mother never said, "Where were you?" [pause] Ken,
no' like what's going on nooadays! … Because everybody trusted
everybody! There were never any, I don't remember ma mother
locking her door in Benwhat! Every door was open!

When asked about play, Jean Wilson, who also lived in Benwhat, born in
1932, did not seem to have the same freedom of her peers:

Further up the hill because we used to go up and play hooses with
wee bits of thing wee bits of things we would find we would go up
there and play wee hooses with wee bits of china and stuff.
YM: What kind of games did you play then when you were wee?
All the usual skipping ropes and hide and seek and whatever. We
were very protected we werenae oot much unless my mother had us
by the hand.

Agnes Auld, known as Nan, born 1932 in Lethanhill where she lived until
aged 10 in the Diamond Row, recalled:

25: School play, Dalmellington.
By kind permission of East Ayrshire Leisure Trust/East Ayrshire Council

> It was a great place to bring up weans! It definitely was because I mean, they had, they had everything that they could ask for an' they were nae in ony harm [background noises], you could let them oot t' play an' they were nae in ony harm ... Oh, we played peevers an' boules an' skipping ropes an' rounders an', makin' a things, that was, that was w'or entertainment. ... and wheel and girth – that's a circle.

Money was tight so toys were a luxury:

> Christmas, we got a, in oor stocking, we got a new penny, an orange and an apple an' that was it ... I never had a doll in me life! ... No. We could nae afford t' buy toys. Just them that had, er, was higher up in the pits, they were the yons that could afford it but we...

Kids swapped comics to keep costs down. Robert Hall recalled of his childhood in the 1940s:

> Oh, ah used tae get the *Dandy* delivered tae the house, aye ... we swapped the *Beano* and the *Dandy*. One would get the Beano, one would get the Dandy and one would get the *Hotspur*. Aye, we only bought one each, it wis a' we could afford [laughs].

Similarly, Felix Todd remembered:

The *Dandy*, and we had yin … it wis … the hero o' this comic wis a man who … he wis invincible as a goalkeeper. Cast Iron Bill they ca'ed him. [laughs]. It wis jist like everythin' else: it wis aboot your turn. Ah got the *Hotspur* or the *Dandy* and ah'd pass it on tae Jim Frew. And vice versa … That's how it wis done.

Others recalled being passed toys down from elder siblings, sometimes after a repaint. For example, Hugh Hainey, born in 1921, remembered being given a hand-me-down Meccano set when he lived in Lethanhill. His elder brother also built him his first bike in 1931 to replace the scooter he had previously got about on. And in the mid-1930s Hugh got involved in the Scouts, enjoying many local trips. Nan Auld remembered enjoying local dances and the 'cantatas' – locally produced concerts, with plays and singing. Mrs Currie, born in 1897 in Benwhat, recalled playing an old washerwoman in a cantata at the Benwhat church hall around 1910. The cantatas were held in the school hall in Benwhat and in Lethanhill. School halls were a vital community space for socialising.

Alice Wallace reflected on the school as a social space:

Most o' the events were in the school. Any big events or a big headcount. Concerts, they were held in the school as well. And weddings, wedding receptions were at there. In fact, the whole weddings, they were there. And the band played at most o' the things

26: Cantata inside the school hall at Lethanhill, c. 1930s.
Courtesy of Cox family

as well. And the concerts, if there was gonna be, say, a big headcount at any event there and children were allowed, we had all t' go an' sit up at the front, cross-legged on the floor because there was nae enough chairs for people or benches even. So, but we were quite happy to do that. I mean, it was great to get into these things! And we felt quite kinda grown up, 'oh, we're getting into that! This is great!' Aye.

In Lugar, the Institute (situated next to the village store) was described by David Murray, born in Lugar in 1930, as: 'the centre of the village.' One feature was a swimming pool but no one could recollect ever swimming there. David Murray recalled:

> And the water for the swimming pool came from the Ironworks up the top [laughs]. So the baths had swimming pool and I think the foundations of the swimming pool leaked or something. They put a floor in and made it a dancehall. You could go under the floor and that's where they stored all the chairs and tables for the functions would take place, and also Lugar's silver band instruments were all down there for a while. Stored under the floor in the tiled [empty pool].

Another woman from Lugar remembered other important social events at the Institute and that eventually it was turned into a factory once the community was moved to Logan:

> There was actually a swimming pool in it but then it got emptied an' closed o'er but there was weddings in it, there was a dancing class in it. We went tae Highland dancing in it an' the baby clinics were in it. That was afore Falmer's bought it o'er an' it was, Falmer's made jeans in there! That was turned in to a Falmer's factory! But the baby clinic was in there. We went, there was billiards in it. Erm, we went tae the Highland dancing in it. Well, you just went to onything that was on! You would hae went tae onything just t' … [laughing] … just t' get oot somewhere!!

Alex Kirk, born in 1941, was in a mining family and lived in the Briggate Row, Lethanhill then Polnessan Row, Burnfoothill. He recalled of his childhood:

> Och, we used t' play. There was a bit where we used t' play at … the rocks …

65

We used t' build dens and God knows what wi' old bits of corrugated iron an' things like that that we found lying roond aboot ... that was oor hidey-holes! [both laugh]

YM: And was that just the boys?

Aye, boys, aye, the lassies, they were usually running aboot playing wi' their dolls and prams – if they had prams.

Nan Auld, who as we have seen 'never had a doll in me life' would dispute this assertion!

Mary (May) Baird, known as May, born in 1954 in the Highhouse Rows, also recalled the freedoms of childhood in the 1950s when there were few restrictions or restraints. However, there were some places that were out of bounds to the kids. One of her earliest memories was of being told the places she was not to go:

I've, I've got a vague memory of ma mum ... giving me a, [chuckles] instructions! The front doors were always left open ... An' we were playin' just around the door an' she would say, "Now, where have you no' t' go?!" I had nae t' go to the washhouse! Nor had I t' go near t' the bing, which was close by, an' obviously very dangerous but, er, that's really the only kind of memories that I have.

May continued:

Er, aye, grew everything! Everything he [her father] could get his hands on! Grew tatties, leeks, you name it – he grew it all, didn't he?! ... Aye! An' when we went out t' play, we were told, "Don't be goin' in among the veg!"

Kids being kids, these parentally-imposed restrictions were sometimes ignored. A Craigbank miners' row resident (anonymous) recalled:

We mainly made our own entertainment! [pause]. Kick the can bedlam, you know! Three or four, five kids playing aboot ... but you were never far away frae a bing! A pit bing, which is dirty, an' you were always up it, sliding doon it ... So, you went in, you were dirty, wasn't you? An', er, many a hard skelp I got fer it! Goin' in in a state like that!! But that was the, that was the way wur parents lived in they days.

Another Lugar resident (anonymous), commented that her friends ignored the perils of the bing:

> We used t' run aboot together an' we were up where we should nae hae been! Up the bing! We'd no right tae be there but that's where, you were tellt not t' go is where you went! An' we were playing at hide and seek and he jumped into an empty hutch where, where the coals are an' we did nae really see somebody along an' the hutch, he was in the hutch and the hutch stairted moving!
>
> An' oh my God! The blood was running oot his ears an' everything! Oh! We, [chuckling] we all ran hame an' somebody ran fer his Mum an' Dad an' they come up an' all the rest o' us run hame – "Oh, he's deid! The blood's coming out his mooth! The blood's coming out his ears!"

While many recalled swimming in the burns on the hills, Barbara Alexander singled out the dam by Glenbuck as a danger in her childhood. This was her response when asked what she did as child:

> And walked an' … we'd mebbe walk doon t' the dam but we were never, that's one o' the things – I never ever knew a child in my generation that would go near the dam! Never, never!! An' there was a lot o', em, pits, em, disused pits, just up the hill frae the council houses wi', erm, barriers round them and if you dropped a stone, it took absolute ages before it would hit the water. But we would never ever go near these things. I don't know why. You know how kids now get drowned in swimming an' things? We never, ever heard of anybody being in the dam.

Another restricted area was land that belonged to the local laird. Fishing was another local pastime – though usually for food, rather than for pleasure! Tam Hazel, born in 1927 and a resident of Glenbuck for twenty years, recalled one fishing expedition: 'Some people call it 'tickling trout'. I called it '*guddling*'! They called it guddlin' where I came frae! And, och, we had a … I don't know … I must hae had aboot twa dozen dead *troot*! At least!!' Another Scots expression for fishing – used by Tom Wilson, Benwhat resident (1926-1940) – was 'gidlin' for fish: 'yin a ma favourite pastimes'. Tom recalled:

> We'd a different game for every month in the year. Marbles, ye know, kick the can, as they talk aboot. Ah see them talkin' aboot bar the door, skippin' ropes for lassies, and rounders and … Hounds and

hares and burnin' the moors, and ginlin' and bird nestin', dookin', we never wearied as children.

Sam Purdie told the following story about illegal fishing in the Glenbuck Loch, owned by the local coalowner:

There was a big house. The big house was owned by [...] the local coal owner and famous black sheep breeder and he was the laird. And you weren't permitted to, you could go on the road when you were out of Glenbuck but you were not permitted to go in the fields. If anybody saw you, back on the, back on to the road. "You've no business here!" Especially when you got anywhere near the big house. [...] Glenbuck 'Loch' - there were some nice fish in there so, naturally, we learnt to fish! [chuckles] ... the River Ayr starts there as well and the big river ... so there's plenty of fishing and we spent a lot of our youth fishing for trout. That was one of our main hobbies ... In the rivers, in the rivers it was OK but, er, it was very much illegal in his dam with his trout!

But nevertheless, we got, er, well, you know, there was kind of communication – when the gamekeeper was going to be spending an afternoon away somewhere and then, there we were. But the other interesting thing about that is, the police were part-time gamekeepers, at our expense, of course, they were getting a tip off from, from the laird and they would chase you from the dam! It was none of their business *but* Glenbuck dam is *half* in Lanarkshire and *half* in Ayrshire and, in those days, there was a demarcation of the police forces. So, if you were fishing and a policeman would come along, you would quickly determine where he'd come from and then you would cross the dyke onto the other guy's jurisdiction and they couldn't touch you! [laughs]

So, um, and we occasionally, we had a wee argument occasionally with the policeman. Of course, the trick, didn't hae anything but waders because some of the, the areas of the dam was quite a, a gentle slope. So, the trousers got rolled up and you went in. So, here would come the policeman and the argument would start. And he would have a choice – either to calm things down or get wet. So, they decided not to get wet invariably! [laughs]

The fruits of their labour would be consumed, or gifted, as Sam recalled:

We knew where the fish could be got, we knew where the rabbits could be got. We knew what doors to knock on. It was a complete community! If I went to the Glenbuck dam and caught several trout, I'd knock on a pensioner's door and say I've got too many or, if I'd one or two rabbits because there were quite a lot of them, I'd put a rabbit into somebody. Clean it on the hill and hand it in clean! That's what you did.

In the first half of the twentieth century, religion played a greater part in miners' families lives, and for some, church and chapel had a recreational function. For the kids, this could provide opportunities. Nan Auld remembered:

> There was a church and we went to Sunday School every Sunday …
> An', er, once a year we went on a Sunday School trip! On the horse and cairt!
> *YM: Where did you go?*
> Patna! [All laugh] That was as far as we went! But that was a guid day oot fer us! Going to Patna. [laughs] Doon the hill!

Tom Wilson, who lived in Benwhat, remembered:

> Ah don't remember much, as ah say, about ony religious life, apart frae the fact that ma mother insisted we … we never missed the Sunday School. You know, in fact we got a prize, we got a bible for perfect attendance, that kind of thing, ye know. We never missed … we were never allowed tae miss it.

Alice Wallace remembers when the Rechabites, a religious group that promoted temperance, moved into one of the empty houses in Benwhat:

> Er, an' on a Sunday, it was used for Sunday School and it was the Brethren that had it. Now, we had latched on to the Brethren [laughing] very quickly in Benwhat. There was nae a church there but there was a Sunday School for the children in the school but if adults wanted to go to the church, they could walk along the line to Lethanhill, they had a church or walk down to Dalmellington to the church, you see? But, there was – see, I've lost my track of what I was saying there – aye, now, the Happy Clappys, as we called them, the Hallelujahs, they came to Benwhat an' they used one o' the empty houses for a Sunday School an' we started to go just t' see what there was because wor parents were, sort a, laughing up their sleeves, a wee

bit o' ridicule, ken, the happy clappys, er, "Right, we're no' going!" but they frowned on drink. Very sorely against drink. They were teetotal an', er, they had all this, you know, "My cup's full an' running over" and they did all these actions an' The wise man built his house on the rock and the rain come tumbling down' an' you're doing all this, so we loved doing all these actions! This was good. But, the best bit was, they had cookies, an' everybody that went got a cookie! You know these big cookies with the sugar lumps on them?

YM: Aye! [laughing]

They had a bag o' them! An' we all got a cookie so that was the only reason we really went! And then, in Bellsbank on a Sunday, there was the Sunday School and it was similar, it was the Brethren that had it so we went an' we got wur cookie an' stuff up there!

With some exceptions – like Sunday School – recreation was gendered with girls and boys tending to separate to enjoy different activities (at least prior to courting). Football was important for boys – as a Pennyvenie resident (anonymous) from 1938-1954 noted: 'When you got home frae school, it was, er, just football'. Burnton man, Henry (Harry) Kennedy, born in 1932, elaborated: 'An', er, played a lot o' football in the fields out there. At the back, what we called the back field, that was behind the houses, like, an', och, every night you'd about fifteen aside! An' I'm talking aboot schoolboys up

27: Lethanhill Mission Church.
Courtesy of Cox family

tae aboot near about forty or fifty!!' Hugh Hainey recalled playing football in the 1930s in Lethanhill even at night as long as the moonlight was strong enough! Girls were almost always excluded. Glenbuck resident Ella Reynolds, born in 1930, recalled:

> *An*' there was a *foot*ball pitch at Glenbuck! … Yes, there was. An' there was a Glenbuck *team*! [laughs] But *I* never ever went an' watched it! We *were*, we were nae allowed t' play. *Kick* a football! … *No*!! We were nae allowed t' do it!! … I, I would nae dare kick a football! [laughing] No! You were nae allowed tae do that!! But *there* you are – women are doing it now!!

Barbara Alexander, who lived in Glenbuck from the 1940s to 1970s, came from a footballing family on both sides. As well as the most famous member of her family Liverpool manager Bill Shankly, a number of her other uncles on the Shankly and Blythe side of the family played professionally at some point. When asked whether she ever played herself, she replied: 'No!! That was nae, maybe though! Maybe nowadays, if that had been the thing now!' Barbara implies that her gender prevented her from playing and that perhaps given the changes today she might have given it a go. She continued: 'Em, mebbe, mebbe nowadays that would hae, I, I look at the women football players an' I think, '*mebbe* I could hae done that then! But there was nothing like that in these days. Aye!'

28: Lethanhill School Football Team, not dated.
By kind permission of East Ayrshire Leisure Trust/East Ayrshire Council

In response to the question: 'What kind of games did you play?' Alice Wallace recalled:

> Ohh, peevers! Beds, they were called. You know, the chalk on the road? The boxes with the numbers. An' your peever was like a polished tin filled wi' mud tae make it heavy. Oh, a wee bit o' marble, maybe broken off at the butchers, off their counter, they would save the marble for the lassies to play at beds. Skipping ropes, things like that. Daisy chains. Sittin' making daisy chains. A lot o' the time we just went for a walk an' we sat on doorsteps an' we talked and played about on the grass. The boys, they would, er, there was a wee, a wee burn … they would make wee boats and sail them down. Now, the wee boats were like matchboxes, but they had their own identity on them and they could run down beside them and watch them going and, er, they got fair excited! To see who had won! I mean, there was no prize or anything, it was just fun! Aye! So, they did all that kind o' thing and played wi' marbles and stuff. Peashooter an' all that.
>
> *YM: Did the boys and girls play together ever?*
>
> No' very much, no. No. Maybe hide and seek, things like that, they might join in but no, no the girls were together and the boys were away doing their own thing.

29: Inside Lethanhill School, 1918.
Courtesy of Cox family

PUB, FOOTBA' AND THE REST: MINERS' RECREATION

Social class, income (and its distribution) and gender continued to pattern the ways in which adult men and women enjoyed their leisure time in mining communities. The coal companies encouraged certain forms of 'rational' recreation – activities that were 'wholesome' and not damaging – hence, for example, the banning of the drinking spirits in some villages. There were entrenched ideas about what was acceptable and 'respectable' for men and women to do; spaces for each and lines that must not be crossed otherwise transgressors were considered outcasts and shamed. This was tied up with notions of masculinity and femininity that had hardly changed from the Victorian times. Women's leisure time was much more prescribed and limited, with the home being the site of much of housewives' recreation, whilst the pub, pigeon loft and football field were the domains of the village men.

The 'beer house' or the village pub remained a focal point for miners' recreation in Ayrshire mining communities, as elsewhere. This relied on the tradition of men withdrawing for themselves 'pocket money' from their wage packets, something which could impact adversely on family finances. This was money for beer, cigarettes and perhaps a bet on the horses or the football. John New told a story passed down to him and referring to Commondyke:

> The Store Row … the men would all sit around or stand about … and she [grandmother] said they had a big, enamel bucket there and they would just, erm, have a wee cup and just, all just help themselves to the beer. It was sold in these big, kind of, er, probably like a flagon or a, er, so there was, emptied into a ceramic bucket and just drink away at it, you know. But, she said, you, you either went one way or the other. A lot o' them, drink was, they were bad with the drink…

In response to the question: 'What did the men do for their leisure?', Alice Wallace recalled:

> They went to the pub, most o' them. Some of them did nae drink and that would certainly help their wives and their income, how they managed their money. But most o' the men got their pocket money an' I think they would all get roughly the same an' it was quite a good portion o' the wage. Because, at one time, er, my Mum was good at managing because she was so thrifty and good at making stuff an' a good cook an' she could make a meal out o' nothing. Er, but, if she was a bit short, she would say to ma Dad, an' ken at this particular

time, the boys needed new shoes an' she says, "The boys are baith needin' new shoes, Jim" an' he says, "Well, you get the pay, it's up to you how you work it! You get them! It's you tae do that! I've gied you the pay, I've done ma bit!" And she was really hopin' that he say, "Well, I'll dae without ma pocket money this week an' that'll help" but no, he did nae, you see? But that was the attitude of most o' the men, I think, at that time. Aye. They did work hard and they knew it and they knew they were entitled to a break and if they wanted to go to the pub that's what they did. Aye.

YM: Where was the pub?

There was a pub in Benwhat, they called it 'the store' and it was quite a big building and it was actually two businesses under the one roof. Er, there was the beer store for the men. It was only beer they sold, they did nae have spirits, no whisky or anything. And, er, women were frowned on for going in! That just did nae happen. But there was a wee, kinda, quiet corner if it did happen, if a woman had a drink, she sat in the wee bolt hole, they called it, this wee corner kinda screened away, I think. Anyway, the other part of the store was for the women to buy their food and provisions and everything else,

30: The Runnin' Dog Western Club (undated).
By kind permission of East Ayrshire Leisure Trust/East Ayrshire Council

so it did nae just sell food. It had, er, pails, shovels, paraffin, er, tools – everything else you could need for living, kinda style.

Alex Kirk testified to the provenance of this recollection referring to 'the Hill':

> There was a store that was owned by the company that owned all the mines and that at that time. An' there was a beer store so that the men could go for a pint.
> *YM: Did the women go to the beer store?*
> No, very, very … you never ever found a woman going to there.
> *YM: So, what did the women do then?*
> I don't think so many o' them drunk, not like there is nowadays because, plus they would nae have the money t' do it! The wages were nae high in they days.

Another interviewee (anonymous) recalled the Lethanhill beer store and

31: Jack Young (with the apron), last manager of the Lethanhill Store, c. 1948.
David Young Collection

how it was a focal point in the village:

> The pub which was called the store, the beer store and the grocery store was in one building but the beer store was at the back and the summer ah remember on the Saturday would be the store would come out at nine o clock at night there were a bit called the square it was grass oot the front and ye used to get the kids ontae a circle and there were a man … canny mind his first name … he used to play an acordie and he used to get the accordion and there was a wee man … used to live in that house across the road actually afore he died, and he used tae dance on his hands … he could go about on his hands as well as you could go about on yer feet and he used to dance about, and you used to be in a circle and he would in the circle dancing and that and … everybody passed an hour after the pubs came oot at nine o clock.

Communal events in the village hall or miners' institute involved both sexes; dances, concerts and the like were common, recurrent events. John New recalled a story told to him which related to the dances in Commondyke:

> Ma father always talked of the lock-ins. He said they had great dances in the church hall and, he said, they would, erm, they would make an announcement about eleven o' clock – to all those who wanted to go, go *[YM laughs]* and to all those who wanted to stay, stay! Erm, because of, probably, licensing laws, they did a lock-in, so they just locked the door, and everybody would then just keep merrymaking till, probably, four or five in the morning, you know, and then … probably go into a shift! [Both laugh] We've all done it!! [both laugh] But they were, erm, [pause], he said that they were *fantastic* … great, wee hoolies, you know, they had! … And, erm, a lot o' the time it was … lemonade. You know, if it was run by the church, very often they wouldn't condone alcohol. It was lemonade or soft drinks. The drinking would be done outside beforehand, maybe a beer or whatever … a way out in the middle o' the countryside, they weren't bothering anybody, you know, the music would just carry on right through. So, these were the, kind of, [rustling paper] gleaned stories over the years that people told me.

Another pastime of the men was a betting game called 'pitch and toss'. In Lethanhill this often happened after the beer store closed. Another recollection was of betting on horse-racing or football via a 'bookie' in the store, using the only public telephone outside the store to check on the racing results.

For a long time, the pub was a male-only space and 'pocket money' or 'drinking money' represented male advantage and the mal-distribution of scarce resources. That said, this inequality was mostly accepted within mining communities, and rarely challenged, at least prior to the 1970s. It was the way it was, and always had been. Waterside parish priest Eddie McGhee recalled:

> Yeah, a lot o' them were, there was a lot of hard drinking done among mining communities, you know. Erm, it all depended, I mean [pause], you know, for example, ma Dad [a miner] came home, he would open his wage packet, count it, make sure it was right and it was handed untouched then to ma Mum! For lots o' women, though, that was not the reality! [pause] The guys took what they wanted and gave the rest and that was for their housekeeping, you know? Erm, so there was a very definite kind of inequality [pause] that I was very well aware of there! Because, erm, I mean, the kids would talk about, even at school, you know, their Dad's being drunk. Ma, ma father was basically a non-drinker, you know, erm, and going to the pub and drink was, drink was a big [pause], a big part o' it!

Apart from a drink, miners enjoyed a wide range of other social and recreational activities, including competitive sports. Football was popular amongst the younger men, perhaps because it offered a release in the fresh air after working underground in the pit. And pit work, especially in the labour-intensive pick and shovel days, honed strong, lean and fit bodies (at least before middle-age and whilst miners were fortunate enough to avoid accidents) and inculcated the kind of team work and collective responsibility that worked well on the pitch. Camaraderie characterised the mining community, but there was also a surprising degree of competitiveness at the coal face, as we have seen, with men individually and in work groups wanting to out-produce others and be known as hard grafters: 'workers not wasters' as one anthropologist (Daniel Wight) nicely put it. Almost all villages had their football team (or teams) and there was a healthy rivalry in games played between villages, which scaled up to Junior Football competitions and cups in which teams like the Glenbuck Cherrypickers and Auchinleck Talbot became notorious. Kames miner Dick Boland recalled:

> Big Jock Dalziel, it used to be when we finished our shift, when we were dayshift, we'd get bathed and changed and a bit of dinner. We

*32: Benwhat Heatherbell football team c. 1910 on the pitch in front of the miners'
rows at Benwhat.*

By kind permission of East Ayrshire Leisure Trust/East Ayrshire Council

went up to Dykeside and there were two football teams played. Big
Jock used to play in his pit boots. It was frightening when he went to
kick with his boots on.[1]

Tragically, Jock was one of those killed in the Kames pit disaster in 1957 (on
this see Chapter 4).

Alice Wallace commented on Benwhat:

We had a football field. Now, er, before the pits were mined for coal,
it was iron ore and part of the procedure for that was to lay out this
hot iron ore on a field so there was a big, level bit o' ground and that's
where they laid it out. And the end result was a good football field.
It was all nice and level then. So, er, they had a football team. It was
the Benwhat Heather Bells and all the villages had their own football
teams an' they all had their names so there was quite a few matches
all arranged. Some were up there and some were at Dalmellington,
some were at Waterside, Lethanhill. They all had their teams there

---

1 Interview with Dick Boland, Kames Colliery Disaster Project, http://www.muirkirk.org.uk/
minersvoices/dick-boland.htm.

for that.

Sam Purdie recalled of Glenbuck:

> The village itself had a tremendous history because it had generated
> a football team, called the Glenbuck Cherrypickers, which is rather
> a famous name in football history and even more famous is the
> fact that fifty-four of those miners, who worked in Glenbuck in the
> pits, went on to become professional football players, some of them
> professional managers, like, like Willie Shankly [Liverpool manager]
> so, for a village of a few hundred people, the contribution that they
> made to football was tremendous. So, that was one of the sports that
> we, we had.

He continued:

> But Glenbuck, at that time, had a terrible reputation because we're,
> we're hillbillies. We're completely divorced from Ayrshire and it was
> a long recognised fact that if you went to play football in Glenbuck
> and won, you'd better have your running boots on! [both laugh] It
> wasn't unknown for the referee to find himself in the burn! [both
> laughing]

Unusually Sam himself did not play: 'I have a distinction! I'm the only guy
in Glenbuck that *didn't* play football!'

At the centre of the heritage site which is the village today is a
memorial to the ex-Liverpool manager Bill Shankly, born in Glenbuck, to
which Liverpool fans travel to pay their respects to this legend of a football
manager. The memorial to Shankly is swathed in football scarves, shirts
and memorabilia. Tam Hazel spent his first twenty years in Glenbuck and
lived next door to the Shanklys. Tam recalled:

> But *all* the men that worked in the pit, that's, that's why probably, why
> there was as many good players in Glenbuck – they were desperate
> t' get oot the pit! An' the only pastime at night was ... kickin', kickin'
> the ball aboot! Football.

If football wasn't your sport then there were running and athletics clubs,
quoits and other sports. Alice Wallace recalled:

> And, er, there was, er, the Doon Harriers. That was a great running

33: Sombre but fit looking Doon Harriers.
By kind permission of East Ayrshire Leisure Trust/East Ayrshire Council

team and they had some really great runners. There was a man, Reid, who was really good an' made a name for himself at this! An' wi' him running in our team, that brought other good runners from other places so they had a great event with that every year! The Harriers.

Hugh Hainey similarly described the range of recreation on offer in Lethanhill in the 1930s and 1940s:

The Primrose was a very successful football team. Lethanhill Pipe Band was a grade 3 band. Lethanhill Quoiting club was moderately successful in the Ayrshire league. Lethanhill Flying Club was a pigeon club and a member of the Kyle Federation. There was a male voice choir and the Orange Lodge had a flute band. The Church had its organisations including the Womens Guild and there was the Womens Rural. Evening classes were available in the school during the winter months. Open all the year round was the Miners Institute containing a library and reading room with daily papers, a billiard room with two tables and carpet bowls, chess, draughts and dominoes were also available and one room was a small shop selling sweets, lemonade and biscuits. Most houses had gardens available and the two families I knew concentrated on Pansies and won several prizes at the Southport show, which was a leading British show at that time. Church and religious activities were the only thing permitted

80

on a Sunday. On a good Sunday it was common for families to be seen out walking.

Sam Purdie recalled that Glenbuck wasn't only famous for its footballers:

> One of the interesting things about Glenbuck was, we had, quoiting, as some people call it, as a sport, in addition to our tremendous concentration on football. And one of our interesting characters was a guy called, er, Thomas Bone. Everybody had nicknames in Glenbuck and he was 'Tuds'. Tuds was the British champion and so there were only quoits played in Britain, he was the World Champion. And he was a case in point. Tuds was working for all them years in the pit while he was playing quoits and, er, at the height of his career, he lost an eye! [pause] Well, that virtually put an, an end to his career.
> *AM: Was that lost in a pit accident, Sam?*
> Yes, he lost it in Grasshill Pit an', and, er … he was, Tuds was like a lot of men of his generation – he never saw fifty summers. [pause] It ruined his career and it ruined his health!

Other miners indulged in pigeon racing. Lethanhill resident Hugh Hainey recalled in his hand-written (and unpublished) autobiography assisting as

34: Dalmellington quoiters (showing the round 'quoit' that was thrown a distance aiming for a fixed post).
By kind permission of East Ayrshire Leisure Trust/East Ayrshire Council

a young teenager in the mid-1930s:

> I helped with the checking of the time clocks for the racing pigeons and retrieving the capsules containing the numbered rubber rings that identified each bird. The rings were fitted to the legs of the pigeons before they were put in a Wicker basket usually holding twenty birds. There could be around 150 birds for the short races, Dumfries, Carlisle or Penrith. The longer races saw a reduction in numbers with probably 20 for the races from France. Arriving home the bird would have the band removed from its leg and placed in a brass thimble-like capsule. Then a good running member of the family circle would run with it to the nearest club time clock, insert the capsule in the appropriate place and pressed the lever that dropped the capsule into the clock and functioned the clock dial to record the exact time of clocking in. To decide the race winner all clocks were checked for accuracy then each capsule and time in recorded. When all clocks were emptied and times recorded the calculations for the winner began with allowance for overfly time between lofts and running time to the clocks be considered before the winner and placings were announced.

When Waterside parish priest Eddie McGhee moved to the Doon Valley

35: The Lethanhill Flying Club members celebrating the awarding of the pigeon cup, including Diane Cox's relative Tommy Kelly.
Courtesy of Cox family

in the 1980s he recalled becoming part of the Lethanhill Flying Club with former 'Hill folk:

> I have a personal connection because I participated in the ultimate sport of the mining communities. I was a pigeon fancier. And [pause], with ma brother, Jimmy, we raced pigeons in Cumnock but as soon as I moved to Waterside in the Doon Valley, I built ma own pigeon loft [pause] and there were two pigeon clubs ... I applied to Lethanhill Flying Club, erm, and was accepted straight away as a member so, and Dalmellington Club told me I was out with their boundary for membership so that was fine. So, I raced pigeons for the few years that I was in the Doon Valley in Lethanhill Flying Club and I was the Secretary, following in a great tradition of secretaries. [pause] But I had a wee guy called Johnnie Gibbons, who had lived on the 'hill and had kept pigeons up on the 'hill and – see, being a Parish Priest is a bummer for doo racing because sometimes the pigeons are held over and you've got Sunday Mass and, I mean, it was a total nightmare if I had a holdover but wee Johnnie, wee Johnnie came to me, oh, shortly after I'd been accepted, erm, for membership. He came and he said, "I'll look efter your pigeons, son, on a Sunday if you can nae make it! I'll sit oot the back." An' he came every weekend, then. Every weekend he was out the back and he would tell me about, erm, the days when they had pigeon racing on the 'hill [pause] and, I don't know if you know, understand pigeon racing. You don't actually race pigeons at all! You put a little, rubber ring onto its leg. [pause] When the pigeon comes home, to its own loft, you take that rubber ring off off its leg and it goes into a thing a bit like a thimble and then it goes into a timing clock, you turn the handle and it stamps the time and it's only when that handle is stamped, has your pigeon arrived. [pause] Now, on the 'hill, they had only one pigeon clock for the seventeen or eighteen members who raced pigeons so, all the wee boys who could run fast, were given a thruppence or something by the pigeon fanciers so that when they timed a pigeon, they gave the ring to the wee boy, who would run like stink to wherever the clock was kept and it was, it was then timed in! So, even if you knew nothing about pigeons or cared nothing, for that thruppence you were prepared to run your, your hardest on the 'hill t', t' time in the pigeons. Erm [pause], an' that's just, again, it's [pause], it's indicative that the whole community was involved in what the community was doing so, if doo racing was part o' the community, yeah, if you could take part, you took part!

As noted in Chapter 1, gardening was another common pastime in Ayrshire mining communities, again mostly undertaken by men. Eddie McGhee thought this reflected a competitive culture amongst the men and, perhaps like football, a chance to rise above the grim conditions of work and the housing:

> They had to create an environment that somehow lifted them out of that [pause] kind of harshness and grinding poverty and that's where all of the things that happen, you know, the guys who grew the biggest cucumbers and the biggest leeks and the guys who had the best pigeons or the best canaries...

Singing and music were other popular leisure activities, with music embedded in mining communities, from the miners' choirs of South Wales to the miner's bands of Northern England and Scotland. Nanette McKee, born in 1949, recalled a story told by her father (who lived in Commondyke and Darnconner):

> My Dad was a good storyteller! I think a lot o' the miners were! … Well, a friend o' his was actually an opera singer! Aye. Tommy He used t' sing to them doon the pit! And Dad said it was wonderful … Aye, he used t' sing to them.

Ayrshire prided itself on having a long tradition of pipe bands, silver and brass bands. Tom Wilson cut his teeth in the Benwhat band in the late 1940s and then went on to play third cornet in the Dalmellington Silver Band. Alice Wallace also recalled:

> All these wee villages had their own band and they were at every event in the village and really involved in everything … And at the likes at Ne'er Day the Benwhat Band was going round about, just about the time the bells were going. See at that time, what happened was, just before twelve o' clock, the women are all cleaning their house an' everything is spotless, no' a bit of dirt anywhere! An' the cloth that was used to wash the fireplace an' have it all sitting nice an' clean, is popped into the fire so there is no dirty thing anywhere at all! That's burned and it's away. So, the house is immaculate and they're waiting on the bells. The men are at the pub and they're coming back and then, the pits wor sounding their horn and the church bells in the village were ringing, just before twelve. And then everybody went an' opened their front door and opened their back door an' this was to

let the New Year in and the old Year out and the Band started playing an' they were walking all round all the rows playing their tune and they were stopping to get a wee drink here an' there an' they were getting really quite drunk [laughs] as they went further on!

Family dynasties developed in the bands, with fathers passing down their interest and knowledge to sons. Henry (Harry) Kennedy (Burnton resident, 1932-1953) recalled 'ma dad was in Benwhat [Benquhat] Band fer years an' years an' years … Ma oldest brother, he was in Dalmellington Band fer, oh, I think it was aboot fifty year!!' Iain Hutchison had a Glenbuck connection via his grandfather and he recalled:

My grandfather's generation and, indeed, my father's generation, they all learnt musical instruments! Erm, my grandfather was a trumpeter, er, and my father also played the trumpet but certainly, you know, when he was in his sixties an' retired, I know that my grandfather passed his trumpet onto my father because he could no longer, er … draw the breath to play the trumpet. So, the miners' lung must have been affecting him for a while. He probably didn't even recognise it as being related to, er, lung disease from the pits! Erm, but it must have been affecting him, certainly, by that time as well.

YM: So, did he play in any, like, was there a miners' brass band? Did he play in anything like that?

Yes, there was. Yeah, there were colliery bands, er, and I know that, er, certainly my father, er, played in a colliery band. Er, it was the Hamilton Palace Colliery Band. Erm, and it was, kind of, based

36: Dalmellington Band, undated.
By kind permission of East Ayrshire Leisure Trust/East Ayrshire Council

in, erm, another lost village, er, Bothwell Haugh! Yeah? You know it? Which is now under the Strathclyde Park loch! ... Erm, er, and anyway, it, it had a band and, er, as I say, it was the Hamilton Palace Band and my father played in that. And I've got a couple of pictures, er, you know, where they'd maybe be playing at Gala events or whatever and they all had a uniform and everything, you know! Erm, and er, I'm, I'm guessing ma, ma grandfather probably played in similar kind of, er, er, band. You know, a lot of the collieries and the iron foundries and whatever had these things, and it was a way of, you know, ensuring that their employees engaged in 'rational recreation' on their days off rather than, er, engaging in pub culture and idleness, you know!

Inter-village and wider competitions kept pipe and brass players on their toes. Again, though, banding was traditionally a male-dominated recreational activity. In her PhD thesis on music in the coalfields, Marion Henry explores how gendered the bands were at mid-twentieth century, though she notes how women played a vital role behind the scenes.[2] Sanquhar resident Margaret Wilson recalled:

> The women all worked behind the scenes em raising the money em ... making sure the men were presented and tidy and doing their uniforms and things like that [...] [T]hey raised a lot of money just... having coffee morning em... and my mum sold tablet em just things like that they did yeah, they were the backbone without the women, they wouldn't have had no funding, they wouldn't have been able to do it.

Margaret was one of the female pioneers in Ayrshire, playing cornet in the Sanquhar Silver band in the 1980s (where she met her future husband, Rab Wilson). The Dalmellington Brass band was amongst the most successful and famous. One of its most celebrated band leaders was Hugh Johnstone, awarded MBE for his services to the Brass Band movement.

The outdoors also provided miners with a wide range of recreational activities in, which included walking, rambling and cycling in the beautiful Ayrshire hills. Parish priest Eddie McGhee reflected:

> Lots o' them were BIG, big gardeners, you know, an' of course, there

---

2 Marion Henry, "'Every village would have a band": Building Community with Music: A Social and Cultural History of Brass Bands in the British Coalfields, 1947-1984' (PhD thesis, Sciences Po and University of Strathclyde, 2021); p.222.

were all of these [pause], like, competitions. You know they would
have flower shows and vegetable shows an' I mean some o' them
were unbelievably talented! That's where you saw it! Not so much
in the day-to-day fact that they went down the pit, did their shift,
came home but they, they had these other hobbies like the doos, lots
o' them kept greyhounds or whippets, you know. They grew stuff,
generally stuff to feed the family, you know, so they'd, they'd plant
a few tatties, a few leeks, a few carrots, cabbages – I'm just trying to
think of all the things that ma Dad grew! Eventually, ma Dad got two
greenhouses but initially, I mean, all the stuff that ma Dad put in the
ground was to feed us!

You know, in the fifties. Erm, and I mean that fifties now sounds
like a long time ago! Well, it is, it's seventy years ago! Erm, [pause]
so, all o' this was done and then there were other [pause], erm,
bird fanciers in the mining community and they, they would catch
bullfinches, goldfinches, chaffinches an' they would cross 'em wi'
canaries! You know, these were the Fine Feather boys. There were all
of these hobbies which, which engage, I think, engaged the people
who took part in them [pause] and it gave them a wider dimension
of just going into this hole in the ground every day and, and earning

*37: William and Maggie
McClelland in their garden
in Burnfoothill in 1940s,
Courtesy of David Young*

enough to survive!

Many of the miners were self-educated, but lacked the opportunities to get further formal education because they were required to work from an early age for the survival of the family. In this context, choices were limited. Sam Purdie (Glenbuck) recalled:

> My grandfather Purdie was a very well-read man. His, his house was full of books and I was encouraged from a very early age to read. And he was a lifelong atheist, but he insisted that I went to church, went to the kirk to see what was going on. There he says, "You'll go and hear what they've got to say and you'll make up your mind!" Because he was a very, very fine, like most of these old miners, a very fine man. Very … world conscious.

Felix Todd spoke of how well-read the men were in his village of Crosshouse, especially on Burns:

> In the raw, what ah wis telling you aboot whaur we wis born and bred in the 19 hooses, every hoose ye went intae there wis a Burns book and a bible. These men were a' experts on Burns. They never spoke tae Burns … never spoke aboot Burns at a public meeting in their life, and they could have telt ye the … everythin' aboot the man.

The miners' welfare club or 'Institute' provided the space and the amenities to promote such self-development, often housing the miners' libraries, as well as being the place where miners could play billiards, bowls, dominoes, darts and other games. Often the Institute was the focal point of village indoor recreation; the place where events and parties took place. A resident from the Pennyvenie miners' rows from 1938-1954 described (in an interview with Kate Wilson) how the Institute was positioned in the middle of one of the rows and what went on:

> Pennyvenie Institute. Where all the miners – it was a miners' institute! … Where they used t' go an' play [pause] bowls. Carpet bowls. Billiards and snooker, on the big, snooker table … Periodically, they held a social in there 'cause there was a big hall, you know. That's where we played the carpet bowls. [Clears throat] Sunday School was held in there. … Parties. Sunday School parties. Err … an' that's where … at the Queen's Coronation, that's where the activities were held – in the Institute, you know? All the celebrations.

He told a story of an early experience (in 1952):

> I went there when I was fourteen. … I played billiards … they had a
> *tournament*. An annual tournament. An' if it was your, if *that* was the
> first year you'd been in the tournament (it was *mine*, at fourteen) an'
> they played to … the first to reach a hundred. Who's the winner. So, if
> it was your first year entry, you got a start of fifty! [chuckling] So!!! I
> … hed fifty as a start an' I was quite good. As they say, it was a young
> man's game. An', er, I won the cup! …The man I beat, of course, was
> nae too happy because you got fifty [chuckling] o' a start!! [Both
> laugh] He *din* nae think that was very fair!!! Anyway! *That* was the
> Institute, there!

Whilst not exclusively so (for example for celebrations and events, like gala
days), the Miners' Institute in most villages was predominantly a male-only
space in the first half of the twentieth century. Alice Wallace recollected of
Benwhat:

> There was also the … er, God, what's the word for it?! Now, it's
> left me! Ah, it was a room fer reading, the … Institute! Sorry! The
> Institute was actually just two houses that had been sitting empty
> at the end o' a row and they made the two o' them into an institute,
> which was a, sort of, reading room. An' it was used just by the men
> and the big boys an' actually, a lot o' the men up there would have
> been clever, well, they were clever but they just never had the chance
> t' get a good education. An' some o' them were good speakers and
> clever men and apparently, in the Institute, they would have talks
> about, er … you know, how things were maybe no' done properly
> at their work and they were cheated out of certain payments and
> there was nothing they could do about it! If they spoke up about it,
> it went against them. There was a Union but they did nae want t' go
> on strike, no' for the least wee thing! Because, I mean, if they go on
> strike, that's their wage stopped. There's nothing at all coming in. The
> women did nae work outside their home. There was only one wage
> going into the house. Well, some o' them, I mean their grown-up
> sons maybe working in the pit but it's the same thing if they're on
> strike, there's no wage going in. And there was actually a waiting list
> to get into this membership o' the Institute, er, because they had t'
> be discrete and careful about who they spoke in front of. Now, most
> o' the men were all for one another an' get things done together, but
> they did nae want any stories going back to the pit bosses in any way

so they had to be careful.

But, as I say, that was used mainly by the men and the bigger boys and they had plenty o' books there an' they had newspapers delivered up from the village and they could sit an' have a read o' the paper. They had dominoes and cards, a dartboard, even inside carpet bowling in there! It was good! But they had t' pay fourpence a fortnight that one was, from their wage. My Mum told me all these things years ago. And that fourpence a week off every miner's wage paid for this so the men wanted to get good use o' that because they had paid fer it – and they did. An' they started up wee clubs and things an' they had meetings up there for different things. They even started a Burns Club, which was good because they did nae have good education, I mean, it was very basic because the families could nae afford t' send them to college or university and that was it.

Later in the interview Alice returned to the topic, recalling 'The Institute was really for the men an' newspapers an' stuff an' books. Aye, they did nae encourage young kids in there, it was a man thing. A man cave!'

MAKING THE MOST OF IT: WOMEN AND LEISURE IN AYRSHIRE MINING COMMUNITIES

Women's enjoyment of leisure in the miners' row villages was much more

38: Women involved in amateur dramatics, Dalmellington.
By kind permission of East Ayrshire Leisure Trust/East Ayrshire Council

39: Benwhat Ladies Burns Supper Committee, undated.
By kind permission of East Ayrshire Leisure Trust/East Ayrshire Council

prescribed than men's; they usually had less time because of family and household responsibilities, as well as less financial resources to devote to themselves, putting the family's needs first. As mentioned, women were also denied access or had only limited access to many spaces and activities which were monopolised by men, including the pub, Institute and the football field. Much of women's recreation was therefore centred around the home and the neighbourhood and much of it blurred into work, such as sewing and knitting. We discuss this further in the next chapter. Alice Wallace recalled of her mother during wartime:

> Well, they had a blether and that with their neighbours and their friends. Er, they made time for that. I mean, they were busy but they still made a wee bit o' time for one another. And they would go along to see somebody else was alright and take something, something nice for them to eat. A couple o' slices of cake, things like that. I mean, they could nae give, like, a full cake! They were all working wi' their rations, their flour and dried eggs and you name it! But they would make what they could an' take a nice couple o' slices o' that and some pancakes and that was a nice tea.

Recalling Lethanhill, Agnes (Nan) Auld mentioned women going into close neighbours and friends houses for a cuppa and a 'gossip'. And there were 'transgressions'. In an interview John New told a story passed down to him referring to Commondyke in the interwar years:

> Ma wee Great-Great-Granny … she would go in [chuckling] to the, the lobby and she kept a, a tin there, an enamel tin, a paraffin tin and she would always have a bit of beer in it and she would, over the day, get more and more chatty as she was going [both chuckling], sipping at the beer! And she said it was, kind a … an open secret that she was always going in and having a wee, a wee fly drink but nobody would ever say, "Where's the beer?!", you know!

And going to the cinema was an important leisure activity, especially for younger women and men, from the 1930s on. Alice Wallace recalled of Benwhat women:

> They all had their friends, groups o' them, an' they would arrange to go down to the pictures in Dalmellington. There was a picture house and they loved going down and they would arrange who all was going to try and get enough to make it worthwhile getting transport if they could. And whether they were going to have to walk it. I mean, they would get a bus down but I don't think they would get a bus back up at that time. But they did things like that. Er, they loved going to the pictures, I know my Mum did! An' they loved seeing all these glamourous women an', er, there was the bit where ma Mum used t' say, "These women go to their bed and they get up in the morning and they've got all their make-up on and their hair's sitting beautiful! How do they do it?!!" [Laughss] It was hard for them to believe all this. I mean, it was fantasy and they loved it!

Nanette McKee also recalled the magic of the cinema as a child in the 1950s:

> Our treat on a Saturday night was the pictures. When I was wee … Auchinleck. The Picture House … and my mother and I would get a bag o' chips … And ma father would get a pint o' beer… in MacLeod's. So, he would hurry on up. We would go in and get our chips and he would hurry on up and get his pint and by the time we'd got back, he had caught up wi' us!
> BG: Aye! And erm, was it two films or a single film you went to see?
> Oh! Two! *And* a cartoon and a Pathe News! And Currie's Lemonade at the shop! … and an ice lolly, aye! I think they bought me that just

to shut me up so they could get to watch the film! … They took me to *Gone with the Wind*! I did nae manage to sit through that though! Aye, *Gone with the Wind* had come oot at that time, too!
BG: Well, unless it was re-released 'cause it was originally done in 1939!
Ah well, b' the time it got to Auchinleck Picture Hoose that would be right!!
Och, there was cowboys. Cowboys and my Dad used to tell the story about, they would shout, "Come on, the guid yons, the bad yons are winning!!" [BG laughs] [*NM laughing*] … And in Auchinleck, the chucker-ooter was Alex Roach! And he was famous, Alex Roach! Aye, wi' his torch an'… He was the boss, right, aye! Aye, he would shine his torch on you if you made a noise or you talked or anything an' he used t' turn round (I remember it as well), he did it in ma Dad's day – "Shurrup! It's no' outside you're in!" [Both laugh] So, that's what Alex Roach was famous for!

Tam Hazel recalled a taboo being broken when the local Muirkirk cinema that he went to started opening on a Sunday:

It was one o' the first [pause] picture houses … t' show pictures on a Sunday! Sunday night. Some o' them come *oot* the chapel an' queued up tae get into the pictures! Mmhmm Ah ha. On a *Sunday*! … Oh, heavens! Heavens! Oh, *that* was during the war.

Tam Hazel also had a paper run as a young lad and recalled:

The main thing that people were looking fer that paper was [pause] Muirkirk had two Picture Houses so baith, baith programmes was in it, so they were waiting about t' see what was on at the pictures! We just said, it was nae the cin …, it was the pictures! An', um [pause], we, we got home tae Glenbuck wi' Rowe's bus because we would be, er, mebbe … eighteen o' us, you ken.

Felix Todd, born in 1917, recalled going from Crosshouse to Kilmarnock for the cinema as a young man in the late 1930s with his 'pocket money' after handing over his miners' wage packet to his mother:

Well, ah went and ah halked roond wi' ma friend, Big Rab Hood and me. Rab died a young man, tae, Rab. We went tae the pictures on a Seturday night. … In Kilmarnock. We went frae Crosshouse station tae Kilmarnock station, which wis 3d. a return. … We come out, and we went intae the café up at the station in Kilmarnock and got a fish supper, which wis fower pence. … The pictures wis 6d. … We were left wi' a shillin' for the Monday night, and we walked tae the pictures on a Monday night and back hame. Goes tae the pictures twice a week. … Different pictures. Oh, there was whit, there wis the George, the Imperial, the Palace, the Empire: there wis six or seeven picture hooses in Kilmarnock at that time.

Taking holidays anywhere away from home before the 1950s was rare – and holidays with pay only came after Second World War. Tom Wilson recalled never having a holiday as a youngster before the 1940s:

A holiday, I ah can put that intae perspective for you: ah remember when ah wis a wee boy, we used tae … we used tae try tae see the put ponies comin' up Chalmerston. We used tae see them. They got up for a week, and the miners were off for a week. But it wisnae paid, it wis jist a wee o' idle time for the miners. The put ponies wid benefit mair than the mend wide … But it wis … it wis difficult times and, ah mean, naebody thought aboot a holiday.

40: Dressed in their best! A 'Primrose Tours' charabanc' (early motor bus) outing in the Doon Valley, Fair Holidays, July 1928. Few miners' families could afford such luxury in the hard times of the Depression.
By kind permission of East Ayrshire Leisure Trust/East Ayrshire Council

In response to the question 'Did you ever, kind of, go anywhere as a family? … For a day out or a holiday?', Agnes Auld recalled 'No. Could nae afford to go onywhere'. Felix Todd, interviewed by Ian MacDougall in 2001, recalled of the 1930s:

> Ye maybe think, say the likes o' the Fair holidays, when everybody should have been happy, ma mother dreaded it because it wis idle time.
> *IM: Aye, exactly. Unpaid holidays?*
> Unpaid. It wis idle time, ah mean …
> *IM: I mean, I take it as a family you never got a holiday away from home?*
> Oh, no.
> *IM: You were never away from home as a laddie?*
> Never. Never.

Felix added that his mother got her first ever holiday (to relatives in Portsmouth) around 1947-8 when she was 70 years old!

41: A rare break? The completed bonfire on top of the Dunaskin slag heap to celebrate the coronation of George V in 1937.
By kind permission of East Ayrshire Leisure Trust/East Ayrshire Council

Others managed a holiday at the annual 'Fair' break in the 1930s. Every year, Jean Wilson from Benwhat went on a camping holiday with her family at Loch Doon. In an interview with researcher Yvonne McFadden and Jean's daughter, Ann Temple, Jean told us about her holidays:

> Aye we went up Loch Doon every year at the fair a lorry came and the year before that or since the last one we'd been saving up and we had two cupboards my father's made and they were in a cupboard like that and it was filled up for the year. So when this lorry came for our next holiday they cupboards were foo of stuff for our holidays. We had tilly lamps, we had fires primus stoves, we had everything and great big tents and our beds went the double bed and the single beds went in this lorry up to Lamdoughty.
> *YM: Lamdoughty?*
> Lamdoughty that's the wee farmhouse halfway up the loch and we got parked and the folk fae 2 doors up fae us, 3 doors up fae us they used to go tae we all went at the same time with these great big tents.

42: A school excursion 'doon the water', 1938. By kind permission of East Ayrshire Leisure Trust/East Ayrshire Council

YM: And how long would you stay there for?
A fortnight. Wur holidays just wur holidays hen but then the co-operative vans came up the vans would come up of course they would come up there to…there's farmhooses ken and the hooses at the top of the row they had to deliver up there anyway so they stopped at us in case they needed something so there you go. We could hire a boat for the day, we could hire a boat for the week […]
AT: What was on the floor of the tent?
Wooden floor, ken it had a wooden floor with 6 sections, 2,4,6, it would be the size of this room … Aye and then we had a wee tent for washing, washing and drying and toileting
YM: A wee separate tent?
A separate tent. Ye ken the toilet tent.
AT: I think that's what my mum means when she says she was spoiled.

Throughout her interview, Jean calls her family 'weel aff'. She attributes this to several factors: the fact that they only had two children compared to other families; her mother being a skilled household manager; and her dad making toys and other items from wood to supplement the family income. Her neighbours from the row also came with them on holiday for the two weeks, so they were not the only family to holiday like this.

Savings were difficult to accrue for many miners' families and few had the disposable income to afford longer trips away from home, except perhaps for the occasional trip to the local town (for the cinema and sometimes shopping), or exceptionally to the beach. Nanette McKee recalled a story of her experiences in the 1950s and 1960s:

Well, we could nae afford holidays either, erm, but ma Auntie Liz, my Dad's one and only sister … erm, she ran *bus* trips … at the miners' holiday which would only be a week. And there was, maybe, five different trips and you would choose what you could afford to go, maybe *one*? *Day* trips! Or you would maybe afford t' go *three*! But that was the miners' holiday. And it would be St. Mary's Loch or Loch Lomond or Girvan … Or, erm, the beach, erm, Croy beach! And they used to take primus stoves on the back o' Davy Liddell's bus! An' boil the kettles! [laughter] An' steal tatties out the field! An' gather whelks [Laughter] an' they all got fed! Whelks, tatties an' a cup o' tea!

When asked about holidays, Jean Burns, who grew up in Trabboch in the 1930s and 1940s, replied: 'No holidays!... Too expensive! No, there weren't!

No. No. Playing at the ... *burn* – that would be a holiday!'. Jean remembered the village daytrips to the seaside:

> Yeah, that was on, the Glasgow Fair was when, er, men got their holidays and we'd, we would have a day out. That would be *it*!! You know?! That would be a real treat! [pause] Getting *one* day out! At the beach. Edzell *that* was popular and there was, erm, a, a, a *bus* in the village. Er, Holdin's buses and he would hire a bus. Somebody would organise the, a trip to Croy Shore. And we did at Maybole and we would all get in and go to Croy Shore.

Sheila Crosswaite's mother was sent to the 'Hill to stay with her father's family for her holidays. Her mother died when she was only ten and her father was in service:

> My mother said we all went to Granny Anderson's for holidays and there was a whole rake of them because there was the children of

43: Enjoying Ayr beach. By kind permission of East Ayrshire Leisure Trust/East Ayrshire Council

these sisters and there was a whole batch of them, all round about, I used to think it sounded like Enid Blyton, my mother used to say because Jim Wiley and Jim McKean were both, and my mother, were all born within, oh months of each other and they all had a younger brother or sister who were not much younger so there was a whole gang of them and they just used to run around Lethanhill up the moor during the school holiday time because my mother, my mother's mother, as I said was sickly and eventually died when my mother was 10; I never knew her obviously.

Women then were also involved in a range of 'public' activities, albeit in more sporadic and episodic ways than men in the mining communities. Alice Wallace recalled:

Aye … they made their own entertainment. I mean, they had concerts, they had whist an' they had … everything under the sun you could think of! I mean, when it was Halloween there was a party. When it was Ne'er Day [means New Year] there were parties, Christmas it was parties.

She told another story involving her Mum:

They would let out the sports ground. Aye, and Hunter sports, that was an annual event and it was held between Benwhat and Dalmellington alternate years and the man Hunter, who organised these, was the local bookie and he financed everything an' he paid for everything that happened that day. Refreshments for everybody as well an' all the prizes and he was just a kind-hearted man that gave them a treat once a year.

There was races for all age groups – children and adults – and, er, a lot of the funny races, you know, where you're three-legged, sack races, paper hat on your head, paper plate, sorry, on your head, egg and spoon, they had all these things. And, er, they had a women's race, like, you know, for the married women and one for the men, the older ones as well. And ma Mum, she was good at running an' Jeanie [chuckles], she did nae have sand shoes or anything to wear on her feet. Now, I don't know if you know what sand shoes are. We called them gutties. Aye … She had t' go to a friend, a man, a friend o' hers an' say, "Gie me a wee lend o' your gutties till I run in this race!" [laughs] And she won it! And her prize was a teapot and she loved it! And you were honoured t' get a cup o' tea out of her prized teapot. That gave them all a good laugh, things like that. And she said once that she had knitted a swimsuit. Er, she had got a pattern an' she had knitted this swimsuit and it's the usual thing, if they're knitted an' they're wet, they're dragging down! [laughing] So, she never ever wore it again when she realised that!

Alice's testimony confirms that there were some exceptions to women's exclusion from public life, and a range of experiences among women. Indeed, it should also be noted that were less restrictions on young women compared to married women with families. Nonetheless, up until the 1940s, women's leisure was mostly family-centred, and enjoyed in private spaces like the home, and largely episodic compared to men's participation in similar activities. As mentioned above, holidays with pay only came after Second World War, and transgressions into sport were relatively rare for women before the post-war period.

CHANGED DAYS: LEISURE PATTERNS IN THE 'NEW' AYRSHIRE COMMUNITIES
In the second half of the twentieth century, and notably from the 1970s on, patterns of leisure and recreation in Ayrshire mining communities changed, with women increasingly able to access a wider range of activities as gender inequalities were challenged and boundaries transgressed.

Agnes (Nan) Auld married and moved to live in the miners' rows at Pennyvenie. She reflected that lives were getting 'better' for women in the 1950s, when they were allowed access to the Institute:

> It was good 'cause we'd plenty to talk aboot an' then we had the Institute at the bottom of the row. Er … which were, like, women's groups. Er … an' they played whist some nichts. It was quite good … Oh, it was a good life in Pennyvenie. Er, we used t' have some good laughs. Did nae do an awfu' lot. We went into Dalmellington an' maybe to the pictures once a week or something like that. We went in to do anything we wanted, fer our shoppin'.

Alice Wallace recalled babysitting her younger brother allowing her Mum to go out on a Friday night to the Bingo in Dalmellington and how the family started to go on 'real' holidays:

> I don't know whether this had even happened previously – but the men went into a holiday pay scheme and a pound a week was deducted from their wage, er t' give them fifty pounds for their two-weeks holiday of the year. An' if we didn't go a holiday, it was used for

something maybe kinda big for the house. That's actually what paid for the television set when we got it and it paid for a washing machine for my Mum and things like that. So, if we didn't get something new for the house, it was a holiday and, er, it was usually caravan holidays at first to Ayrshire resorts. Never far away. Then they went a holiday to Morecombe Bay Holiday Camp. Now, that's just over the border in England and this was me going to a different country and this was going to be great! It was something to talk about wi' yer pals because some o' them had been abroad, so this was me! And, er, mind you, it was a lovely holiday, we all enjoyed it. It was entirely different from what we'd had before because you were going into a dining room to get meals all made for yer. My Mum did nae have t' cook them in a caravan, you see? An' there were events and prizes and things like that. We loved it. Aye, that was good! But mainly, it was caravan holidays or a chalet. Wee chalet holidays down at the shore. Things like that. Nothing very extravagant but good. We enjoyed it.

44: 'Doon the Water':
Advertising boat trips, which
became popular from the 1950s.
By kind permission of East
Ayrshire Leisure Trust/East
Ayrshire Council

45: The Waverley steam ship.
By kind permission of East Ayrshire Leisure Trust/East Ayrshire Council

Families being able to buy their own cars (usually on hire purchase) in the 1950s and 1960s facilitated these shifting leisure patterns, liberating families and enabling day trips and holidays further afield. Women taking paid employment and bringing in an extra wage was increasing and this could make a difference to family disposable income. Nanette McKee recalls the family's first car:

> My mother [a midwife] started working and then we became wealthy!! Aye, we were in another league then!! She was earning more than a miner! So, we were the first folk in the street to have a car! An Austin A30 … first television in the street as well! 'Cause my mother was earning good money!

At the same time, pioneers were challenging male monopoly over recreation, such as Margaret Wilson in banding and Rose Reilly in football. Despite becoming Ayrshire's (and Scotland's) most celebrated and successful football player, Rose Reilly, was forced to leave the country to develop her career in France due to a lack of opportunities for women in the sport. Most notably, Rose excelled in Italy in the 1970s and 1980s, where she played for the Italian world cup winning team. Margot McCuaig's wonderful documentary for BBC Alba tracks Rose's story.[3] Latterly her achievements have been recognised, with Rose having a sports centre in her home of Stewarton named after her and being inducted, albeit belatedly, into the Scottish Hall of Fame at Hampden in 2007.

Concurrently men's lives were becoming more home and family-

---

3 See Margot McCuaig (Dir.), *Rose Reilly* (documentary for BBC Alba, 2019).

centred, aided by larger homes, smaller families, TV, home Do-It-Yourself and changes in male identities associated with the idea of the 'new man' and a less 'macho' image and identity. As a result, the gender gap that existed in recreation and leisure had significantly eroded by the end of the twentieth century.

46: Woman shown working a hand-cranked wash drying mangle.
By kind permission of East Ayrshire Leisure Trust/East Ayrshire Council

3
WORKING LIVES: THE WOMEN

In the first half of the twentieth century, the prosperity of the mining family was dependent upon the miner's work. While the comfort and wellbeing of the family firmly rested upon the shoulders of the women. The mining communities reflected wider society in Scotland at this time with experiences of home and work divided along the lines of gender. While husbands, brothers, uncles and sons toiled in the pit, wives, mothers, aunties and sisters took on the burden of work within the home. As we have previously seen, the housing conditions within the miners' rows required a great deal of hard physical work and creative housekeeping to look after the family. Women have always worked. However, in contrast to men's work, this work is not always valued in traditional sources or within a capitalist economy. Equally, unlike men's work, women's labour and reproductive work remains largely unrecorded unless we ask women and their families what they did. As a result, oral testimony is a key method for uncovering the 'hidden' work of women. As the twentieth century progressed, the entry of women, particularly married women, into the labour market marked social and economic changes in gender equality, the family and standards of living. In this chapter, we will look at women's work within the mining communities from girlhood to widowhood, charting changes in women's lives.

WOMEN'S PAID WORK IN THE EARLY TWENTIETH CENTURY

Earlier in the century, female workers in paid employment were mostly younger single women. As the century progressed, increasingly married women re-entered the workforce once their children were older. In rural communities, such as the mining communities, young women and girls had limited choices for work, the two most common being either farm work or domestic service. Harry Kennedy, born in 1932, remembered his mother telling him about working on a farm before she married. He recalled: 'I think she milked the cows. I, I mind her telling aboot that somebody flinging a dog or something onto the back o' the cow when she was milk, when she was milking it! She just did general work, ken, and that on the farm.' His mother also worked in a 'big house' nearby. Domestic service was the most common option for young rural girls. The perception that domestic servants declined between the wars is not supported in the census data for Scotland. After an initial drop after the First World War, by the 1931 Census the number of domestic servants had increased.

Entering domestic service often meant leaving the family home around fourteen years of age. Hugh Hainey, who was born in Lethanhill in 1921, remembers all his sisters leaving their home to work in domestic service, often one, if not all, came home to the villages on Sundays. In 1939-40, he recalled where two of his sisters worked: 'Peg was cook to the family of the JA Coats of Paisley thread mills. Anne was a servant to the family of Flight Lieutenant McIntyre of Everest fame, being pilot of the first plane to fly over Everest.' Similarly, Sheila Crosswaite's grandmother who later lived in Lethanhill, was a lady's maid and her grandfather a footman. They met in service at Coodham House, owned by the Houldsworth family who owned the mines around Lethanhill. Tom Wilson's oldest sister Jean was given an exemption from the Benwhat school to leave at thirteen and enter domestic service to supplement the family income. Tom was one of nine children; here he remembers Jean and one of his other sisters, Ag, who had joined her in domestic service, coming home due to the outbreak of war:

> Ag and Jean were up tae Glasgow, up at Whitecraigs in Glasgow, in private service there. This is one of the things about it, and that wis – remember the war started in September 1939. And both these sisters were in Glasgow at Whitecraigs workin' tae a big house, a lawyer, and they were very good tae us. But then the war started. Ma mother brought them both home immediately. Ah think ma mother thought the Dorniers would be over bombing Glasgow the next morning.
>
> So they were brought home, and what a shock to their system. Brought home - by this time we lived in Dalmellington, of course - and brought home and seeking local employment. Where did they go? A brickwork! Both of them.

Tom is referring to his sisters' 'shock' of returning to a social housing scheme after having lived in a middle-class modern suburban housing. Mary (May) Baird reminded her mum and aunt that her gran, who lived in Glenbuck, worked cleaning houses. Her aunt Ella Reynolds then picked up the story:

> An' it was nae a different house she went. She went t' the same house fer a long period of time an' they got t' know … the, the family an'

all the rest o' it. An' they relied on her! She could be trusted! An' that went a long way! Er, an' she did their cleaning for them. Cleaned their houses an' all the rest o' it! That was the only help she got, was out working. To bring a wee bit extra money.

Barbara Alexander lived in Glenbuck and her mum was one of the Shankly family of five boys and two girls, with her uncle, her mum's brother rising to fame as Liverpool manager William (Bill) Shankly. Before marrying and having Barbara in the 1940s, Mrs Alexander worked in service in Cambuslang, Glasgow. In Lugar, one woman remembered that her mother looked after the children of a doctor in Auchinleck and cooked for the family.

Some young women of the villages had some opportunities for work other than domestic service by the interwar period. Alice Wallace's mum Sadie Douglas, born in 1920, was an 'in-between' housemaid when she left school at fourteen and then once she was old enough worked in a hospital as an assistant nurse. Barbara Alexander's aunt Belle worked at the picture house (cinema) at Muirkirk as an usherette and later as a librarian. Barbara emphasised that her aunt 'had to work all her life' due to her husband being held as a Prisoner of War by the Japanese, before dying at

*47: Female workers employed at the Smith's box factory in Mauchline, c. 1900
(with a few men looking on in the background).
By kind permission of East Ayrshire Leisure Trust/East Ayrshire Council*

the age of fifty. John Neil's mother born in Lethanhill worked in a restaurant in Ayr, where she met his father.

Jean Wilson lived in Benwhat and left school at twelve in 1944. She started work as an apprentice dressmaker in Ayr until she around sixteen years old. A bout of appendicitis changed the course of her working life. After experiencing her own ignorance about her body and being exposed to the hospital environment she decided to train as a nurse:

> When I was 16, I realised I was stupid went into the hospital for an appendicectomy and I was asked if I was a virgin and I said no. I thought a virgin was a nun and I kent it wasnae a nun but I didnae ken the difference and I heard them laughing and I went into the duty room and because it was an emergency I was in the bed next to the duty room I could hear them all laughing. What are they all laughing at. I was lying there in mortal agony but I then realised that well because of that answer I got a laparotomy I didn't get an appendicectomy I got a laparotomy and what's the difference.

She continued:

> And then I says you will go and do your training and learn what everything is aboot we didn't even ken the difference between a bloody boy and a lassie. We were 2 lassies and I think we were sheltered we must have been.

The Second World War expanded women's opportunities, like nursing, and unlike the First World War the number of women in the workforce did not dramatically drop after the war ended.

Like their brothers, in working families girls and young women were expected to contribute to the household, as we saw in the case of Tom Wilson's older sister leaving school early. In the 1950s, Alice Wallace, encouraged by one of her teachers, hoped to go to further education doing art at college:

> Aye, well, I was good at art at the school an' I won the art prize for the school every year that I was in the Higher grade, that's like three years. And the art teacher was Mr Brown an' I thought he was wonderful an' he gave credit where it was due an' he said to me, "Alice, you've got a talent there an' it should nae go to waste! You should go to, talk to Mum and Dad about going to College. You could go to Jordanhill College. You could be an art teacher or you could learn

fashion design, there are loads of different varieties of stuff you could do!" An' I said, Do you think I could actually do it? He said, "You could do it no bother! Now, talk to them about it and I'll ask you tomorrow." So, I went home and I said to them, we were all sitting at the fire at night, Mr Brown said to me … an' I came out about this, er, "You'll do nothing of the kind! You'll leave the school at fifteen and hand in a pay, the same as the rest, that's it! No more talk about it! That's it, finished!!" The decision was made, you see?! And I went to my room an' I cried an' I cried an' I was in a bit o' a state er, but I had to accept, I had to accept it! And, er, that was it, end o' story. So, you were still having to do as you were told […] I got a job in a shop and after that, I got a job in a factory sewing garments. I quite liked it, mind you, I did it for quite a few years. And that's about it, after that I was married.

'THEIR LIFE WAS A TRUDGE': DOMESTIC WORK

Until the mid-twentieth century, most women left paid work upon marriage. The combination of formal and informal policies around married women working, a lack of formal childcare and the reproductive and domestic labour of family life made remaining in the workforce difficult. The living conditions in the miners' rows created physically taxing work for women. The continual labour of maintaining the family water supply from the spoot alone meant multiple trips from morning to night for washing, drinking, cooking and cleaning. A common thread in stories about the rows was how hard women's lives were living in these conditions. Here an ex-miner James Whiteford born in 1938 observes:

> The man was the head o' the family an' the wife, ma granny fer instance, who came from Lanarkshire, a mining place, an', er, they'd no life whatsoever! All they had, ma memories, were all they had was – cooking; washing … dirty pit clothes; drying them round the fire an' the place was steamin', of course, because they came hame very wet sometimes; an' having kids! An' that's, that's ma assumption. In fact, ma gran came through and that's the sort o', it sort of carries on t', t' my parents. Especially ma mother! No' ma dad.

The patriarchal family was the dominant model at this time with rigid gendered divisions of labour. Similarly, Agnes Auld, known as Nan who was a child in Lethanhill describes her mother's generation: 'Their life was a trudge. 'Cause it was the, trying to keep the house clean wi' the coal fires an' trying t' keep a washing goin' an' make food – their life was really nothing.' Later, in 1956, Nan moved to a row in Low Pennyvenie as a young newlywed after having lived in a new house in Dalmellington for a couple of years. This row had more 'modern' conveniences than the 'Hill. It had internal cold water, an outside flushing toilet and electricity supply (though this was unreliable). While it had its challenges, Nan reflected fondly on this time as being hard but enjoyable due to the shared comradery with the women around her:

> An' the majority that were in it were all young an' married. [...] Two, three o' ma family there. Er … an', like, we were all on the same, kind a, parr, do you know what I mean? There were nae any of us that well off. Just, well, existing, put it that way, wi' the wages we were getting, we were all existing. But never mind. It was good! It was, er, mair friendly. [pause] Made some nice friends there […]
> *YM: So, what was that like then, like, with all the women, an', like, what was that like having a lot o' young women in the same area?*
> It was good 'cause we'd plenty to talk aboot .

The contrast between her life with running water, electricity and a twin tub with her mother's on the 'Hill highlights the difference that housing conditions can make to quality of life. The women who lived and worked in the miners' rows in the 1920s and 1930s are no longer able to speak for themselves; we are reliant on others looking at their lives and reflecting on what they saw.

Alice Wallace was a young girl growing up in Benwhat born in 1945, she was only five when the family moved to Bellsbank, Dalmellington in 1951. Her recollections are a combination of her own memories and that of her mother. They allow us to access stories of women's lives in the mining villages from the perspective of Alice's mother's generation, as well as Alice's childhood memories. The oral tradition of storytelling was continued as time went on. Alice Wallace reflected poignantly on the importance of memory transference across the generations in keeping alive the traditions and stories from mining communities. She told interviewer Yvonne McFadden:

> I used to get my Mum and Ethel and take them up to Jeanie's [her Mum's friend] because she was, kinda, housebound. She was in a house wi' a lot o' stairs going up an' she could nae manage these stairs. So, we went up there and I made pancakes – that I carry on these old traditions, I'm telling you. And I took them up for the tea an' the lassie that lives next door come in, made the tea, buttered

the pancakes an' that and we had the wee plan, that they would sit an' talk about everything, everything that they did! An' that's how, I do remember an awful lot meself, Yvonne but they've refreshed my memories and added more an' that's how I know and remember as much about Benwhat. Because we used to sit, I mean that was every Wednesday and that would go on for many, many months before they died and it was great entertainment! An' the lassie when she made the tea, she would sit and laugh, we were all sitting, laughing and … it was great! Just enjoyed the company. And some o' the things that they did, I could nae actually repeat and they would nae want me to, but we sat and talked about it, and laughed all the time! Aye, it was good. They were quite daring in their own way. Aye.

Women's lives in the miners' rows may have been prescribed, hemmed in by patriarchal attitudes and restrictions. However, Alice's testimony (and other voices) speaks to the ways in which women in Ayrshire made the best of this and pushed back against societal constraints and conventions, transgressing norms – 'quite daring in their own way' – enjoying life and affecting change. Storytelling was a tradition that was embedded in the community, for the men and the women. It was something that Alice Wallace cherished. She became a living repository for the memory of Benwhat – for the intangible heritage of the miners' rows and mining communities. Alice and other narrators were living witnesses to how children and adult men and women in mining communities spent their working days and their leisure time in the miners' rows and the 'modern' communities that followed.

Margaret Sim, who grew up in Lethanhill between 1924 and 1950, commented on the miners' wives work between the wars and identifies the war as a significant watershed:

Oh yes. The Second World War, as far as the women in the 'Hill were concerned, almost became, um, I don't know what, how would I describe it? Up until then, all that they did was raise children and wash pit clothes, as far as I could see, because, of course, they were all miners. And they didn't have baths and things. They came home black um, there was no, there was no bathing facilities and they had a, they had a wooden tub. So, the water was carried from the tap, it was put into a big, um, quite often there were these great big pans, you know, and they were put over the coal fire. Now, we were never short of coal! Because we got cheap coal, there was never any problems with that. But then they had to heat the water and it was, I mean, these women hadn't time to do anything else because

48: Women doing their washing in Lethanhill, Mrs Allan, Jeanie Henderson and Mrs Kelly with children Margaret, Tom and David Allan, undated Courtesy of Cox family.

they were either carrying water, heating water or washing them, you know! And cooking and cleaning!

It was not only wives who did the work but also other women living within the home. Sheila Crosswaite's mother told Sheila that her Aunt Meg did the housework in the Anderson house in Lethanhill:

> I remember her telling me that she, well as I say she was the one that was doing all the washing and the ironing, because my mother, and cooking and everything. My mother said Granny Anderson sat in her chair, she was very erect, so in her chair and she had lovely long

hair and she said, we used to brush and comb her hair, you know, and things like that. And she said, when I think about it, she would sit there shelling peas and that Aunt Meg was diving around, you know, making soup, checking everybody and doing all the washing and everything.

Margaret Sim commented in her taped interview in 1998 with her daughter, that there were unmarried women in the village and suggested this was because they were looking after the family.

Female interviewees were still quite young when they lived in the miners' rows, and few remembered having specific duties in the house. Jean Burns, born in 1936, lived in the Trabboch rows for thirteen years before moving to Drongan. When asked by interviewer Rosanna Brown about work within the house she replied:

> [Exclaims] Ahhh! [Both laugh] My goodness!! *Everything!!*
> Everything! Because my mother was nae a *bairn* person so, but also,
> as I said, she was a very Victorian woman and she thought *children*
> should be seen and not heard! So, I could say, I was pretty scared
> of her. But I had to do what I was told and that was whatever she
> wanted done, and I would have to do it. Erm, [pause] like … go for
> the paraffin. Go for the paraffin. Go to the shop. Er, that was it.
> *RB: Did you have to do house, like, a lot of housework as well, yeah?*
> Aye. Ah. Hmm. Yeah, I did it. And more so when I got past, er …
> thirteen but that all happened slowly. But I had to do what she told
> me! Very much, you know. Anyway, that was it.

Jean equates this to her mum's strict nature but acknowledges that it was not until she grew older her work around the house increased. John Neil's mother Margaret McBride was born in 1927 in the village of Lethanhill and helped her mother with the washing. An accident with the mangle, resulting in the loss of the top of her finger when it became trapped.

When asked about household chores, Alice Wallace, born in 1945 in Benwhat, reflected on the gendered nature of domestic labour. As Alice grew older she was given more work around the house, while her brothers did mostly outdoor tasks:

> Not when you're wee but as I grew up, I got a lot o' domestic work
> to do. Now, the boys didnae have to do it because that wisnae men's
> work, it was women's work! An' my mother did all the housework, all
> the cooking, all the looking after children, the men didnae do that,

they went t' the pit. They worked hard at the pit. They earned their pay and that was them, they'd done their bit. Er, so when I grew up a bit, we had moved to Bellsbank and then down to Dalmellington, to a bigger house, an' it was my job at the weekends to clean all the way upstairs. There was three bedrooms and a bathroom upstairs and my mother never touched them, it was me, I had t' do that, that was my job. Do all the bedrooms upstairs. I did the dinner dishes every day and, er, I did all the ironing for the family. And that was a lot because there was, like, four boys, my Mum and Dad and me! No, three boys, sorry, four o' us altogether. Aye.

YM: And did the boys not have to do anything?

AW: They were boys! Oh, well, they did actually, they would split the sticks. You know, it was coal fires at that time and they would get wood that they would chop into sticks for starting the fire so they would chop the fire sticks up and fill the coal pails and that was about it. Maybe help in the garden a bit. But no housework, no! [pause] [laughs] That was terrible, eh!

KEEPING CLEAN IN A MINERS' ROW

Pithead baths were not commonplace in the mines until the late 1930s. Jean Burns was born in the Trabboch rows in 1936 and remembered when the men came back from their shifts:

> And they didn't have a *bath* at the pit. They came home on the train and they had to walk a mile down the road t' get home and everybody was *filthy*. Filthy! I went to meet my dad on the, and I was quite *shocked* because I thought, 'all these folk look the *same*!' [chuckles] I didn't recognise him! Er, but he was there. But that, the next day was, come home, wash and dinner was, was sometimes soup, meat, something.

Around the villages of Lethanhill and Burnfoothill (also known as the 'Hill) the first pithead baths opened at Pennyvenie mine in 1936 followed by the nearby Houldsworth pit in 1939. Many of the 'Hill men would have toiled in these pits and taken advantage of the new facilities.[1] Before this luxury, women had the labour of getting the hot water ready for the miners return. When asked about his mother, Alex Kirk from the Hill reflected the work involved in keeping his dad and brothers clean:

---

1 McQuillan, *The 'Hill*, p.44.

> Well she was, er, as I said t' yer earlier on, there was no baths at the pit at that time. At Houldsworth pit. An' ma Dad an' them, they were coming home from the pit an' [rustling in the background] they were in their working clothes an' all the rest o' it. There was nae where, where they could keep them at the pit so it was a case of, when they came in, they came home, my Mum had to wash all their working clothes an' that, for the next day again! 'Cause they were covered in muck an' God knows, coal dust and God knows what all! [pause] And she done all the cooking.

While Alex's family worked the same shift at the pit, some women had to manage multiple shift ends to ensure the men had hot water and hot meal at various times throughout the day. In Lugar the men washed in the washhouses before coming into the house. Here David Murray, born in 1930 and the son of baker living in Lugar, remembered the men coming off their shifts:

> Then the miners at that time, the miners did not have pithead baths. So they come home dirty and whoever day it was for washing, the washing was always finished for the time the miners were going home. So the last thing she does is fill up the boiler up again with water and get the fire going so that there was a boiler for hot water for the miners going home [laughs]. So the miners washed themselves in the washhouses after the washings had been done. It worked okay.

Reflecting on the gendered nature of life in the mining villages, Jean Burns related this directly to the pithead baths with some strong language on women's work:

> Sometimes in my lifetime, five boys coming in from the pit – *Dirty! Filthy!* And having to *work* and the woman of the house might have been a bloomin' slave You know?! *That's* the bit I don't *like!* Yes. No, some of my friends had big brothers, the likes of Anna, she had brothers, and she was from about *nine* children! And *all* them and there was no *bath* facilities!! And *that* was in *my* memory!! And when they got baths at the pits, life was so easier erm, for the *women!* You know? The men came back and come home *clean!*

The miners' rows generally had no internal running water. The job of collecting the water from the 'spoot' or pump was a constant daily task for women. Here Alice Wallace describes the labour of fetching and emptying water:

> Aye, well, my mother would bring water in. You see, down at the end of the rows, that's where the water was and it wasn't even a tap that you turned on, it was a pump! An' the women had to get their pails, two at a time, right, up there, pump the water into the pails and carry them back up to the house, two at a time, and back down with another two so it took them a while to stock up the water for the needs for the day! I mean, they'd have to go back down later and get some more fresh water but this water was fed from the hillside. It was, sort a, routed down wi' a pipe to this pump, and the women had to pump it there to get the water. So, it was only cold water, carried up to the house and that's where they had t' use this stone sink. So, they would heat the water up for getting washed an' doing their dishes and things like that. But when they were … by with the water, they could nae pull out a plug and let it run away, there was no plumbing! They had t' bail this water back into a pail and back out the back door an' there was a, a trough that went down. It was made of bricks, I can remember that. Er, and you threw your dirty water into that an' the rainwater flushed it away so, that's what happened to your dirty water. Aye.

The 1943 film 'Mining Village' captures a day in the Ayrshire mining village of Mossblown. It provides a unique snapshot of village life and focusses on the lives of the women as well as the men. A woman is shown carrying two pails at a time to collect the water, as Alice describes above. The 'trough' in the road, also referred to as 'syver', is shown being maintained by the women. Later, we see a woman washing her pots outside over the trough to drain the water away.[2]

DOING THE WASHING

Inside the washhouse, the equipment was standard for that time. In Lugar, the building had the dry toilet and the 'scullery', and the equipment in addition to the boiler was two sinks. David Murray described how they were used:

> Aye, but the scullery had two big sinks, ah well, a big deep sink and the shallow sink. The big deep sink was for doing your washing in. So that the brick row had wash houses and you'd get your day. You'd

---

2 'Mossblown: Hard Times', 1943, Paul Johnson, Production Group, an Ayrshire Educational Film. Accessed at: https://youtu.be/0iBP4LhNWiE.

a get a certain day every week and wash.

Sometimes, if the miner was on an early shift, he would light the washhouse boiler on his way out for his wife. Alice Wallace talked about her mother's difficulty getting the fire lit for wash day:

> Aye, the whole row had maybe about, say, four washhouses to service them. Spaced out. Aye. Do you know the easiest way to kindle a fire underneath? My Mum would go into the house an' come out wi' a shovel of hot coals from the fire an' take it out the back and put it in there and that started it off. It was the quickest way o' doing it. So, they had a lot of hard work to do. Aye, it was heavy, because they had to build it up a bit and keep it going until the water was all warm enough and then scooping it back out – that must have been hard as well!

Isabel Hendry remembered doing the washing and balancing her caring responsibilities in the wash house at Highhouse Rows in Auchinleck as a 'nightmare':

> This … washhouse … oor May was just a baby! Aye, you were just a baby at the time! An', er [pause], you'd tae kennle the fire underneath an' t' water on the top. [pause] It was a nightmare t' … I did nae ken how, how I was gonna dae it, but I managed it!! [chuckling] But, eh, no, it was, it was a nightmare. [pause] An' then you hed tae empty it oot fer the next body! You hed a' your ain, your own turn.

From these descriptions, the word 'hard' is used frequently. Women in the mining communities were the first up to feed the early shift miners and school children, then the last to bed between feeding babies and late shift miners. Their work revolved around the rhythms of the reproductive labour and industry.

The problems of living alongside a working mine for women's work were apparent. The tracks for the pug, the train that transported the coal, could be next to gardens of the houses. James Whiteford who grew up in Connel Park, described how near they were to pithead:

> An' when I stayed in the Rows. Every Row, every Row in Connel Park had a nickname. Oors was the 'Washa' Row. 'Washa' Row 'cause we were just o'er the fence frae the, the pit washer that washed the coal! There was nae distance! [pause] When the train come up wi'

the empties, t' fill the coal … yer mother hed t' take the washing in! You'd t' time it t' take the washin' in! 'Cause o' the steam an' the dirt an' the filth that's going on, ken! That's how near we were t' that [pause], t' that, er, that, eh, pithead. Very close t' it!

When Nan Auld moved from the family's new council house to her marital home in the rows next to Pennyvenie mine, she encountered the same problem. Though at this point she had a twin tub washing machine, here we see the competing needs of domestic work versus industrial work:

> We'd put the washing oot on the line, all right doon the row. Lovely, white nappies, right doon the row. An' then the tug would come along the Waterside, do you ken what the tug is?
> It was a shuttle train.
> An' it would come along the line an' stop just at the back o' the pit an' I don't know what the hell it blew but they blew something an' w'or washin' was all spotted wi' soot!
> So, we'd t' tak it all in an' wash it again! We kicked up hell about that but it did nae work! Naebody listened. So, we'd just t' keep going. Bring, put the worst o' them in, back into the washin'. [chuckles] Shouted our faces off fer weeks but nah, naebody listened!

The women felt ignored in this case and the fact they had to repeat their work deemed unimportant as Nan put it: 'naebody listened'. Alice Wallace described the work involved cleaning the heavy blankets from the bed. It reveals the challenges of washing with no spare bedding and the Scottish weather:

> An' you were depending on good weather to get your washing dried. An' the likes o' the blankets, they were really only washed maybe once a year! I mean, they must hae been really pretty bad! But they were heavy, big, thick, woollen blankets. They talked about the Skeldon blankets. Now, Skeldon is maybe about, er, eight, ten miles down the road from here an' they had a blanket factory and they were great blankets, you see, an' everybody had Skeldon blankets. An', but they were heavy when they were wet an' they had t' ease them up out of this an' this big, mangle thing that was sitting outside, they had t' turn the handle. I don't know whether you've seen the kind of thing that is?
> Aye. So, they had to work two together at a time because it was so heavy an' then you'd carry all these up to the rope to peg them out.

But they had to wait for a good day to do their blankets an' the reason for that was, they didnae have any spares! They needed them washed and dried and back on the beds the same day. Aye.

YM: That must be hard in the Scottish weather.

I know. They had to watch for a good day to get them done. An' of course the women are all wanting to use the boiler and the big mangle an' all that at the same time! But they can work it out.

YM: Do you know how many women shared the boiler, like the washhouse?

At least two at a time, aye, they worked in pairs. Er, Jeanie, my mother's next-door neighbour and her best friend, worked with her and they did all these things together. See some of the other blankets that they had, Yvonne, er, they had these patchwork blankets and it was like an old, thin blanket that was nae much good anymore and they sewed all these patches onto it. Now these patches of fabric could be from old pyjamas, shirts, pinnys, dresses, anything at all! Any kind of fabric! If it was quite good and serviceable, that was cut up and stitched on. Some bits were big and some wee and they stitched these on. A lot o' them had sewing machines, my Mum always had one and that was the easiest way to run them through. But it was still a lot of work, you can imagine, I mean, stitching all these things onto a blanket. And then, they did the other side as well!

49: Women doing the washing at the river possibly Dalmellington, undated. By kind permission of East Ayrshire Leisure Trust/East Ayrshire Council

So, that was a heavy blanket! But it was quite good as a, sort of, over-blanket. Heavy.

The sharing of this large task of washing the blankets supports other testimonies that the mining communities 'helped each other out'.

Women were not only in charge of the cleaning of clothing but also some made the clothes for the family. Hugh Hainey describes the clothes he wore when starting school in Lethanhill:

Going to the village school for the first time I was accompanied by my sister Williamina (Minnie) and my brother James. I was attired just like him, a close-cropped haircut with a front fringe, faces scrubbed and dressed with a hand knitted woollen garment as pants and vests rejoicing in the name of combinations, over this was a woollen jersey with a fancy shirt type collar to permit us to wear a tie. My mother knitted all my underwear as well as making my trousers from old coats and lining these with the material from bleached cotton flour bags. She also knitted all our stockings as we always wore short trousers the woollen stockings fitted to below the knee with a patterned turn over at the top and held up with garter elastic, leather boots complete with steel toe plate and heel shods and three rows of steel tacks. This form of dress was common in most

50: Lethanhill School class, 1916.
Courtesy of Cox family

mining villages.

Alice Wallace's mother made much of the fabric for the house. Here she describes the women making rag rugs:

> I know they were stone floors and they didn't have carpets unless they made them theirselves, they made rag rugs and this was from faded jumpers and things. And, er, well, aye, the style. They would cut them into strips and they would make rag rugs from these and the backing for this rag rug was like a, say, a tattie bag. Any old sacks. They were washed and dried and that's what they used for the backing. And the women would sit at night, at the fire, if they wurnae mending or doing something else, they were making rag rugs and they had a, kind of, gadget fer pushing and pulling this wool stuff through, all these big strips. So, they were quite colourful and some o' them made really nice designs and things like that. Er, so, they never really wasted anything. Any old clothes were used up one way or another. If they were just too done to wear and could nae be mended, they were cut up for rag rugs. But that's what the floors were. I mean, it was a hard stone floor. I think they were kind of flagstones and the women swept them and scrubbed them and put their rag rugs back down.
>
> YM: *So, you were saying that your Mum would sit in the evening, would she, what kind of things would she be doing? Would she be relaxing or…?*
>
> AW: No! [laughs] Er … things at night, she would be knitting. She would be sewing. She would be making rag rugs. She'd be preparing things for the next day. She was always busy, always very busy and that used to annoy me sometimes because…my mind was full o' questions! I had a great imagination and I was always wanting to ask things. And she kept saying, "Where do you get all this frae? See all these questions, away and play!!! I'm too busy!!" [laughs] So, she hudnae much time for sittin' playing wi' us. Unless the weather was wet and we were really, it was really bad and we were stuck inside. Er, she was quite good at sitting drawing wi' us an' we all became quite artistic! We've all been fairly good at drawing and painting as the years went by.

Alice's story reflects the constant nature of housework and its impact on women's leisure time (as we discussed in the previous chapter). Around the mid-twentieth century, access to new housing and a home-centred culture in Britain saw the emergence of new domestic roles for men, particularly the

121

rise of the Do-It-Yourself movement. This meant that men were expected to do more tasks around the house. However, unlike the relentless nature of women's work, these jobs were often one-off projects or outside chores, like taking the rubbish out. It was not uncommon for women to spend their evening knitting, sewing, or ironing while listening to the radio or later watching television.

WOMEN'S WORKING LIVES AFTER 1945

The miner's wage fluctuated depending on the prosperity of the industry. The testimonies suggest that money was usually tight in the villages. Informal economies helped boost the family income. Women sometimes operated a shop from their house. In Benwhat, Tom Wilson recalls Mrs Jean Dick's store:

> Well, the village... there were nae shops as such as we know. But auld Jean Dick, I describe her affectionately as auld Jean Dick, when you're a wee boy, auld Jean Dick had in her house, she'd a wee annexe and there wis a postbox outside her door oot on the raw, and she'd this wee annexe and she'd a wee sweetie shop and she did the post office part, ye know, that sort o' thing.

Mrs Dick in Benwhat was related to a Mrs Johnstone, a widow, who sold jam and eggs from her home in Commondyke. David Murray, born in Lugar in 1930, recalled Miss Kelly having a sweet shop:

> There were a lady down the Brick Row. Away down here in the Brick Row, Mrs Kelly, Miss Kelly. She ran a wee shop from her kitchen [laughs]. She had her table across the door as you go in. You just went to the door and table was there and she sold sweets.

David continued describing Mrs Mearns who ran the chip shop:

> Aye. She knew that some people liked their chips well done nice and brown and other people didn't want too brown, want them white, and she [laughs]. Sometimes people would try you over and send you up, when you get up to the chip shop and get me a fish supper and something then Jean would say "who's it for?" so-and-so, right, she knew how to make the chips [laughs]. Aye it was quite a happy wee place, actually.

These informal economies for women became problematic once they

51: Jane McHattie on her last day as postmistress at Benwhat.
Courtesy of Ann Hunter

moved down to the new public housing. All shops from home now had to have the approval of the county council. The housing committee minutes often featured a woman applying for a shop in her home and being refused permission.

During times of hardship, such as male unemployment, women took on seasonal work. Grace Bradford from Auchinleck recalled to our interviewer Allison Galbraith going tattie hawking with her mum when she was thirteen while her dad was looking for work after leaving the pits:

> My mother had a hard life. And that's why I telt you we went to the tatties, tattie hawking because that's hard. A van picked us up there was maybe about 4, 5 women all thegether that went to the tattie fields.
> *AG: And what age would you have been then?*
> I was thirteen. It was quite, aye it was hard
> [...]
> *AG: So did it hurt, did it physically hurt?*
> In the beginning it was I mean you just got used to it.
> *AG: And earned lots of money?*
> No not much money, no. I think you would be lucky if you had £1.50

or something at that time.

AG: So why were you doing it then if it's so hard and you weren't earning much?

Because my mother needed to do that.

AG: Was your mother out there in the field with you?

My father didnae work to get oot the pit, he didnae like the pit so he got oot of there and he had to wait a while before he got another job so it was quite hard and my mother … my father didnae go he stayed there with the rest of the weans and my mother and me went.

AG: So it was the only work there was for you? Did you get to eat any of those potatoes?

Aye, aye it was called a pickling, a pickling of tatties when you were going hame when you finished.

AG: So what was that a bag?

Wasnae a great big bag just a wee bit.

AG: But enough to give you...

But enough to get chips and things like that, cut the chips and that. We always had plenty of chips.

Whilst the closure of the mines around Scotland undeniably affected men's working lives and identities, women were impacted by closure as well. Barbara Alexander worked for the National Coal Board:

> I worked wi' the *Coal Board* at Kames an' then I went t' *Lugar* t' work with the Coal Board an' the Coal Board at Lugar, their offices eventually closed and it all went to Greenpark at Edinburgh, so I applied for a job in the social work as a home-help organiser.

When asked if she was made redundant, she replied: 'I was in Marketing and then Marketing went to Greenpark in Edinburgh an' then I was moved t' another department an' I thought, "Och, time. I need t' get something … *different.*"'

From the mid-twentieth century, working patterns were changing, with a larger proportion of married women taking on part-time paid employment. In Scotland the number of married women in occupations increased by 185 per cent between 1931 and 1951 and by 1971, two fifths of married women in Scotland were economically active. The proportion was somewhat lower in mining and ex-mining communities (because of limited alternative employment for women), but the trend was similar. The main employment sector for all women in Scotland was the non-manual services sector, including occupations such as teachers, nurses, secretaries, retail assistants and clerical administrators. By 1971, seventy-five per cent of Scottish female workers were clustered in these occupations in the banking, insurance, and public sectors.

The movement of women into the care sector was common at this time. With the continual growth of the National Health Service in the decades after the war, followed by the expansion of care within the community, women found work in these sectors. Barbara expands on this:

> So that's when they were taking on a lot o', that, that was actually the start o' community care, then. As far back as '88 [1988]. We were involved in community care with housing an' the nursing service an' the doctors. It was, nothing in writing but we were doing community care.

While heavy industry was in decline affecting largely male workers, this was to some extent offset by gains in the public and manufacturing sectors for female workers. In many places the workforce was predominantly female. Factory work offered shifts and part-time opportunities to allow women to balance domestic responsibilities with some paid work. Margaret Hynd was born in Muirkirk in 1947 and lived in Glenbuck from the 1970s until 1995 when their house was demolished for open cast mining. She remarked that when the pits did close around Muirkirk, the impact was slightly lessened by the availability of women's work around the area. Margaret worked in a factory just outside Muirkirk, which was where she met her husband. The Hynd family bought Barbara Alexander's house in Glenbuck from Barbara's parents in the 1970s:

> Aye there was more factories. The women didnae used to go out and work but when the factories came it gave the women a lot of work but the men were still working in the mines, the pit for a while and then they kind of closed down one by one and the most of them went away down Scunthorpe different place, Doncaster.
> *YM: So was it mostly the women that worked in the factories at that point?*
> Aye it was mostly women and I think that's what's actually brought the village up money .
> CH: Gave it a boost.
> Everybody was poor and it gave it a boost it definitely did.

WOMEN SUPPORTING WOMEN

Throughout the testimonies we can see glimpses of support networks and friendships between neighbours and extended family members. The role of the woman as household manager was essential to working-class households. Their labour was extensive: managing the household budget, making their food reserves last, ensuring their families were clothed, their houses were clean and everyone was fed. Other oral histories reveal there was a pride in this role for women. Being a successful household manager was essential to the idea of working-class respectability. The miners' had their long johns, heavy coats, caps and tackety boots for work and the women had their working clothes as well. Tom Wilson remembers his gran in the 1920s and 1930s, 'Ma mother's mother, I remember her quite well, jist an old lady wi' her hair turned up into a bun and she always seemed to be in her peeny, ye know, workin', workin' garb.' The peeny, or pinny, was an overcoat that women wore to hide or protect their clothes while working in the household. Alice Wallace from Benwhat described the significance of the pinny for women's work in the 1940s to interviewer Yvonne McFadden:

> I mean, they got on mostly wi' one another but there was one or two o' the women who were a bit funny or a bit lazy and, er, one o' the sayings was, er, "Look at her, working outside already as if she's finished inside! I'm good sure she has nae all her inside work done! [laughs] If she does any at all!" [laughs] That kind o' thing. Aye, this woman, she always wore the wee, front apron. Most o' the women wore the crossover, I think an' I think mainly, Yvonne, that was to hide maybe the old clothes down below. Because they wore their old stuff, right, and this hid all these, it was a crossover and tied and everything! Er, one o' the front aprons that pulled over your head, right, with the bib thing here and tied behind your back. My Mum wore that most of the time. But this woman just along a wee bit, she wore this wee front apron, a wee daidily. "An' look at her! Huh! She has nae done much work, that ain!" Because she was quite nicely dressed an' a wee, fancy apron on. A wee frilly apron, you see!
> *YM: Aye. I was actually gonna ask you about the peenies so…*
> Aye, aye, a lot o' style, aye! Most o' the older women wore the big crossover. Aye. Because they were all covered. Aye. They didnae have sleeves on them, mind you, but, er, they had a jumper on underneath.

This detailed description of the peenies that women wore during their working day in the home, seen in the photograph below, also touches upon the meaning of clothing within the village. The woman with the wee 'daidily', which would have only covered the bottom half of her clothing was therefore associated with not working as hard. Also, that she was

126

52: McBride family photo at Lethanhill.
Courtesy of John Neil

doing her 'outside' work so early suggested to the other women that she was not working as hard. Perhaps, she wore a different peeny in the house. Similarly, we see the older women wore one that completely covered their outfit while her mother and other younger women wore one that went over the head and tied around the back. Clearly demarcating a new 'style' among the younger generations. Many working women throughout Britain wore this 'uniform' to tackle their daily chores.

What emerges from Alice Wallace's testimony is the friendships and support that women built into their daily lives to make their hard work more palatable and less isolating. Alice told us her mum's memory of when Alice was born:

> Aye, apparently, when I was born, er, the women went to their bed for ten days to a fortnight and that was their, sort of, ante natal care and their neighbours came in and helped an' the nurse was coming up every day to see that things were OK an' Mrs McBride, that stayed at the other side, had came in an' my Mum never liked margarine, she liked butter. She hated margarine an' would nae eat it kinda style! If she'd nothing else, she would just spread it on so thin that you didnae get the taste. But she loved butter and she would have it as thick as she could but it was on ration, you see? Now Mrs McBride had a bigger family and she'd more butter in the house so she came in with a wee tray an' a nice wee cloth over it an' a cup o' tea and a plate wi' just bread and butter but nice thick butter! "Here you are, Sadie, I thought you would like that!" And my Mum says, "Oh, my God, that's lovely! Oh, that's good!" She said, "I never enjoyed anything as much that day!" It was just that nice that somebody came in wi' that, something that she liked. An' she was so happy! An' she talked about that afterwards. I mean, that was a nice thing. Aye, the looked after one another. They had a bond.

Life in the rows was hard for the families but the stories told tell us that people were resilient and resourceful. The informal networks women form within working communities are both practical and social. One interviewee recalled her mother's reflections about the people in the row at Auchinleck:

> But my mother said the *kindness* in the rows at that time when a baby, if somebody was in labour. One neighbour would be making a pot o' soup! Another un would take the weans in! Er, you know, they all helped!

Alice Wallace talked about how they would support each other in difficult times:

> An' they always helped one another out. I mean, they would say "Mrs so-and-so up there, you ken, he's not at his work yet, no, it's a shame!" And they were all making pancakes and stuff and handing them in. They always helped their neighbours because they knew what the position was and it could happen to them just the same. They were

very good at looking after one another.

Sheila Crosswaite who was told stories by her Aunt Meg, who lived in Lethanhill then Patna, recollected a story of her aunt's about the village women pooling resources to clothe the children:

> But she used to, she told me she went with one of the other women, it just seemed to be the two of them, but there might've been more for all I know, and they used to go into Ayr and they would walk down the hill and I fondly imagine they got a bus into Ayr but when I think about it there maybe weren't buses, maybe it'd be a cart or something, I don't know how they got there.
>
> But they went into Ayr and they went round textile warehouses or something, there must've been, I don't know, cloth making or something in Ayr and they got, I presume for nothing; now this might've been the Depression maybe, maybe in the 30s I'm not sure, I never thought about it until, you know, doing something like this. But she said, we went round all these and we got ends of, you know, ends of runs of stuff, cloth of all kinds and I think they gave them to them and they cut them all, tied them all in a great big bundle and they'd come back.
>
> Now I don't know how they knew because they didn't have mobile phones, but people would come down from the village to help them carry these bundles of cloth up and she said, and we made, you know, we made shifts and wee shirts and shorts and skirts and wee dresses and things out of all this material and it was from, from Ayr, they went into Ayr and did that.
>
> [...]
>
> *YM: Was the material like for the village, like would everybody get a bit of it?*
>
> It was for everything I think, ah-ha, they'd just, and those that, you know, could sew made things, they made clothes. I remember her talking about making them for children but they made them for everybody because it'd just be simple sort of shift dresses or shorts, or something, but that was where they got it, they went down, I remember her telling me about that, so I don't know.

Industrial unrest during the interwar period was marked by strike action in the mining sector and during these times the village women shared resources. Sheila's aunt Meg's story of clothing the children supports other stories. Margaret Sim, interviewed by her daughter Sorrel Weaver in 1998, grew up in Lethanhill from the age of two in 1924. Her dad was the village joiner, not a miner. His role was to maintain the houses within Lethanhill and the surrounding villages for the company. Their house had running water, a dry toilet in their garden and the kitchen was extended with a coal store. During the 1926 general strike her dad continued to work as he was not technically a miner. In the 1930s, Margaret recalled her mother supporting their neighbours:

> There was another tricky time about 1933 but I don't, I think the miners had learned very hard lessons and they didn't try it again. It was um, I can't remember it, except that I can, I can remember people coming to our door and asking if they could borrow … not money … food. And I do know for a fact that mother used to look out clothes that we'd outgrown and she passed them on and nothing that was, now that was interesting, nothing that was, that was noticeably have come from us.

Throughout the interview she infers that her mother was an outsider, while her dad, who was more outgoing, assimilated well into village life:

> She didn't. She was never happy. That's not strictly true. She was never comfortable at the 'Hill. She really didn't join in with the others. Because it's pretty unique, how they, how these women, erm, and my mother had great difficulty. Erm And she smiled and [unclear], but she had very little to contribute.
> *SW: sounds quite lonely*
> It was. But, see, her parents were in Patna. The lived in Patna and although they were miners and lived in Patna, they were superior to the 'Hill.
> *SW: What like the people in Patna were, the miners in Patna?*
> The miners, the women felt they were, because there was so … [pause] the hill was rough. It really was. And if it hadn't been, if it hadn't been for my parents that how's I would have grown up. [unclear?]. You see mother cleaned and washed and, and dressed me and baked. We were always properly dressed. You know I think I was the only girl my school who wore a school sl … no there was one other girl, who wore a school slip.

Margaret's mother established the family's social mobility through careful housekeeping, maintenance and presentation of the children. These symbols of working-class respectability were important to Margaret's mother. Coming from a mining family in Patna, the tensions between the two localities are clear here but also found in other stories about the 'Hill folk moving to Patna. For Margaret, an incident during the 1926 strike is a pivotal movement in her realisation of their slightly elevated social status within the community:

And I went to school when I was 5 and that would be 1926 and that was the miner's strike. 1926 strike. [pause] We didn't have, um, I, I wasn't aware of being any different from anybody else. But of course, my father was not on strike, he was still working. And, he must have been pretty brave, or he must of dealt with it very well because we were not ostracised because he was working.

SW: Well I suppose because he wasn't a miner … I suppose his job, in some way, supported the community if he was doing repairs

[...]

That's right

SW: which they, people themselves will tell you [unclear]

That's right, the mining system. And so therefore, he was not, he was not looked on as a, as a scab. Certainly not as far as we were concerned anyway. And the only anxiety, I think I told you before, was when I was 5, I just started school and they had a soup kitchen, for the children. And I, um, they used to queue up with their, they had a sort of, some of them had a tin mug, some of them had an enamel mug, and it was, they got this thick soup. And it was, it was full of beans, thinking about protein, you know made with marrowbones and beans, that was their main, the little children. And I, there was one wee girl there and she used to save all her beans and peas she would put them in a bag and she would bring them out to eat. And I thought that this … So I didn't see any reason why I shouldn't go and have some but I was only 5 and I didn't have a mug and I just stood in the queue with all the others. [The women were] giving out soup in the kitchen and I was standing there and I didn't even have a mug to hand over, all the others had, so I mean, I don't why I bothered to be even there! And [one said, 'What are you doing here Margaret Sim?'. So, I said, 'I've come for my soup.' And she said, "You can't have soup! Your faither's workin'." [Interviewer laughs] So I didn't get the soup. And I felt … I felt a bit put out!

SW: Yes!

All the others.

SW: Yeah. Is that the realisation, when you go to school that people could be different?

> That's right … I mean it didn't matter to me. [unclear] I mean, I didn't
> know that was all these children had to eat. [unclear][3]

For Margaret, she was aware latterly that her father was still working but
felt this was accepted by the community given his role. As a young five-
year-old, she had no understanding of the politics or social implications
of waiting for some soup. The woman who told her to get out of line also
did some cleaning for her mother, another indication that the family were
different from the miners. When Mr and Mrs McBride, grandparents of
Janis Chambers moved to the village of Lethanhill in the early twentieth
century they were regarded and outsiders:

> I did hear though – from ma mum – that erm, because they weren't,
> they were kind of interlopers, the, it, it was quite hard for them to
> begin with, when they first moved up there an' I think, you know,
> kinda, but anyway, they did, they did settle into life there. You know,
> they seemed to be quite happy with their lot up there, yep.

In a small tightknit community, it can take time for newcomers to be
accepted. This was the case for the McBrides and the Sims in Lethanhill.

KEEPING A MODERN HOUSE

The hard labour of the miners' rows was left behind to some extent as the
villagers were decanted into the new houses. Moving to a new modern
house transformed women's lives. From 1918, housing design in both the
private and public sector initiatives placed housewives at the centre. New
social housing considered women's daily work: hot running water meant no
more multiple trips to the water pump at the end of the row. Double sinks
in the kitchen with a boiler ended waiting for your weekly turn at the wash
house. Some new prefabs had fitted kitchens and a refrigerator.

In the *Planning Our New Home* report in 1947, the housewife's
work was consistently referred to throughout. Considerations for new
houses included kitchens with additional sockets for new domestic goods
that tenants might potentially purchase such as washing machines or
refrigerators. In their new house in Bellsbank, Alice Wallace recalled her
mother's delight at having modern facilities in the house:

> Ma Mum loved it. It had a cooker in it, which had two rings and
> a big square for cooking on as well. But you could also make your
> pancakes on that. And, er, it had a grill and an oven. All worked

---

3 The tape recording quality made complete transcription difficult.

53: Two women on doorstep, possibly Lethanhill.
Courtesy of Cox family collection

by electricity. And she experimented with all these things, it was great. And there was a boiler. Now, they used t' boil their clothes. Everybody's underwear at that time was white, the sheets were white, things like that, and everything was boiled. In Benquhat as well, you see? Er, but here there was a boiler installed in the house an' you just filled it wi' water frae the tap. You had a hose going in so you had t' feed it in. This was magic! And switched on the control an' it heated up without a fire on down below it. So, she could boil all the clothes there, that was great. Didnae have a washing machine for many years, mind you. But, er, there were two sinks. You had a deep sink an' a shallow sink wi' a frame in the middle and you could fix a ringer onto this frame so, she would do the washing in the deep sink with a scrubbing board and put it through the ringer into this sink t' get rinsed and then back through the ringer again. And, er, oh, she loved this! That was great. I mean, that was state o' the art stuff then, hey!

As the second half of the century progressed, new homes and modern appliances altered women's work but did not necessarily free up time. More rooms equated to more space to clean. Higher standards of cleanliness were expected within the home, promoted through advertising but also the images of home now on people's television screens. By the mid-1970s, televisions were almost universal in Scotland and eighty-eight per cent had a refrigerator.[4] While physical labour within the home was undeniably reduced due to modernisation, the responsibility for the home remained with women. Girls and young women could take advantage of the growing public sector and manufacturing industry between 1950-1970 offering opportunities their mothers were unable to access.

Women's domestic labour in the rows was referred to as 'hard' and they were referred to as 'trudges' and even 'slaves' in the interviews. The poor conditions and basic facilities were navigated by the women with skill and some muscle. Some villagers were moved to the same or nearby streets in the new estates; others were not so fortunate, and the transfer to the new houses undeniably involved some dislocation away from neighbours left behind into a more diverse and wider community. However, for women these new houses transformed the physicality of their daily lives. This brought new challenges: how to furnish these rooms; more rooms to now keep clean and tidy; and keeping up the appearance of respectability within the new consumer society. Hot water, a modern cooker, electricity, vacuums, refrigerators and eventually washing machines transformed the lives of the mining families in ways inconceivable to the previous generation.

---

4 *General Household Survey,* 1976 (London: HMSO, 1976), Table 5.36, p.148.

4
WORKING LIVES: THE MEN

This chapter focuses on the working lives of those men who lived in the miners' rows and were employed in the mines in East Ayrshire in the twentieth century. It draws upon their personal reminiscences and those of their families in newly conducted interviews for this project and a series of previously completed and archived oral history interviews of Ayrshire miners by other researchers, including the doyen of oral history in Scotland, Ian MacDougall. The joys and the misery of working in the Ayrshire mines were recalled by eye-witnesses in great detail and what emerges is a real sense of attachment to the job, despite the evident risks; of identification as a miner and the pride that went along with this. Of course, the lived experiences of working in the pits varied enormously, in part because of the occupational hierarchies and diversity of the pit. Jobs ranged from manager through to the supervisors, deputies and firemen; the craftsmen like the pit electricians; the 'colliers', themselves divided between surface

54: Memorial to lives lost at the Barony colliery, at the A Frame memorial site near Auchinleck. Courtesy of Margot McCuaig

55: No 1 Pennyvenie Colliery, late 1890s (showing the various trades associated with mining work – note the bowler-hatted managers/supervisors and flat capped workmen). By kind permission of East Ayrshire Leisure Trust/East Ayrshire Council

workers on the screens and working underground; the haulage workers; repair and maintenance crews; and the 'elite' coal face workers (the 'hewers' or 'strippers'). Miners also narrated their working lives differently. Some for example were (understandably) angry 'activist narratives', whereas others more subdued, fatalistic and nostalgic. A minority loathed the job and did it for the money and/or because there was no feasible alternative. Recurring themes in the oral testimonies were the authoritarianism of the private coalowners and the importance of trade unionism to protect workers and push back against the exploitative bosses. Miners recalled how central work was to their lives and how important it was to their identities – as coal mining anthropologist Daniel Wight put it as 'workers not wasters'. They spoke of the camaraderie of the mining workforce; the hard graft of the pick and shovel 'hand stripping' era under the private coalowners; and the transition to mechanisation and what nationalisation of the industry in 1947 meant – the changes and the disappointments. And the miners frequently attested in their stories to the dangers, accidents and ill-health caused by the job – the 'blood on the coal' – with almost all accounts including emotive stories or anecdotes about the impact the work had upon miners' bodies, speaking, sometimes quite reluctantly, of friends and family severely injured or killed in the pits. Ayrshire mining communities suffered

Pennyvenie miner c. 1900s.
By kind permission of East
Ayrshire Leisure

a heavy toll of injury, disability and death from their employment, more disproportionately perhaps, than any other working-class communities.

JOB CHOICES, TOIL AND TROUBLE IN THE DEPRESSION

Introductions to work for boys in Ayrshire mining communities were rarely directly into mining. At twelve or thirteen, many kids from the miners' rows did part-time jobs, including working on local farms and doing newspaper deliveries or milk rounds to get a little cash, usually handing the earnings over to their mother and getting a bit back as pocket money. Poverty necessitated this in the early decades of the twentieth century. David Murray, born in Lugar in 1930, was a message boy for the village shop for a time when he left school, before he got an apprenticeship as an electrician in the pits. He was paid five pounds per month, when asked how long it took to spend his money he laughed: 'Oh I don't know I gave it to my mum. I never take pocket money either. Because I was getting more than five pound in tips from the people I was serving. More than five pounds in tips so I never took a penny back from my mum.' Before starting in the Mossblown pit, Robert Hall had both a milk round in the morning before school and a paper round in the afternoon after school

57: Bobby Jackson, blacksmith at the Pennyvenie Colliery. By kind permission of East Ayrshire Leisure

finished. His earnings (usually around 10 shillings – 50 pence in today's money) were handed over to his Mum and he got 1s 6d – less than 10 pence - back as his pocket money – though he admitted 'Ah used tae keep the odd shillin' now and again!' Like many, Robert's father suffered from bronchitis and emphysema and had to give up working in the pits prematurely. These ailments were usually put down to smoking and not officially determined to be occupation-related until the 1990s (after a long trade union campaign), so he got no financial workmen's compensation at all.

It was normal before Second World War for miners' sons to follow their father into the pits – indeed it was expected of most of them. Tom Wilson (Benwhat 1926-1940) was asked what he wanted to do when at school:

> Ah don't think ah gave a lot o' thought tae what ah wis goin' tae do. As a matter o' fact, as ah say, like loads o' boys, we jist went tae the pit... I think ... ah think they [parents] were that harassed ekin' oot an existence and workin', and they were ... Ye know, they werenae... It wis such a hard life for parents. ... we who were brought up to it, we turned automatically to the pit, because we were aboot pitheads when we were boys. And it wisnae foreign to us.

58: Highhouse Colliery miners, including very young-looking boys, c, 1900,
By kind permission of East Ayrshire Leisure Trust/East Ayrshire Council

Felix Todd, born in 1917 in the Crosshouse miners' rows, recalled:

> Ah mean, it wis aye in ma mind even at twelve-year-old sittin' in the
> school and sayin', 'Well, ah ken where ah'm goin': ah'm goin' tae the
> pit.'

James Whiteford, born 1938, from Connel Park rows, next to
Knockshinnoch, recalls how he ended up working in the mines:

> I started in Knockshinnoch when I was fifteen. I got a phone call
> frae … frae Hunter's shop that I was wanted at Knockshinnoch fer a
> medical, so I went an' got ma medical. I was asked to stay in Hunter's
> shop because I was doing well … an' I was only aboot thirteen.

He reflected on his decision to leave the shop and go to the pit: 'Well, I got
that phone call t' go fer the medical…an' I was asked t' stay on at Hunter's
but didn't do it. An' I didn't regret it, 'cause, er, ma time in the mines, I
enjoyed them!'

David Murray recalls the day he chose to change careers:

> One of the ladies I went to, her husband was a manager up in the
> works, the coal board works. And she says "my husband says there a

139

job going David, would you like to change your job as an electrician in one of the pits?" And I was standing at her door with water running out me and I said aye [laughs]. So I went into the pits and served my time as an electrician.

The first job at the pit for boys was usually at the surface. What stuck in Ayrshire miner Alec Mills' mind about working on the 'screens' sorting coal at the surface as a youngster was the dust and the noise: 'The noise was horrendous'. Tom Wilson described his experience at the Pennyvenie pithead in 1940-41:

Ye know what pithead's like, a screening plant, tables and … Well, we went… Your first job invariably, every boy went in among a' the auld men, what we cried craw pickin'. It wis jist a phrase, that's jist a phrase. Everybody knew what craw pickin' wis. You're … you're separatin', you're pickin' oot the dirt as the tables were moved, elevator moved slowly, and you're pickin' oot the dirt, you throw it tae the side, then you shovelled it doon a hole tae another cross elevator took it away tae the dirt lift. That wis craw pickin'. Well, because ah wis a wee shaver, and this other boy, Jimmy Fairbairn, and I we were started in the July. And there were boys left the school later on, two or three

59: Chalmerston, Houldsworth pit in the 1930s, showing the headgear and surface buildings. By kind permission of East Ayrshire Leisure Trust/East Ayrshire Council

60: Houldsworth Colliery, undated.
By kind permission of East Ayrshire Leisure Trust/East Ayrshire Council

months later on, and they were in the craw pickin' for one day and then they were up on tae the pithead where the tumblers were, where they cowped the hutches. And we were annoyed aboot this, because … we were that wee, we were wee boys. We were kind o' kept under surveillance, and the old men took care of you. That wis one o' the features aboot mining, of course, especially when you're very young, as a wee boy you're startin', the auld men took care of you, ye know, ah mean, one would sort o' focus on ye, and see that ye werenae…

Tom Wilson went on to training as an apprentice electrician after a year or so based at Pennyvenie pits, then Beoch. He commented:

It wis a kind o' elevated thing for a … if ye were a tradesman. And ah'm very cautious, when people talk tae me from different walks of life, ah say, 'Ah'm a miner retired.' Ah don't say, 'Ah'm an electrician in the mines … Ah'm a miner and proud of it.

For some, choices were very limited. John Rodie was born into a mining family living in the miners' rows at Mossblown. His father died when he

141

61: Pennyvenie mine electricians in their workshop, c, 1976-7,
By kind permission of East Ayrshire Leisure Trust/East Ayrshire Council

was 8 years old and as the eldest son he was expected to work in the pit in order to retain the company house. He started aged fourteen in January 1939, recalling with evident pride: : 'That wis a great day when they gie'd ye a helmet and a lamp. [laughs] … A hard hat, aye. You're makin' your way.' John recalled that from his first wage packet the house rent was deducted, as well as a charge for an allowance of cheap coal. At a lot of the Ayrshire pits, like Mossblown when John worked, the method was still pick and shovel, with little or no coal face mechanisation.

Where miners worked depended upon what pits were operational in the locality and as coal seams in pits were exhausted (or pits were deemed to be uneconomic) they closed and miners had farther and farther to 'tramp' or cycle to work. Sam Purdie was from a fifth generation of miners in Glenbuck and he recalled:

Now, this was a tiny hamlet which, by the time I was born [1936], had suffered the loss of its only remaining pit and there would probably be four or five hundred inhabitants. The men who had worked in the local pits were split between working in the Kames Pit, which was four miles away in Muirkirk, and the Kennox Colliery, which is five

142

62: Young miner with pit pony at Chalmerston mine, 1900s.
By kind permission of East Ayrshire Leisure

miles away in the other direction in Glespin in South Lanark.

Tom Wilson (Benwhat) recalled a story about his father:

> Ah remember ma mother sayin' tae me in these days they'd tae get up in the morning so early, he'd tae walk from Benquhat across tae Lethanhill and down the brae to the Houldsworth pit where he worked, and she says he never saw daylight in the winter time. He'd be walkin' four mile - maybe two and a half miles tae Lethanhill frae Benquhat and a mile tae the Houldsworth … Doon the pit in the dark and back up it wis dark.

In the 1920s and 1930s Ayrshire coalminers and their families were ruthlessly exploited by the private coalowners (who were invariably also the landlords owning the miners' rows) – the likes of the Kenneth's, Baird's and the Dalmellington Coal Company. The interwar Depression facilitated such oppression. The powerful miners' unions were defeated in the 1926

63: Three Dalmellington miners photographed on the day the war broke out 3 September 1939. Matthew Dempsey (on the left with the pipe) fought in the First World War and his son Matthew was killed in the Second World War. By kind permission of East Ayrshire Leisure Trust/East Ayrshire Council

General Strike and subdued for more than a decade thereafter. Poor demand for coal meant rising unemployment for the mining villages and this drove wages down and empowered the bosses. This was the time of soup kitchens and the Hunger Marches, when union activists and militants were punished by the colliery companies with sackings, blacklisting and mass victimisation. Managers could discipline and punish by determining who might be laid off when orders were low and who might be favoured. And miners could be evicted from their company-owned homes if they did not toe the line. A regime of fear and intimidation prevailed. And these times were remembered and passed down as folklore in mining communities. George Montgomery started in the mines in 1940 and he recalled: 'Feared, feared, aye – aye, blacklisted. But ah think the main fear wis gettin' their overtime stopped. 'Ye're a nice boy - overtime, you'll get it.   You'll no' get it.' That wis common.'

The loss of work in the 1920s could have a devastating effect on the health of miners' families. A Scottish doctor reported a case of 'semi-starvation' of a miners' wife, and two cases of malnutrition amongst his practice, with one boy aged six dying and one case of a girl aged five

64: Miners working on cutting a new roadway through stone at the Chalmerston mine. Drilling for shot firing. By kind permission of East Ayrshire Leisure Trust/East Ayrshire Council

recovering after treatment. He reported the diet of the girl thus: 'Breakfast (at school), cocoa to which condensed milk was added, bread and margarine; dinner (at home), soup from soup kitchen containing over-cooked vegetables, with now and then a slice of bread added; tea (also at home), bread, tea with condensed milk.'[1]

John New recalled an experience his grandfather had in the Depression years and his sense of the mine owner's oppression of the workers:

> You got good times and then hard times, erm, because I know my, Arthur told me that my, my Granda, he was, like, the quiet man, he hardly ever said much. But he says, in his early days he was, erm, he was quite a wee firebrand. He said, there was a strike at some pit along the road and a whole group of them went along to support the strike but they got ambushed by the police, who were just, who gave them a hammering and, he said, he managed to jump in the, the Lugar river and escape them, you know. He said, but erm … he said,

1 J. Boyd Primmer, 'Medical Impressions of the Miners' Strike', *British Medical Journal*, 2:3163 (1921), pp.260-261. http://www.scottishmining.co.uk/478.htmlhttp://www.scottishmining.co.uk/478.html

they were tough times, you know. He said, they were, they were up for it at the time, you know, they had to fight for their cause because, er, the mine owners ruled … you know, they ruled their whole life!

Margaret Sim recalled this story about her grandfather during the industrial unrest of the 1920s and 1930s:

My grandfather. My mother's father, he was, he worked a mi … he worked in the pits but he was, um, the equivalent of a, an under manager […] Now, when they went on strike, his strike team, my grandfather used to give them so much a week out of his own pocket because he, he, he felt responsible for them. They were his, they were his men and erm, I think my grandmother eventually took a bit of a dim view. But at the end of the strike my grandparents said nothing and neither did the miners, they were really good.

Felix Todd was interviewed by Ian MacDougall in 2001 and recalled his elder brother's experience:

65: Highhouse miners. By kind permission of East Ayrshire Leisure Trust/East Ayrshire Council

Now John took an awfu' active [part] in the miners' union. And durin' the '26 strike - ah wis nine year old then - he used tae get Sam and me up in the mornin' and we'd two' these bikes wi' the cairriers in front o' them and go over tae the Co-operative and get the rolls and take them to the wee hall where we had for the children ... two rolls and jelly goin' tae school. Now ... when the strike finished, John wis blacklisted. Couldnae get a job. And wi' ma two sisters bein' workin' in the house, he got nae money at a': he got what they ca'ed the Means Test. My God Almighty. And ah remember that day John went away, he went away in 1929 and he wis standin' there breakin' his heart. He didnae want tae go. He wis only in his 20s. And he went oot there and ma uncle Felix, the man ah'm ca'ed for, wis in Canada and he went tae him, and he got him a job as a janitor in a school, which was something then ... He always said, "Fel, don't let ony o' ye say ah went tae Canada." He says, "Ah wis exiled tae Canada. But there wis thousands in the same boat." That day when he wis goin' away he said to ma mother, he says, "This is killin' me," he says, "breakin' ma heart." He says, "But ah'm goin' tae go, mother." He says, "Ah cannae walk in there and ken ah'm no' contributin' tae the keep o' the hoose."

The infamous 'Means Test' meant that as income was coming into the household John's right to any state unemployment pay under the National Insurance Act (the bru' or dole) was denied. Felix grew up with a hatred for the local colliery company. Felix recalled being challenged by an older miner who was a First World War veteran to enlist in 1939:

He says to me, "Ah, well, pal, you'll be gettin' the khaki on?" Ah says, "No' me." "Ah, come on for your country!" And these Kenneths who owned the pits, the three brothers, and they're millionaires ... They were millionaires. And ah says, "Now listen, son. See if they gie me a gun? Ah'll stert ower there. [laughs] So ah ken ma enemies here. Ah'll no be goin' oot and shootin' brother miners the same as masel' oot there."

The 'Kenneths' were one of the group of six smaller colliery companies in Ayrshire nationalised in 1947. The manager of the Kenneth collieries in the 1930s was Willie Reid, who Felix described as a notorious 'tyrant'. Another of the same ilk was Mungo Mackay who hailed from Ochiltree but worked over in the East, as manager of the Lothian Coal Company. Colliery management regimes ranged widely, as Andy Perchard's history of

66: Two Ayrshire miners, with pit pony, c. 1940s. Note the naked flame carbide lamps and the soft caps (pre-safety hard hats), as well as one miner smoking. This indicates that the pit was regarded to be free of methane gas (such as Kames was before the disaster).
By kind permission of East Ayrshire Leisure Trust/East Ayrshire Council

mining management shows, but many across the Ayrshire coalfield during the Depression were callous, autocratic and authoritarian.[2]

Like the 1984-5 miners' strike, the 1926 General Strike and the lock-out of the miners passed into the folklore of mining communities. Both were major watersheds in industrial relations. The miners were defeated in 1926 but arguably their defiance was important in tempering mineowners' actions. Those who acted as 'blacklegs' or 'scabs', continuing to work or going back or replacing strikers, were invariably ostracised within the community. And miners had long memories. Felix Todd recalled:

> Whit we ca'ed the blacklegs. Oh, they got their come uppance. Ah remember them. Some o' them frae Crosshouse who worked durin' the strike. Goin' to the school, and we could hear the crowd comin' - and there it wis: the rest o' the miners who were on strike. Escortin' them hame, ye know. Oh, aye. Some … some they jist never forgive them. The full toonships rendered split. My God, the damage. Oh!

2 Andrew Perchard, *The Mine Management Professions in the 20th Century Scottish Coal Mining Industry* (New York: Edwin Mellen Press, 2007).

It goes on, it goes on yet.

He recalled starting work in 1931:

> That was the first thing that they reminded ye o' ... "He wis a scab." ...
> Some people their families emigrated ower the heid o' it. oh, aye, ah
> remember that, oh, yes, aye. There wis families emigrated because o'
> t. Because they were shut up socially in every wey.
> *IM: Aye. Can you remember a particular family who emigrated?*
> Ah could remember them, and ah'll tell ye, ah widnae like tae mention
> names. Because they're back in the village. Oh, it's a' forgotten noo.
> But the old timers still ... remind ye now and again.

George Montgomery told a similar story about 1926 strikebreakers:

> There were three scabs worked in the Barony pit durin' the '26 strike
> oot aboot 1,200 men. And when ah wis secretary-delegate o' the
> union branch [1970s] there wis an accident away in another district.
> And this oversman wis on the phone tae the pit bottom, and when
> he come off the phone he says, "That's yin o' your members had a bad
> accident, George. He's lost two o' his fingers, gripped in a gearbox
> - Jim Liddle." But before early retirement, men were sittin'. It wis
> piece time, sittin' wi' the Noon Record in here, keepin' theirsel' goin',
> men in their early 70s, and this old boy, kind o' ... [? a word not
> clearly heard], perks up and he says, "Whae did ye say that wis?"
> Says I, "It's an engineer called Jim Liddle." "Where's he from?" Ah
> says, "His faither works in High Hoose." "Oh, aye. Aye." He says,
> "Old Barney Liddle his grandpa?" "Aye." He rolls up this bit paper,
> chucks it across the road. "It's no his finger that should be aff. It's his
> heid that should be aff. His grandfather wis a scab ... durin' the '26."

Given the treatment of the coal miners it is hardly surprising that strong
support for trade unionism, socialism and communism developed in
Ayrshire. This carried on the tradition of the Ayrshire radical, Keir Hardie,
miners' union leader, socialist and Labour Party leader who died in 1915.
Ayrshire poet (and ex-miner) Rab Wilson recalled what he called 'the
subversive history' in his family: how his paternal grandfather had been a
miner and was radicalised:

> My dad is John Wilson. Oh he says do ye ken that your grandfather
> formed a branch of the communist party in Muirkirk. So this is

James Wilson ... That grandfather had fought in the First World War, he had been gassed in the trenches and suffered ill effects after that because of the gassing. So I think he was among the disaffected who came hame from the war expecting the country for heroes and where was it - partly down the pit. And I think he must have embraced the kind of radical politics of the likes of John MacLean and the Red Clydesiders at the time and said no we've had enough of this and he formed this branch of the Communist Party in Muirkirk.

Like other miners, James Wilson would have worked his way through mining occupations, accruing experience from the surface to coal face. Felix Todd started work in the mines in 1931 aged fourteen in the Southhook pit and describes his early experiences working with the pit ponies:

What ah did tae begin wi' wis a pownie driver. The pownies were in the pits at that time. And ah had maybe aboot six months at that. And then ah went tae the coal face. Whit ye did, ye went wi' a face man. He did the work at the face wi' ye, and you wis whit ye ca'ed the drawer. Fillin' and drawin'.
IM: How did you find the ponies? Did you like that sort of thing?

67: Pit pony at the Chalmerston mine, 1937.
By kind permission of East Ayrshire Leisure Trust/East Ayrshire Council

Oh, ah loved it, because ah wis always hert sorry for them.

IM: Were they kept underground all the time?

They were kept underground for a solid year, and they got up what they ca'ed the Kilmarnock Fair Week. And ah can remember goin' tae the pit on the Saturday mornin' and seein' Jimmy Milligan, the ostler, and these men bringin' these puir things up the pit. And there wis a big holm, a 40-acre holm, jist across the railway frae whaur the pit wis, and the horses they got in there. And they were blind for aboot a day before they could see.

The ponies were not the only animals underground. John New recalled a story from his grandfather:

Ma Granda said, he said they used to get quite friendly with the rats. He said the rats lived in mines all the time. He said they would become really tame and they would give them a wee bit of their food, you know, their, their piece! [laughing] Their bread or their cheese! 'Cause that's all, all they had was … was a flask of cold tea and usually a big lump o' cheese or maybe a crust o' bread, that was their … They lived on that as their staple diet down there. Er, so, it was a very, er [pause], a very limited diet, you know.

Felix Todd moved from ponies to the face as a filler and drawer, then to brushing, then on to the coal cutters on the face, working an eleven day fortnight (though Saturday shift was 6-12). By the time he got to the coal stripping on the face he was nineteen. He recalled the elation of the coal face workers' pay packet:

It wis good pay. Ah remember the first time when ah went tae the face masel' and ah come … ah always remember ah had three blue pounds … and a single shillin'. Ma mother jist burst oot greetin'.

Henry (Harry) Kennedy, born in 1932, described his promotion to coal face work at Pennyvenie in 1950:

So, I did, I did go to the coalface. I started, I hed tae get a shovel, a mask, a saw … an' a pick! An' I hed tae trail away aboot a mile an' a half afore I got tae the coalface (we were tied together, like) an' when I got tae the coalface, the fellas … well, the coalface, the height o' the coalface is no' much bigger than that – 2 feet 9 – an' each, well [pause] there'd mebbe be aboot, roughly, gearing up t' twenty men working on the face. Each person had thirty feet o' coal t', t' strip an' b' the time I got ma cut, they were … two oors in front o' me! I was well ahind! There was no way I could dae it, like, an' catch up was impossible, like, because as I say, I was nae, I was mair annoyed aboot keeping ma heid safe! [laughs] You've got t' keep the props up or you get, hmm, you get murdert! I was miles behind them! There was no way I could catch up on them! An', er, as the day went on, some o' them was finished an' when you get finished, you're away t', towards the pit bottom, like. An' I was, I'm, I'm sittin', I mean, it's pitch dark! The nearest body was mebbe aboot half a mile tae me! An' you can nae go away an' leave, you hed t' continue an' get, get all your coal out, like! So, I says, "I'm gonna be left here m'self in the dark!" But here, there were two fellas an' the next thing I knew, the two o' them were heading, heading along there! But two absolute great fellas! They were the best men I think I ever I kennt in ma life! An' they got in aboot it an' we were finished in nae time! An' fer two year, the three o' us went doon the pit together an' up the pit together.

Whether on haulage, maintenance or stripping at the coal face, it was hard physical backbreaking toil and young miners were expected to toughen up and be resilient: Felix commented: 'Ah'll tell ye, ye were always fit! [laughs].' And miner Thomas McMurdo, recalling the 1940s reflected: 'No kidding you, I was like steel. I was a hard man then.' John New also recalled the macho culture: of never being expected to show emotions; never to show fear or to cry:

> That was the way of the miners! You know, it was very much a, kind of, er, [...] you know, that, it had to be sorted out, man to man, and a fist fight, end of story and shake their hand and it was over. So, it was probably common. Er, you know, boys were always fighting anyway at that age group. It was seen as *manly* [laughing] anyway! An', an', er … any dispute was sorted out with a, what we called a 'square go', just a boy-to-boy fight, erm, no kicking, just fists an' a bit o' wrestling, usually, an' that was it, that was it over with, you know? Erm, you shook hands and went away as good buddies, you know! [laughs]

Generally speaking, wages were better in the mines than most other alternative work for unskilled and semi-skilled men in Ayrshire. Whilst never explicitly admitted, this was 'danger money' – a wage premium for the risks taken in working underground. However, mining employment and earnings were unstable in the 1920s and 1930s Depression (when demand

*68: Former
Lethanhill resident
Hugh Hainey, 2012.
(courtesy of Donald
Reid)*

for coal slumped). And there were also significant regular deductions from wages. Hugh Hainey recalled of the later 1930s, when he was an apprentice at Pennyvenie mine:

> Deductions from my wage for rent 2 shillings and 3d, light 9d, doctor 4.5d, ambulance and hospitals 1d, (the company had its own ambulance and paid for the upkeep of three beds in Dumfries Ward in Ayr County Hospital) and approximately every four weeks a bag of coal at 10 shillings.

Felix Todd also recalled the short-time working during the Depression, with bouts of three days work and three days on the broo (signing on for unemployment benefit). He commented: 'It wis hard, it wis hard times. And whiles ah don't get angry aboot it, ah get sad. These should ha' been wir happiest days. But this cloud wis always there.'

'BLOOD ON THE COAL': HEALTH AND SAFETY STORIES
Mining was one of the most dangerous and unhealthy of jobs around and in miners' interviews the bodily damage of working in the pits was

153

often referred to. We might call these accident and disease stories. They told of the ways that bodies were ravaged by their daily jobs; of the risks, dangers and chronic ill-health that could ensue. After a long period of improvement, due mainly to the active role of the miners' unions and state intervention via the Mines Acts – albeit often after major mine disasters – the interwar Depression in the 1920s and 1930s saw occupational health and safety standards stagnate and in some cases worsen. As Jim Phillips has shown, Scottish mines were statistically more dangerous than the rest of the UK, and more rapid mechanisation of coal getting in Scotland than other coalfields was implicated in this in the 1920s and 1930s.[3] Ayrshire had more than its fair share of pit disasters and a steady daily drip-drip of disability and premature death from accidents and respiratory disease. The causes of such accidents, injuries and fatalities were varied, but managerial negligence and the condoning of a risk-taking culture to maximise production (and hence wages) lay at the heart of the issue. Roof supports were neglected, for example, to speed up coal production. As Ayrshire miner Davy McCulloch recalled: 'If there was an easier way to dae it, you done it', whilst miner William Dunsmore commented on putting up roof supports: 'Sometimes you'd to improvise.' And George Devenne reflected: 'We were out for the money … You're cutting corners.' Having said that, miners appear to have rarely taken unnecessary risks and respected the dangers of working underground. However, where a piecework payment system prevailed there was always going to be an incentive to work unsafely if it could be gotten away with. And sometimes there were management 'cover-ups'. Ayrshire miner Dick Easterbrook recalled how after a man was killed by a roof fall management installed missing pit props prior to the Mines Inspector arriving to investigate the accident.

Before Jean Burns was born in 1936, her dad had an accident underground that left him unable to return to the coalface. Here she recounts the incident and the impact it had on her family to interviewer Rosanna Brown:

> But … I was closer to my dad. Yeah. He was a very quiet man and worked hard all his life. Erm … I don't remember him having the accident, but I know he suffered from it. Most of his life, I think. It was the trauma. You know, the trauma of being trapped underground and he was, er, what can I say? He was shellshocked from the war and had that accident and in those days, anyway, the likes of now would be treated but in those days, it wasn't treated. No. No.

3 Jim Phillips, *Scottish Coalminers in the Twentieth Century* (Edinburgh: Edinburgh University Press, 2019), Chapter 3 'Improving Safety', pp 80-118.

69: Rescue Brigade, date not known. Following the Mines Act of 1911 such rescue units were made compulsory in the industry.
By kind permission of East Ayrshire Leisure Trust/East Ayrshire Council

RB: And did it – if you don't mind my asking – was it like just, obviously mentally, but did it affect him physically as well or…?
No. No. No. It didn't but, you see, he had a fractured skull but the, the pit owners, they, it was before the N. C. B. [National Coal Board] and that was, the N. C. B. came into power when Clement Atlee got in. Before that my dad had an accident and he, the mine owner was … *guilty*. He was, there was a court case about it and he was proven to be negligent and not bothered about his workers' safety and my dad was awarded three hundred pounds for his accident. That was a lot of money then and my mum and dad, before I was born, they set up a shop, in the house. There was, we, sometimes there was, houses had a wee shop in the front of the house. But I don't think *any* of the two of them were money savvy. They weren't money savvy and so the money got frittered away till they had nothing.

The mine owner had to pay compensation to her dad – a system established in 1897 called the Workmen's Compensation Act. This allowed her parents to set up a shop. He was given a job on the surface and the couple were able to remain in the village. It was common for disabled miners and sometimes older miners to be moved from the coalface to the surface to work. This provided some job security, but the earnings were substantially less. Jean's father left for a time during the Second World War but later, when it became the National Coal Board, he was able to return to working in the coal industry. Jean remembered accidents as common in the village of Trabboch, recalling: 'There was always an accident'. She also described the impact on the village:

> Some were fatal and that. Others were not, were not too bad. But it left a … *sadness* in the village when somebody lost their son or their husband in the pit. There wasn't…no. [pause] No, I remember, er … Mrs … Cam, er, Margaret and…and she lost her son, her husband, sorry, and I think then, later, she lost her son as well.

The majority of miners who were injured or killed experienced individual incidents. Felix Todd's grandfather and uncle were killed in accidents in the pits, whilst he had numerous accidents himself and witnessed others. He recalled:

> In 1943 ah wis involved in an explosion … Doon in Oldhall … And whit happened wis this section we were workin' on, there wis a fan which wis extractin' the air and there wis old workins in tae the left o' this fan, and it drew gas, and there wis a … there wis a fau't in the fan, there wis a spark coming aff the wick o' the fan. And it ignited it … Well, I wis aff ma work but ah wis burnt there. See there the skin: they put new skin on, see that yet.
> *IM: It's all scarred still.*
> One o' the boys, one o' ma friends, Jim Watt, he … it burned his eye oot, and it burnt his … the muscle oot o' his right airm … He died about a year or two, jist never wis better again … Ah wis aff ma work for aboot … Ah wis aff nearly a year. Went back tae Newfield, which is on the outskirts o' Kilmarnock there. Ah worked there tae 1956, the year ma mother died … And Newfield closed down then and ah went tae Sorn, and ah finished up. Ah got hurt. Ah wis in the hospital again. Ah wis five times in the hospital actually.
>   The first yin ever ah saw I deeply affected me because because it wis a young boy o' 15 year auld wis killed, and he wis a powny driver. And ah wis talkin' about, ken, the rakes o' eicht, six or eight hutches. In Southhook. It wis in 1937. And he had his horse and he put the tail on tae the first hutch, ye see, and he wis standin' between the hutch

and the horse. And here the first hutch wisnae coupled on tae the rest o' them. Bang! It drew the hutch ower the tap o' him. Killed him … That boy's father and his two brothers worked in that pit. And we a' come up the pit. Ah can see that man staundin' yet, jist … They never even said, "Ye'll get you a car hame." They'd tae walk frae the pit doon here tae Sprinside whaur they steyed. And his boy wis lyin' in the hoose. They'd never even ta'en him tae the hospital. And there wis a case aboot it because the conditions were … were far frae the Mines Act. And they got away wi' it, they got away wi' it. The union brought it to the court. And they assessed the compensation. And his compensation – because there wis a family o' them, he had three brothers and three or fower sisters, a big … [three or four words not clearly heard] – and they came to the conclusion wi' whit that boy wis earnin' … what they did, they gave them funeral expenses, which wis £90. That's what they got.

IM: Aye. The life was worth £90?

That … that… that made me … Ah could never… Ah could never chinge ma approach tae that … The coalowners at that time, there wis sin tae answer for. God knows how they'll dae when they're gettin' judged, God knows.

Henry (Harry) Kennedy recalled being involved in two serious incidents at Pennyvenie – one involving infection which hospitalised him for six weeks and another where he was buried:

I was *in* six weeks in the hospital with that dermatitis, but I managed t' get it cleared up, like. An' then another time, I actually, I got buried! The roof gave way! [chuckles] Don't ask me what happened, I don't know! I had, an' ma wid up, I'd all ma props up, ken, tae support the roof an' then at the next, I just can nae mind, I just, I did nae ken until I was covered in muck an' dirt! An' I was very, very lucky! Of nine times out of ten, when anything fell like that, it was a big, large stone an' you mair or less got killt ootright! But it was all mud an' water! Come o'er me. I might, I was covered in it an' I'm trying t' get oot an' the fella next tae me, Willie Murphy (he stayed in Burnton tae), Willie Murphy you cried him, an' Willie thought that, he says, I thought you had had it! He says, "I mind seeing yer, yer heid comin' up through the mud, the dirt an' that!" An' then, walkin' home the, doon the length o' Burnton that night, he says, "By Jings! You were lucky!!" So, so, so I was, but … there, och, there were a lot o' folk wi'… *injuries* an' that! Some o' them fatal.

Miners working in these conditions witnessing and experiencing such trauma were likely to suffer from post-traumatic stress disorder (PTSD), though this was rarely recognised as such at the time. The mental health of miners was sorely neglected. For a long time it was expected that miners stoically tolerate stress and depression. Few spoke about such things. You had to 'man up'. National Union of Mineworkers' (NUM) President Nicky Wilson recalled that the union had a strong policy on physical disability (with rehabilitation centres and convalescence homes) but that it was one of the failings of the NUM that they were slow to address mental health issues.

Waterside parish priest Eddie McGhee reflected ruefully on the toll taken on his ancestors of mining work:

> Ma Grandfather McGhee, ma Dad's Dad, was killed on 2nd November 1929. Erm, the roof collapsed on him. Erm [pause] and … Grandpa Mahoan was very badly injured when he and a few other miners were thrown out of the cage at the Kames Colliery in Muirkirk and he never worked again and, subsequently, as a very young man, thereafter died of a heart attack. But I think it was related to, t' the injuries that, that he had received in that incident. So, I never knew either of my Grandfathers … ma Uncle Phil … Phil lost his arm. He was 17 years old, ma Uncle Phil, and his arm was ripped off by a belt [pause] in the pit. But he continued to work! I mean, latterly, before he retired, he was the Manager's Clerk at, er, the Killoch … Deaths all the time, you know, and doing the family tree, you find there's lots of gaps.

Sam Purdie (Glenbuck) reflected on work and its hazards before Second World War:

> I have to say that my grandfather, on my mother's side, had lost both legs in an accident in the iron furnaces in Muirkirk. My grandfather on my *father's* side had his back broken in Grasshill Pit so, they were both crippled with the mining industry, so nobody needs to explain to me the price of coal! And, er, the conditions for the compensation men were abysmal. They were paid practically nothing [pause] and just paid off.

The latter comment refers to the ways that the colliery companies exploited the statutory Workmen's Compensation system that was supposed to provide miners and their families with some financial security for injury or a fatality. Like many other employers' associations (the bosses equivalent of the trade unions), the Ayrshire Coalowners' Association formed the Ayrshire Employers' Liability Company to challenge and fight workers compensation claims, aiming to minimise the amount the bosses had to pay out. Ayrshire miner George Montgomery, born 1926 (family from Burnfoothill and Lethanhill), told the following story about his father:

> He got buried in the pit in 1934 when ah wis eight years of age. They were enlargin' a junction underground, him and another two men and the three o' them got buried. They were buried for aboot nine or ten hours. Come oot badly injured. He wis off for aboot two year … we were now living in Skivington Place, that's on the road to New Cumnock, council houses facin' the main road. And there were nae propriety. So when people came tae see ye they jist came intae the garden. And this Saturday night this car stopped, and ah I remember it, and this is honest, ah do remember it - a sort o' maroon Wolseley. Two men got oot, one o' them had a pack, the other one wis goin' tae dae the speakin'. Ma dad wis workin' in the front green cuttin' the grass wi' an old hand operated lawnmower. Ma mother wis talkin' tae the next door neighbour, and ma brother and sister and I were there, the three youngest ones. And this guy came intae the garden and said, "Adam Montgomery?" "Yes." "Were you employed at Whitehill colliery ?" … "Yes." "Ye've had an accident?" "Yes." Never asked how he wis gettin' on. "Do you know what time it is?" Ma mother volunteered tae tell the time by lookin' in - we had a wee wall clock: "It's twenty-five past nine." Away. He never got his compensation for twelve weeks, which wis 16 shillins a week. And then he wis advised tae … tae call in tae see Willie Logan, the same as Mackay o' The Green Table [an infamously authoritarian mining manager of the Lothian Coal Co], who gave him a dressin' down and … Aye, the general manager at Lugar, Lugar office. "And ah hope ah never need tae see you here again." … So there you are … They used tae talk aboot Burke and Hare. And ah mind an old worthy once sayin', he said, "It's no Ayrshire they cry this place. It's Bairdshire." Ken, wi' the power o' the coal company.

Scottish coalowners and their insurance agents were driven to challenge and reject claims (for example on the grounds of personal negligence or dereliction of duty) and monitor those on disablement benefits closely (as the above example shows). In some cases, they callously intimidated disabled men in an attempt to get them back to work or on to what was termed 'light work' to minimise compensation costs to the industry.[4]

Hugh Hainey, born in 1921, an electrical engineer in the mines, recalled when his brother John was killed in a gas accident at Chalmerston:

> The shift change over and working day went smoothly and at the end of the shift I was crossing the surface to go home when I met my brother John. He had been working day shift too, but was on his way towards the mine with Willie Galloway another oversman and Robert Travers under manager. I stopped to inquire if they were going back to work. John said there was a small section of gas to be moved. I commented to be sure and keep behind it. Willie Galloway laughed and said the way they were altering the air flow, they would hardly keep up with the gas. As they moved off John said to tell Sally his wife that he would be about two hours late. It was a sunny day and as I turned away I little realised that that would be the last time I saw him alive. When arriving in the village, I had to pass John's house so I told Sally that he would be late then went on home. I had just finished my meal when someone told my mother there had been an accident at Chalmerston. Later the news on the village grapevine was that it was a gassing accident and three men were involved. As usual the village would know who was involved but would not reveal to the families so I decided to go to Chalmerston. I cycled to John's house and told Sally I was going, I would take the motorbike. Going through Benwhat village there were many people out talking but the road was cleared to allow me free passage. When arriving at the colliery there were quite a number of miners and the rescue brigade van on the surface. When the manager saw me he asked me to the office and then he told me that John and Willie Galloway had been overcome with gas. John had been found directly under a gas blower so that he had little air. Willie Galloway and Robot Travers were further into the section but were less affected getting some air after collapsing to the floor. They had been removed from danger and the brigade were trying to revive them for the journey to the surface. The chances of John surviving were not good and he asked me to go home immediately. I went home and within the hour we were informed that John was dead. Willie Galloway was on his way to hospital and Robert Travers was taken home. Willie Galloway

---

4 For more detail see Angela Turner and Arthur McIvor, '"Bottom dog men": disability, social welfare and advocacy in the Scottish coalfields in the interwar years, 1918–1939', *Scottish Historical Review*, 96:2 (2017), pp.187-213.

70: The above-ground cave-in at the Knockshinnoch disaster. The pit bing is in the background.
By kind permission of East Ayrshire Leisure Trust/East Ayrshire Council

died later.

During this tragedy, the villagers protected the families until more was known. As was the custom hundreds of villagers attended the funeral.

Nationalisation (1947) made a real positive difference to safety in mining, with the coal mining accident and fatality rates in Scotland falling by roughly a half in the 1950s compared to the 1930s.[5] Whilst accident fatalities markedly declined over time, the carnage continued after the Second World War. Amongst the post-war mining disasters in the county, Knockshinnoch (1950: thirteen killed), the Kames (1957: seventeen killed) and Barony (1962: four killed) stand out. The disaster at Knockshinnoch pit in 1950 was caused by a managerial decision to mine too close to the surface (technically illegal under the Mining Safety Regulations), resulting in a cave-in and an inrush of peat and liquid moss from the surface flooding the mine. The disaster left an indelible print on miners' memories. Alec McNeish was one of those entombed for two days at Knockshinnoch before

5 Phillips, *Scottish Coalminers*, pp.81, 86, 278.

161

71: *Families gathering at the pit head at the Knockshinnoch disaster, 1950.*
By kind permission of East Ayrshire Leisure Trust/East Ayrshire Council

being rescued. His resolve never to return to mining lasted just two weeks before he returned to working underground.

James Whiteford went to work at the Knockshinnoch mine three years after the disaster. He recalled:

> An' I can remember what's, as I say, the Knockshinnoch Disaster. It sticks in ma mind! I was twelve years old. The village was … it was a wreck! There were a hundred and twenty-nine miners trapped. Thirteen had died. I had an uncle that was actually trapped in the, Jim Carmi, Jimmy Carmichael, he was trapped. One o' the ones that was trapped. An' I've got so many recollections o' that.

Obscenely the NCB denied responsibility and initially offered a maximum payment of just £1,750 in compensation to the Knockshinnoch widows. NUM pressure resulted in a much-improved settlement of minimum £3,000.[6] Ian McMurdo's wonderful recent book, based on exhaustive research, including 60 interviews, tells the full story of the disaster (and the rescue effort which saved 116 entombed miners).[7]

Witnesses' voices from the Kames disaster (a coal dust explosion) have been collected by Johnny Templeton and can be heard (or transcripts

6 Phillips, *Scottish Coalminers*, p.100
7 Ian McMurdo, *Knockshinnoch: The Greatest Mines Rescue in History* (Carn Publishing: 2017). See also https://newcumnockhistory.com/mining-minerals/coal-mining/knockshinnoch-disaster-1950.

read) at http://www.muirkirk.org.uk/minersvoices/index.htm. Dick Boland was one of the first rescuers to go down and he recalled:

> It must just have roared its way through so quickly and burned everything black. It didn't bring down falls but everything was black. I didn't recognise some of the faces, but usually somebody else did. I think that's wee Johnnie Walker or Wullie Hendry or Poops Samson. We discovered who they all were when we came out. But finding the bodies was quite a shock, it really was; that bit is burnt into your mind.

Tommy Mackin reflected on the impact it had on the community:

> The disaster changed Muirkirk forever. The lot of fellows, I don't think wee Jock Bennie the pony boy; I don't think he ever came back. After that you had an exit to the English pits. To Fort William to the pulp mills and to Corby to the steel mills. The village just changed. The new houses weren't long built and the community was quite good at the time because the foalk who were in the houses realised the benefits they had got coming from the Miners Rows into them.

The disaster was the result of a firedamp methane gas explosion ignited by a miner lighting his pipe (followed by a secondary coal dust explosion). The pit was considered safe and smoking had long been allowed. Better ventilation would not have allowed any methane gas pockets to build up. Sam Purdie was a young engineer at Kames at the time of the disaster and has written a damning indictment of managerial negligence in relation to ventilation engineering in the pit. He recalled:

> The effect on the village of the disaster was devastating. Relatives and life-long friends were mourned. Everybody knew the men and their families. Hogmanay that year was a wake. In a community where previously that celebration meant every door had been open to 'First Footers', songs and clatter. There was instead a quiet mutual support for the loss we had all sustained. Like mining communities everywhere affected by tragedy, we mourned together with a common understanding and unspoken grief.[8]

Margaret Hynd, one of our female interviewees, had family members

8 Sam Purdie, 'The Kames Pit Disaster' (unpublished essay), p. 6. Now published, see Sam Purdie, 'The Kames Pit Disaster, 1957', S*cottish Labour History*, 56 (2021), pp.46-53.

involved and recalled the disaster vividly:

> I can remember the pit disaster … Oh aye I was down that night because my uncle and my brother were there [Kames], they were in it and people were coming and saying "this ones dead and that ones dead." I could remember it was dark it was about 9 o'clock at night we were doon there … my brother was there and my uncle was there and my dad and I and my mum and I were all waiting to see what was what and somebody come up and said "Robert Lows was found dead" but that was my dad's brother but his son was also there called Robert. So, he didnae know what one whether it was his brother or his son that was called but it was his brother so it was. That was a terrible time. … That was terrible for a wee village its awful and see all the boys that was killed. They all came about with my brothers oot and in the hoose all the time. They stayed across the road up … on the same street because a lot of them were Glenbuckie people as well just on the same street and going out and in the hoose with the boys and run with them. It was just horrendous aye. My brother luckily enough he was one of the last ones oot that got brought oot but he had to pass all his pals and the state they were in because they were just blown to bits.
>
> YM: *Did he ever go back?*
>
> He left the pits, naw, well he had a broken wrist and everything when he came oot and he started playing the organ too to strengthen his wrist and finished up being a music teacher and that's how he spent his life. But he's 87 now so he is he's one of the oldest that was there ken that's still alive that was actually in the disaster. Terrible time aye it's just that the whole village it was just everybody we knew so it was. 17 of them, terrible, brothers, sister in laws everybody is related really bad it was so.

Kames was Ayrshire's worst coal mining disaster. It led directly to new safety legislation banning matches and smoking from all mines, even those like Kames that had been considered gas free and hence a 'safe' mine.

Accidents, injuries and pit disasters took their toll, but working in the mines amidst the dust and dirt for long hours also led to serious chronic diseases and disabilities, including muscular and joint problems – sometimes referred to as 'beat knee' or 'beat elbow' - eyesight impairment and respiratory ailments. Dust was a major problem working underground. Ayrshire miner Andrew Lyndsay started working underground in 1930 as a road driver (cutting through rock) and commented: 'You were like a baker when you came out the pits at night.' Another noted that when using a mechanical coal cutter 'you just couldn't see' for the clouds of dust: 'I couldn't see the machineman's light for the dust.' Miner John Orr described using a compressed air percussion drill in the mid-1930s which 'threw out clouds of dust':

> There was no form of dust suppression of any kind except that we all carried a big hanky [or] bandanna, which was soaked with water and we tied it around our mouth and throat. And at the end of a drilling cycle the front of your handkerchief was as if it had been dipped in concrete.

Levels of dust depended partly on geology and mining methods. Billy Affleck described a particularly difficult seam:

> We had a seam at Highhouse, and they said it was moon rock … and you couldnae fucking mark it. And we were pumping this with a machine, and you want to have seen the stoor [dust] that was coming off a that. It was nae real'.

It is hardly surprising then that mining villages were full of middle-aged and older men disabled to varying degrees with knackered lungs from silicosis, pneumoconiosis, bronchitis and emphysema. Some like Ayrshire miner William Dunsmore tried to continue to work but admitted: 'I was embarrassed … I tried to get in before the men got in 'cause if they hear me panting, they'd be saying "he's done", which I presume I was.' Whilst only in his early 40s Ayrshire pit deputy Bobby Strachan recalled: 'You could see other folk that wasnae in the pits could dae things that I couldnae dae, ken. They could run about … You were puffed out before anybody else. I mean, your chest wasnae just as good as theirs.' Billy Affleck, who described battering away at the 'moon rock' at Highouse, ended up on full disability in his 50s with silicosis. He described how he felt emasculated – a lesser man:

> I worked a' my life … it was a big blow to me to be told that I'd never work again. Eh, your prides dented, ken. I mean, when you're out and your wife's to come out and say to you, "come on, I'll get that" … It definitely hurts your pride.

These diseases not only diminished lifestyles and made men feel ashamed but invariably reduced life expectancy. Sam Purdie commented on Glenbuck:

If there was any illness in the village, people rallied round. [pause] Because there were a lot of old miners who didn't have good health one way or another. Mining is not the healthiest occupation.
AM: Were there miners with breathing difficulties then?
Oh, absolutely! Both, er, both silicosis and pneumonoconiosis. Now, the mine drivers, stone mine drivers, they, they tended to get silicosis. [sighs] It was a terrible disease and then, er, the coalminers got pneumonoconiosis because ventilation was practically non-existent!

Tom Wilson's father died of silicosis, aged 57, whilst Nan Auld recalled on being asked if working in the mine affected her father's health:

It did so. Ma Dad, ma Dad died with Pneumoconiosis. … It was the lungs [pause] Mum looked after him an' he died at 52 so we were only … Janette must have been a baby. Janette was only a baby at the time.
YM: So, what did your Mum, how did your Mum get by after that?
Well, as best she could. She just had to. An' some of the older weans were workin'…

Alex Kirk recalled: 'My father worked in the pits initially an' he hed t' come out the pits wi' bad health. He got work as a driver, but died early at age 54.'
Breathlessness, coughing and spitting were common in mining communities and black lung was a scourge which, ironically, increased with the mechanisation of coal cutting and conveying because the machines threw up a greater volume of finer particulate dust. Some miners commented that they couldn't see fellow miners because of the dust cloud thrown up by coal cutters, especially if they were working downwind of the mine ventilation flow. Harry Kennedy recalled of Pennyvenie:

One o' the times [pause], the coal-cutters worked on the face while we were there an' you could nae see fer stoor, the dust! An' I was *choking*! I says, "Oh no, I'm, I've had enough o' this!" An' the next, the next day I got a tinker's scarf! You know, the big tinker's scarf?! An' I put it roond there an' I worked like that an' they all laughed at me an' I can assure you – *that's* hoo I'm here!! As I say, there were that many o' them died wi' silicosis, pneumoconiosis an' it was *terrible* watching them, you ken, they had nae a gasp!! I don't think, that's, that's aboot the worst thing you can get!

Statistics show that things got worse in the 1940s and 1950s, the peak years of pneumoconiosis cases, before getting the problem under control to some degree by water sprays on the machines and other forms of dust control and monitoring. And whilst dust and respiratory disability was bad in the Ayrshire mines, it was worse elsewhere. The South Wales coalfield recorded the highest levels of premature death from pneumoconiosis – with rates amongst Scottish miners running at around half the incidence of Welsh miners.[9] Mask wearing also became more common, though these could restrict breathing and communication so were not always worn. As Harry Kennedy recalled: 'They did get masks later on, but they were awful awkward tae work wi'! They were sticking, you were sweatin' an' they were sticking to your face, ken, they were nae very nice!'

With characteristic humour Glenbuckian Sam Purdie commented on the ill-health and risks miners faced: 'That's why we never had any trouble wi pensions … The miners had the good manners to work until 60 and die.' These conditions bred tough, resilient men and an unusual degree of camaraderie and solidarity in the face of adversity, reflected in a strong commitment to mutual support in the workplace and the wider community, and the ideals of trade unionism. For many miners in Ayrshire (and elsewhere in Scotland) this made the politics of socialism and communism popular. Standing together against the coalowners gave the miners their strength and those individuals who refused to join the union, or broke ranks and worked during strikes were widely disparaged, even hated, with subsequent ostracism within the community for years, even decades.

For others, the experience of structural violence, danger and oppression led them to discourage their children from taking on mining work. Felix Todd's parents wouldn't allow his younger brother to work underground. Robert Walker, born in 1952, explained why he didn't follow his grandfather and father:

> It was decreed that it was too dangerous for the kids to go doon. My grandad nearly broke every bone in his body working doon the pits. My father went doon and he said that it got really dangerous by the time he left because in my grandads' early days they weren't working in big thick seams. As the mining companies got more adventurous, they were going into bigger and deeper seams. They could be in a seam that was maybe eight foot high, now if you can imagine being in here and they take the coal oot up to the rock there was always rock falling down from the ceiling. If you got hit by a bit of rock

---

9 See Phillips, *Scottish Miners*, pp.80-116. See also Arthur McIvor and Ronald Johnston, *Miners' Lung* (London: Routledge, 2007), pp.53-58.

coming from eight foot up it could kill you and they did have a lot of debris falling in because they couldnae cover the ceiling in all places. They would put up props to hold the majority of it up but there was always cave-ins, debris falling doon and it got really dangerous. That's when my dad got oot it [late 1940s, after breaking both legs in a pit accident], his brother he worked on for a couple of years after that and he ended up going to the buses in his mid-twenties, but my grandfather he stayed doing it all his days. He finished up his time at the Bank pit at New Cumnock but from when he was born in this hoose and worked at Whitehill pit doon the road there he was in it all his life. He suffered a lot from broken bones and one thing and another and then ended up with pneumonoconiosis and it was just agreed that we wouldn't be allowed to go and work doon the pit that we would need to find work elsewhere which we did.

Robert went on to work in road haulage and, mid-way through his working life, transferred to working in the open cast coal mining industry in Ayrshire. More of his story is told in Chapter 6.

Eddie McGhee's father worked in Mossblown (where his own father had been killed), then Knockshinnoch (just after the 1950 disaster) and finally Killoch, working his way up to shotfiring. Eddie recalled:

Well, interestingly enough, ma Dad would be the first to hold up his hand and say he loved working in the pits! He never wanted any, there are five boys and five girls in my family. He never wanted any of his boys to work in the pit [pause] and none of us did! [pause] Although he loved it, he, I think he also recognised that it was, erm [pause], probably, I mean, it was an option because there was a steady job and so on. But I think he, he recognised it was a horrendous way to live, you know, working everyday underground. And it was high, high risk.

YM: Did your Dad have any, like, health impacts from working in the pits?

Other than, erm [pause] interestingly enough, he'd no blue scars! Ma Dad didn't have a blue scar. Lots o' miners had blue scars when they were hit by falling bits o' coal an' that. Ma Dad never had a blue scar. Erm [pause], I, I don't think, in, in the long term, you know he lived to be 88 an' [pause] really until the last couple o' years of his life, he had no real significant health issues.

Iain Hutchison, born in 1949, whose family came from Glenbuck, recalled:

My grandfather was quite *adamant*, er, that there's no, [changes accent] "There's no whay ony of ma lads are goin' doon the pit!!" Erm, the, ma grandfather, er, er, had three sons – my father was the … middle one – and yes, he was, he was … *adamant*, er, that working underground was not something, you know. He'd *inherited* it from previous generations, but he was gonna break that! So, ma father's older brother, er, er, trained as a, a carpenter; the *younger* brother was a, a painter. Not an artist but painted houses and painted ships on the Clyde as well! In the shipyards. None of them worked down the pits. I *think* my father, when he left school at aged fourteen, I *think* he did work on the surface for a wee while, er, in the, in the office but that was only for a short period.

Influenced by his father's ill-health from working in the pits Alex Kirk was determined not to follow in his father's footsteps. He recalled:

The Houldsworth pit was a very warm pit because I remember when I was at the school, just before we left the school, we got the chance t' go down the Houldsworth pit and, er, we were taken down on the Saturday and the heat, the heat doon, in it was nae real! An' I come home that day and my father said t' me, he says, "Well, what did you think o' that?" I says, "Well, are you wanting the truth?" … There's nae way I'm goin' doon a pit t' work! … I did nae work down the pit. I was a heavy goods mechanic. I got offered a job in the pits doing the diesel, the diesel engines that they had later on, they'd be diesel doon the pits. But whenever the man told me I had t' go down below to do it, I says, "No, no. I'm no; going near it' [both laugh].

Some miners also clearly loathed the work and the conditions in which they worked. May Baird recalled about her father:

But he did nae … he never liked the pit! It was a *job* an' … An', er, it was, it was *hard* times for folk – wherever! An' ma dad just, he, he, he *kind* a reminisced about it but he did nae like it! … An', an' any mention o' the pit, he would say, "Oh, no! That's a, that's a terrible, terrible job! … Erm, an' when I suggested goin' on a wee *tour*, tae a mine, I said, "Would you like t' go?" He said, [Chuckling] "Are you kiddin'?! [*KW laughs*] I had enough o' that!" So, it's no', the *fond* memories are the camaraderie, mebbe, but not the job!

Grace Bradford's father also disliked working in the pit:

> No he had a nickname because he didnae like the pit he worked in the pit but he didnae like it so he was called 'seldom, seldom didnae work' that's what he was called. He didnae like it and he didnae go often to this pit but after he got the council he was cleaning the streets with the council and he never lost the job, never lost a day after that he just didnae like the pit.

There was some ambivalence given the nature and dangers of the work; some pits at some times were particularly bad. Tom Wilson enjoyed almost everywhere he worked, including Pennyvenie and Beoch, but he hated his last five years of work after his transfer to the Sorn mine in 1978:

> But Sorn mine tae me wis, if ah could draw a comparison, tae me it wis like the French Foreign Legion: it wis full o' fellas that wouldnae get jobs other places. In the mining industry we'd a' the different colours and characters and a' the rest o' it. Ye'd have people that didnae do so well. Ye'd the odd scrounger or bad ... bad buddy. But Sorn Mine, there wis a lot o' good fellas at it, ye know. But there were too big a minority o' bad fellas. They would smear excreta, human excreta, over transformers, things like that. Evil people. Ah'd never witnessed anythin' ... Ah'd been born and bred in a wee village like Benquhat, and we'd a sort o' Puritan upbringing and you were brought up tae play the game ... Aye, ah wis very unhappy. Frae the first day ah went tae the place tae ah left it, it wis like a prison sentence tae me - five year ... Ah met some nice chaps there, ye know, ah mean, there's always the positive aspects o' it as well, ye know. But it wis an awful place for me, an awful place ... It wis different in a lot o' ways. Ah don't... There wisnae ... there wisnae the comradeship and the degree o' trust that ah found through ma life in the mining industry ... There wis a ... an awfu' distrust of people there ... Ah would have left it if ah'd been there much longer. Of course, ah'm lookin' for ma redundancy tae get out.

Tom took his redundancy at age 57 and left the industry in 1983 just before the big miners' strike.

Mostly, however, miners themselves attested to enjoyment, satisfaction and pride in being a miner, despite the risks, and derived a strong and enduring identity from it. On being asked what he felt like being a miner, one interviewee (anonymous) reflected:

72: Highhouse Colliery.
By kind permission of East Ayrshire Leisure Trust/East Ayrshire Council

I'm very proud to have been a miner! If somebody was asking me, if I went t' Blackpool on ma holidays or – "What do you do?" I would say, "Oh! I was a miner! And proud of it!" I enjoyed working in the pits. I've worked in some terrible, terrible, terrible, dangerous conditions, I have t' tell you and I took chances as did the rest. We all did things that we shouldn't hae done, ken! Especially when you're [pause], you're, you're pulling the props so that it can fall. You do take chances. You go too far. But on the whole [pause] … I don't regret one bit o' it. I think back on it, an' some o' the things that they did, some o' the things that we should nae hae done an' think t' maself, 'Well, you're…' I'll be eighty-four next month so I'm saying t' maself, "You're lucky!"

One recurring thing that was recalled – evident in May Baird's comment above – was the close comradeship and solidarity between miners – something akin to the armed forces in wartime. Eddie McGhee spoke of his father: 'He loved the pits! He loved working in the pits, he loved the company of miners, he was very happy goin' to his work!' Felix Todd commented on his working life as a miner:

171

And ah wid say, wi' the friendship and wi' the solidarity ah met, ah never grudged a meenute o't. It wis ... The hard darg [work shift] at the pit, the friendship and the solidarity o' the fellas ye were workin' wi', it overcame it a'.

CHANGING TIMES: UNIONISATION, MECHANISATION AND NATIONALISATION
The twentieth century witnessed many changes in miners' working lives and work conditions improved substantially after the 1930s. Amongst the positive forces for change was the Second World War, the revival of miners' trade unionism – which was reorganised with the formation of the NUM in 1945 – and the long-awaited nationalisation of the coal mines, which were brought into state ownership in 1947 under Clement Attlee's radical socialist post-war Labour government. The post-war social democratic political consensus provided a more supportive political and economic environment whilst the Welfare State fundamentally improved miners' health and well-being too. It also brought a radical improvement in the Workmen's Compensation Act, with reform in 1947, building on

73: Miners at Pennyvenie in the 1960s. Note the numbered hutches full of coal (which corresponded to the miner or work team, for the calculation of wage payments). By kind permission of East Ayrshire Leisure Trust/East Ayrshire Council

74: *Coal getting underground using the pick at Pennyvenie. The steel props date
this to the 1960s/70s.*
By kind permission of East Ayrshire Leisure Trust/East Ayrshire Council

the wartime (1942) recognition of Coal Worker's Pneumoconiosis as an
industrial disease for which miners could get financial compensation. The
NHS in 1947 was also a major boon for Ayrshire's mining communities,
bringing free medical treatment and an emphasis on preventative public
health together with improved rehabilitation services. Nationalisation,
moreover, brought renewed attention to health and safety on the job and
an extensive occupational Mines Medical Service emerged in the 1940s
designed to revolutionise the treatment of injuries and disease, and raise
awareness of hazards. This included a pioneering post-war programme to
research the incidence and prevalence of the scourge of pneumoconiosis
across the UK coalfields which continued from the 1950s to the 1970s. The
miners' trade unions were heavily involved in these developments, pushing
back, fighting and campaigning for better health and safety standards and
better compensation, pioneering a progressive and proactive approach to
protecting miners' bodies in the workplace.

Whilst improving, conditions for underground coal miners,
needless to say, remained tough in a job that was still dangerous and with
significant risks to health. Ayrshire miners recalled some of these profound

173

75: *Working a relatively high seam at Pennyvenie, c. 1970. Note the safety helmets and the hydraulic props providing more robust roof support than pre-war. By kind permission of East Ayrshire Leisure Trust/East Ayrshire Council*

changes in the workplace during the war and post-war years. Tom Wilson recalled:

> We were all euphoric a bit when the flags went up on the big day
> …there wis a flag went up when we were nationalised. There were
> a flag up at every pit. … Up on the whorls o' the highest bit o' the
> pit. But no, ah don't think … Ye know, it wis an occasion, it wis a
> big occasion … The manager didnae change his spots like the
> leopard, they didnae change overnight tae be different … it had tae
> be managed and run efficiently … But ah think they got more …
> bigger inputs, they got more scope tae do … tae do things. Ye know,
> there were more money made available for the mining industry in
> total and each individual pit. But what ah dae remember quite well
> is that the changes were … they werenae dramatic. They came quite
> gradually. But then we began tae be … we were gettin' our opinion
> aboot the running o' the pit. The consultative committees came intae
> being and ah wis a … ah wis a member o' that … ye know, we got
> a democratic way of working … But ah think things did become a

bit more democratic. More say, more influence, not so much in the running of the pit, but relationships within the pit, with the men and the management and facilities for the men, to upgrade things for workers … you could see more developing along these lines...

Sam Purdie (Glenbuck) did his engineering apprenticeship and then started at Kames colliery in 1953. He recalled the changes:

Kames Pit, at that time, well, was just about as old as a deep, as a deep pit could be in Scotland. It was sunk in 1872 and, at that time, it was at the cutting edge of technology, which was completely steam … So, the Kames Pit was built in that era. So, when I went to work at the Kames everything was steam and we had horses, underground, to pull the, the hutches. Of course, we called them horses, they were actually ponies…

Subsequently, the pit was modernised and converted to electric from steam, but Sam explained that coal face working remained 'old school' hand working:

But underground, the Kames never advanced. Yeah, the Kames never, had a success of long wall faces. Apart from anything else, Kames coal, in places, was over nine feet thick! So, it didn't, it wasn't susceptible to, to long wall coal production. So, what happened was, they kept a lot of the old, er, pick and shovel production. It was two men with picks and shovels at each coalface producing coal.

Sam then moved to Cairnhill pit in 1960 which contrasted sharply to Kames:

Now, Cairnhill was this new, brand-new mine and what a contrast! Everything was mechanised! Picks and shovels?! Totally redundant! These were machines. And what a contrast that was.

Ayrshire miner Alec Mills commented that mechanisation in the 1960s 'changed the whole composition of coal getting.' Amongst the key changes were the use of steel hydraulic props, mechanised coal cutting or coal 'shearing' at the face, and mechanical conveyors replacing coal tubs on rails (see images above). For Auchinleck miner Billy Affleck still working traditional pick and shovel methods at the old Sorn mine it meant additional workloads as: 'We had to compete. You had to compete with all the other

76: Mechanised coal conveyor, steel pit props and a shotfirer, drilling for an explosive 'shot'. Pennyvenie colliery. By kind permission of East Ayrshire Leisure Trust/East Ayrshire Council

pits in the area with your pick and shovel as against the big machine.' John Rodie moved from Mossblown to the Killoch (via a factory job he took for a few years at Monsanto Chemicals in Dundonald) and was asked what he saw as the differences:

> Oh, aye, there wis difference ... Well, a shovel tae a coal cutter, they say. [laughs] Some difference. But mair stour [dust] than ever. They were sprayin' every pick o' the coal cutter. And lashin' water intae it - and still never subdued it ... They gave you a mask, but how could you shovel wi' a mask on? [laughs]. Oh, it wisnae practical. If the machine wis passin' ye could pit in on, ken ...

Apart from the mechanisation and the resulting higher exposure to dust as the cutters ploughed through the seam at a much faster rate John identified the different shift patterns:

> See, it wis continuous minin' in Killoch, and Mossblown and the wee pits aroond aboot here, day shift wis coal producin', back shift wis

77: The modern pit at Knockshinnoch, rebuilt after the disaster in 1950
By kind permission of East Ayrshire Leisure Trust/East Ayrshire Council

catchin' up and bringin' everythin' and layin' again. Night shift wis
coal cutting, cuttin' it for the next day. So everybody had … Some
old men liked the back shift and that wis … But it wis different in
Killoch, it wis continuous. You jist started frae where you left aff and
…

And reflected on the different social relationships:

In Mossblown everybody knew … It wis known as a family. So wis
Littlemill. Ah worked in Littlemill. But Killoch, the men, before
they went doon the pit, stood in groups in the pit they came frae
- ken, what ah mean? Although they didnae work thegither they
always stood there in the mornin' before they went through.

There was particular antagonism in the Killoch, John recalled, between the
Auchinleck and Cumnock men – partly based on fierce and long-standing
football rivalry. Stuart Burns also witnessed what he saw as the clannishness
in the Barony where he worked for a spell:

I hated it, I hated the Barony. I wasn't in it at a great time. I came

78: Greasing an underground locomotive's wheels (maintenance was an important ancillary job in mining).
By kind permission of East Ayrshire Leisure Trust/East Ayrshire Council

oot it. I detested the place. It wasn't so much the pit it was the men. Auchinleckians take the sugar out your tea and come back for the milk I never liked them.

Mine electrician Davie Higgins also recorded his dislike of the Barony, noting 'I hated the place. Teamwork was an alien concept. Greed and egotism were the predominant philosophies at Barony.'

John Rodie had been forced to go into coal mining because of his father's premature death and had at one point shifted to working in a local factory (for four years). However, when asked how he felt about 38 years working as a miner John emphasised that any divisions based on place or religion meant nothing when working underground. The camaraderie and support were what mattered:

> The great thing about a pit is the men. The comradeship wis terrific, ye know, absolutely ... Danger creates a brotherhood if you're in the navy or the army or a deep sea fishermen or something like that. But that is ... They're very close, the miners – all over the world, it's

79: Diesel locomotive at Beoch mine. Diesel fumes were another hazard to health for miners. By kind permission of East Ayrshire Leisure Trust/East Ayrshire Council

no' just here. Ah'm quite proud that ah wis able tae mingle wi' them and argue wi' them tae, ken [laughs]. See, in thae days if a man wis trapped in the pit naebody asked him what religion he wis or anythin' like that. There were nane o' that doon the pit.

As noted previously, another significant change which began in the late 1920s (well before nationalisation) was the construction of pithead baths (funded by the Miners' Welfare Commission). Amongst the first to be built were at Highhouse collieries (in 1929), Barony (1931) and at Chalmerston. As Tom Wilson recalled:

> The first pithead baths, ah think, were built at Chalmerston when ah wis a boy. Because, as ah say, ma brother got ... John, who wis asthmatic, he got a job at pit ... That wis the first baths. Ah remember the men came tae dae the terrazzo and they lived wi' an aunt of mine, specialists, ken, these terrazzo floors and that sort o' thing. And then Pennyvenie, there wis baths built there. They were there when ah started as a boy. And then the big mine [Pennyvenie] got baths. And then the Beoch got baths ... This became a feature - a' the pits got

baths, ye know. There were a big upsurge in, as ah say, improvements for people which were necessary.

Union activists struggled to improve conditions locally in an industry where working conditions could vary significantly from pit to pit, and even from seam to seam. The Houldsworth mine, for example, was deep, warm and dusty, whereas the Monkton pit, built under Monkton Loch, was notoriously wet. Most of the seams Ayrshire miners worked were between two and four feet, but the Killoch had seams of six and seven feet high – and miners transferred to working there had to adapt.

Different Ayrshire pits had different ways of working, and sometimes action to improve conditions was undermined by sectarian and inter-village rivalries. George Montgomery recalled significant divisions in the 1950s between Catholics, Protestants and Communists in Auchinleck. Robert Hall described how unfair the system at the Houldsworth was in the early 1950s:

> Once we went intae the minin' side o' it in the Houldsworth we discovered that there were very, very selfish men in Patna, guys that had been there for years and years in the Houldsworth. They were movin' in from one section to another hand strippin', which wis gettin' big money. And they were leavin' us tae the wee jobs, bringin' them wood and a' that sort o' thing, ye know, wood boys and that

198: Pithead Baths at Killoch Colliery, Ochiltree.
Reproduced by kind permission of Ayrshire Archives

sort of thing and haulages. And that wisnae … ah wasnae there for that. Ah wis there tae make money. And hand strippin' wis nothin' tae me because ah wis used tae hard work. Obviously bein' on the railway ah wis workin' wi' shovels - no' a problem. And when ah seen what wis gin on doon the pit, ah says, "Ah can do that." So ah became… after about several months and years ah said tae masel', "No, this is an injustice here. Ah'm goin tae stop this." … they were gettin' big money all the time. So ah'm bein' honest with you. Ah had the pit oot on strike … and we were oot on strike, oh, maybe say for aboot four or five weeks until we got it sorted. And Willie Cormie wis the manager. And Willie agreed wi' us. But he couldnae do nothing. Because we felt, and ah eventually got it, a rota system wis introduced where everybody wis gettin' a fair crack o' the whip.

Robert felt many of the Ayrshire pits at that time were poorly managed and full of such injustices. As a young trade union activist (NUM) he set about changing things:

Aye, that's where ah originally started tae take a very interest … a big interest in the union because there were so many injustices up

81: Men operating a hand winch at the Barony pit site (No. 4 sinking). The Barony A frame can be seen in the background. Courtesy of the National Mining Museum Scotland Trust

181

there - not nationally, locally. In the Doon Valley area at that time - and ah'm talkin' about pits such as the Beoch, Minnivey, Pennyvenie, Houldsworth, Five and Six mine, Littlemill, Greenhill and Pilwherin – in all the pits that I've just mentioned there were local disputes, more local disputes than national disputes or area disputes, simply because the men hadn't settled down. It wis … Ah can see this in hindsight. Ah couldn't see it then, ah can see it in hindsight. The men had not settled down tae fair play. It wis dog eat dog.

Part of the problem, Robert felt, was the mining management – largely transferred over from the old regime of private coalowners pre-nationalisation and lacking in ideas: 'Old style', as he put it. But the geological conditions in each pit differed and that created more difficulties – such as the fractured eighteen foot seam in the Houldsworth. Robert commented: 'Ah seen things in the Houldsworth when ah wis a young man that, ye know, would have turned your stomach.' Roof falls were particularly frequent and the instability of the working space was compromised by the wooden roof supports used up to the 1950s prior to their replacement with steel.

George Montgomery became one of two NUM Scottish Safety Officers in the 1960s and 70s, so was at the centre of mine safety management. He noted how things progressively improved because of trade union vigilance. But also commented on the continuing risks, the new hazards of fast-moving machinery, poor management, the heightened accident proneness of older men in the 'modern' workplace, and noted the closures pre-Thatcher as being implicated:

In the '50s and '60s we had a bout o' pit closures, although the industry wis still quite big. But these pit closures meant that you didn't need tae recruit. ... And of course that meant that pit managers had the right tae be transferred, chief electricians, chief engineers. Ah say this quite deliberately, but no' against any individual. The minin' industry then became more dangerous for a while, because mechanisation had been introduced and new techniques bein' introduced when the management had never been used wi' anythin' tae do wi' mechanisation - even the manager and officials had tae do wi' hand work. So they were o' the wrong generation for the new introductions. And much more so, the men that worked in these newly manned up pits like Cardowan - ah'll give ye that as an example. There were aboot 1,200 men in Cardowan, and ah spent a month at Cardowan on behalf o' the union daein' a survey, surface and underground and manpower, at the time I wrote that thesis, and

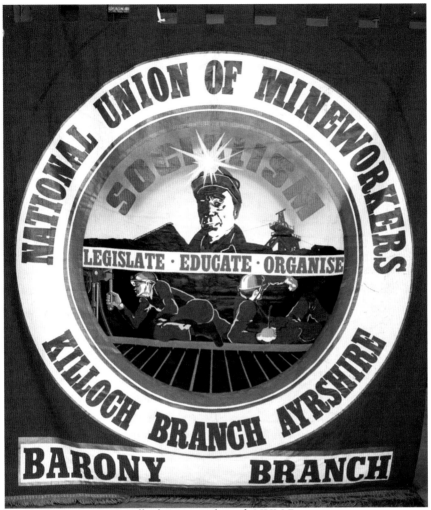

82: Killoch / Barony branch NUM Banner.
By kind permission of East Ayrshire Leisure Trust/East Ayrshire Council

found oot that oot o' the 1,200 men there were 200 o' them over 60, but … 180 over 50. So here ye'd an agein' manpower, more likely tae be injured, a longer time for recovery o' injury, and never been trained at the face - worked on the face before 1947 when the regulations come oot under the Labour government and the National Coal Board. So you had a … you'd an agein' manpower, an uneducated manpower. Now the job ... the accident patterns started tae change. Instead o' men bein' killed in the … at the coal waste, where they were buildin' parks, and they didnae have parks then. That wis tae hold part o' the face up when the roads ... the road up when the face is advancin', they had power supports. And these power supports were moved by mechanical pressure, and a lot o' the men had never seen them, and a lot o' men left the pits. A lot o' men lost limbs, lost fingers. Some terrible accidents happened to their ankle. There wis a bar run across tae link the power support tae the face part o' it, tae the conveyor, and men caught wi' that bar and lost the sole o' their foot. And other men, there were a big scraper brought intae the pit, and they'd an inspection plate and it had four pins on it tae secure it in position, where you could look under the top chain and see the bottom chain wi' this inspection plate off. And men had accidents wi' that. A man got his front o' his foot ta'en off, and a man in Monktonhall got both feet ta'en off, nipped right off, foot and ... in the inspection plate when it wis off. He got his feet ta'en off. So the pattern o' accidents changed, partly because o' the age, partly the lack o' education and schooling. And these were more horrible times than the earlier accidents ah went tae, because it wis quite gruesome. And then there were men got caught on the conveyor, or caught wi' the shearer and mangled. And ah wis at quite a few o' these. And ah remember one o' the ... a painful thing. Ah wis along wi' a government inspector and the safety engineer and the manager, and there were a man had got killed in Castlehill at the coal face. He wis one o' the officials o' the first aid team the chap that got killed, which wis quite strange. And his body wis badly mutilated, and part o' his body had been carried oot on the conveyor and off o' that and on tae another conveyor. Well, the plant had a' been stopped when that happened. And when we went doon the pit - it happened on the afternoon shift - we went doon the pit aboot seven or eight o'clock at night, we were still there at four in the mornin', because we spent a considerable time examinin' the two conveyors while stationary. They had lost ... They were reconstructin' the man's body in the first aid room up the pit, and they couldnae find his right ear and a part o' his jaw. But we got it. We searched the conveyor minutely right through until we got that. These are experiences ye never forget.

In fact, as a matter o' interest, the first fatal accident ah went tae, ah saw the man's body comin' out when ah wis goin' tae the site o' the accident, which wis in 1963 in Lingerwood pit ... that left an indelible mark in ... in ma mind, aye.

When interviewed in 2002, Robert Hall recalled (somewhat reluctantly) a number of fatalities at the Killoch in the 1960s and 1970s, when he was a

Workmen's Inspector and branch secretary:

> Ye know, it's something that you don't … you don't talk about in great detail because you don't want tae … Ah mean, any miner, jist one fatality. And ah had … Ah've witnessed quite a few in Killoch. Some friends and, ye know, it hurts. It hurts … as an example, and ah don't often talk about these things, but there was a fella, a young boy, [...] He wis a Rangers supporter, and he had taken … he'd changed shifts tae go and see the Rangers and he went out on the day shift. He wis originally back shift, ah think. And he got buried and he got killed. And the personnel manager John Scullion at Killoch colliery, who was the best of a bad bunch of personnel managers, let me tell ye. We … had the task, him and I had the task tae go down and tell his wife and unfortunately it wis round about Christmas time, about the 12th or 14th of December, and when we chapped the door, ah was in a dil … ah didnae know whit … where ah wis goin' tae start … So we went tae the door and the two kids came tae the window and they thought, "Oh, ma daddy's home early, ma daddy's home early!" And if ever a lump has went tae anybody's throat it went tae mine. Ah mean, John Scullion and myself had the terrible task of doin' this. They had tae be notified. Every death in Killoch had tae be notified, and we always made it possible: one from the union and one from … one from management went and seen them… When we went out the house ah looked at Scullion and Scullion looked at me, and ah've never seen two men so close tae tears in a' ma life. And that affected me, that Christmas and New Year. Ah remember that … That's how you hear so many stories from miners, "Ah wouldnae let ma son down the pit."

A little later in the interview Robert reflected on how health and safety in the pits was not as bad as previously and how nationalisation and the activism of the union were the key things that made a difference:

> But wi' the new safety records comin' in, the death rate in the pits went down, ah'm pleased tae say, it went right down. And in all fairness, in all fairness tae people in the pits, the safety departments from the Coal Board, the National Coal Board, changed dramatically along with the safety comin' from our Executive in the NUM, SCEBTA [The Scottish Colliery Enginemen, Boilermen and Tradesmen's Association] and COSA [Colliery Officials and Staffs Area, NUM]. They were pushin' for safety and it went down well.

Robert added to this referring to what happened at the Killoch, where he worked from 1961 until it closed in 1987:

> And we … we were organised in such a way that we developed something that wis rather unique in mining. We formed a safety committee where it wis involved wi' the HM Inspectorate, under-managers, SCEBTA union, COSA union, and the NUM had two people on it. And NACODS [National Association of Colliery Overmen, Deputies and Shotfirers]. And each and every one o' us went round the whole pit and all the outlyin' mines under the jurisdiction of the National Coal Board. That's what we done. And reported… you had to put everythin' in a report, and filed, and wis brought up at the committee meetings on safety. And when we went intae a section we had the power tae say, "Stop. You're not doin' that" - over gaffers, shot-firers, the lot. We decided that that wasn't right, it wis a … If it wis breakin' the Coal Mines Acts or anythin' we had the power tae stop it. If we didn't stop it we asked that man tae report tae the manager as soon as he went up the pit - but not before we stopped it.
>
> We had that power. We had also accident site observers where there wis people injured. They went in right away to … They were there immediate. If you were maybe, say, about five or six miles away and you couldn't get to the surface, you reported it and the accident site observer of that section went in and took an accident site observance of what happened, which wis an asset incidentally, because he made sure that nothing wis touched and nothing wis altered, ken, serious reportable accidents and that.
>
> And we had a hell of a lot o' them, I can assure ye. And our system union wise slowly built up, and although ah say it maself and self-praise is no honour, the union at Killoch were well organised. We had wir differences of opinion political wise, bein' Labour, Communists, and SNP, and guys that sit on the dyke: we had a' that differences. But we overcame that for tae get the policy. And that wis a good thing.

Robert's eloquent testimony speaks volumes about the continuing, persistent risks of working underground, but also how things changed for the better in the post-war decades and how the miners' unions were at the centre of this transformation. They were the driving force behind the improvement in miners' working lives, ensuring respect and dignity at work and a civilised living for their families and communities. These post-war decades from the end of the war to the late 1970s are often described as a 'golden age' for workers. But Ayrshire miners, like others, had to mobilise, fight and struggle for improved conditions. Much of this union activity happened at national and pit level, though notably there was no big national strike until 1972 – the first since the General Strike of 1926. Ayrshire miners shared in these post-war workplace improvements, reforms in occupational health and safety and rising real wages, the product of strong trade unions and sustained demand for coal. And in the main, pit closures in this era were managed with sensitivity, with many miners transferred (for example to the Barony and Killoch) or moving to other alternative jobs in a period when demand for labour remained relatively high. This has been referred to as a period of 'managed decline'. This was to change dramatically from the mid-late 1970s, through the 1980s and 1990s, with Thatcher spearheading market-driven deindustrialisation and accelerating the pit closure programme with a vicious attack on the miners' unions amidst mass unemployment and deepening deprivation in Ayrshire. We turn to that story – the end of coal mining in Ayrshire through the lens of those living through it – in the next chapter.

83: The Houldsworth mine which operated from 1900-1965.
By kind permission of East Ayrshire Leisure Trust/East Ayrshire Council

5
'THE SCRAP-HEAP': THE END OF DEEP MINING

At nationalisation of the coal industry in 1947 there were 42 collieries in Ayrshire and in 1951, 11,569 men were employed in the industry accounting for around a fifth of Ayrshire's male workforce. Well over 50 mining villages accommodated this working and retired community in 1950s Ayrshire; some still thriving, others in terminal decline, as we have seen, with miners and their families decanting the old traditional miners' rows and moving to better housing in nearby communities, often to council estates, as at Patna, Muirkirk, Dalmellington and New Cumnock. Pit closures happened progressively, as in the pre-war period, as seams were worked out, with miners often moving from pit to pit, following the work (see Appendix 1 on pit closure dates for Ayrshire mines). Throughout the later 1940s, the 1950s and 1960s, 29 of the Ayrshire collieries closed including Bank, Beoch, Chalmerston, Houldsworth, Kames and Knockshinnoch. At 1970 there

84: Miner heading home from the Houldsworth mine. By kind permission of East Ayrshire Leisure Trust/East Ayrshire Council

were only thirteen Ayrshire collieries still running under the auspices of the National Coal Board (NCB), with production increasingly concentrated in the major collieries, such as the Barony and Killoch.

Ayrshire SNP MP Jim Sillars was amongst those who voiced their concerns at the precarious position of mining employment in Ayrshire in the mid-late 1970s. In an address to Parliament in February 1977 he painted a grim picture of the prospects for coal mining in Ayrshire unless there was significant state intervention:

> In Cumnock and Doon Valley district, the mining industry is at one and the same time our pillar of strength in respect of male employment and our Achilles heel. What is good for the coal industry is good for Cumnock and Doon Valley, and what is bad for that industry is very bad for the people living there.
>
> In Kyle and Carrick we have the mining village of Dailly whose life is presently threatened by the possible closure of Dalquharran colliery. Dailly lies within the Girvan employment exchange area where unemployment among men is already 14.3 per cent. The closure of Dalquharran would push that rate up to about 18 per cent. if no alternative jobs are made available.
>
> In South Ayrshire we have many of our industrial and employment eggs in the coal basket and, given the continued decline in the number of collieries and mining jobs, this has been a constant source of apprehension and anxiety for all concerned with the well-being of the community.
>
> Due to crass errors of judgment over the availability and possible price of oil, both Tory and Labour Governments ran down the coal industry in the late 1950s and throughout the 1960s, and in Ayrshire that decline has continued. In recent times we have lost Littlemill, Cairnhill and Minnivey. Now Dalquharran is threatened, and Pennyvenie in Dalmellington is known to have a limited life. There have been no new sinkings, and no indications have been given that the National Coal Board, the Government, or the strategic planning authority, which is the Strathclyde Regional Council, see anything but a declining future for the industry.
>
> The Ayrshire coalfield is, of course, extremely vulnerable. Our major markets remain electricity generation. Seventy per cent, of total Scottish coal production is burned in South of Scotland Electricity Board power stations, and the manpower requirements of the future will greatly depend upon the coal requirements of the SSEB. In geographical relationship to the coal-burning power stations in the

190

85: Pennyvenie colliery, c. 1978, around the time of its closure. It was the last deep mining pit in the Doon Valley.
By kind permission of East Ayrshire Leisure Trust/East Ayrshire Council

East, the Ayrshire coalfield, in the West is at a disadvantage.[1]

Apart from the issue of supplying power stations, Sillars went on to lay responsibility on entry to the EEC (1973) for the loss of coal markets and to castigate the Government and the Scottish Development Agency for lack of aggressive enough intervention – for example in the creation of new 'alternative' sources of employment for ex-miners, including factories. Unfortunately for Ayrshire and other coal mining communities, two

---

1 Hansard (record of Parliament); HC Deb 02 February 1977 vol 925 cc704-16704-705
Mr. James Sillars (South Ayrshire). Accessed at:
https://api.parliament.uk/historic-hansard/commons/1977/feb/02/coal-mining-ayrshire

years after Sillars' comments in Parliament Margaret Thatcher was elected as Prime Minister in 1979, leading a radically Conservative, neoliberal government which was implacably opposed to state intervention with subsidies and other support, and crusaded for the termination of what they saw as 'lame duck industries.' This triggered a new, devastating era of politically-driven accelerated deindustrialisation which completed the decimation of deep coal mining in the country, neutered the coal mining trade unions and prompted the end of underground mining in Ayrshire by the late 1980s.

Only a handful of collieries survived into the 1980s in Ayrshire, with deep mining in the county ending with the closure of Killoch in 1987 and the Barony in 1989. Open cast mining proliferated for another couple of decades or so, under the auspices of Scottish Coal and a plethora of private mining companies, but the open cast employed a relatively small number of workers – initially with most workers brought up from England in the 1980s. The work was very different to underground mining, akin to quarrying, involving earth moving from the surface and working massive diggers and dump trucks, and a very different skill set. Very few ex-underground miners appear to have transitioned into open cast mining. And there was much resentment against the industry for taking miners' jobs and despoiling the beautiful Ayrshire landscape. We discuss the open

86: The last shift from Pennyvenie at closure, 6 July 1978.
By kind permission of East Ayrshire Leisure Trust/East Ayrshire Council

cast era in more detail in the next chapter.

Having to adapt to pit closures was built into the DNA of mining communities, as the villages were built near coal reserves which had a finite life. 74 coal mines in north Ayrshire closed between 1900 and 1939, including the Kenneth's mines in Dreghorn, Springside and Drybridge and Baird's mines in Kilwinning, Irvine, Galston and Hurlford. Many coal miners and their families subsequently moved south and east to find work. However, the Depression affected East Ayrshire too, with 25 mines in the region closing in the 1920s and 1930s, including 11 mines run by Bairds and Dalmellington Iron Co. in Auchinleck, Dalmellington, Ochiltree, Cumnock and Glenbuck's Grasshill mines. After Grasshill closed Glenbuck miners tramped several miles to work in the Kames mine near Muirkirk, or over the county line into Lanarkshire to the Kennox colliery in Glespin.

James Whiteford recalled moving from pit to pit and village to village chasing work:

> Ma time in the mines, I enjoyed them! And, as I say, I was in seven different pits. [pause] … Ma first one was Knockshinnoch, the disaster pit. I done ma training in the Kames, another disaster pit. [pause] I got married an' then I come over to the Beoch Mine [coughs] an' then, Littlemill, Pennyvenie, the Barony an' the Killoch. So, I could nae blame Margaret Thatcher fer shutting them all! Ah ha. So, there you go, that's, that's ma, an' five, five villages, er, five miners' rows as well.

That said, pit closures and job losses accelerated rapidly from the 1970s and the difference then in a period a widespread economic recession, plant closures and mass unemployment was that there were far fewer opportunities for getting another job. Rab Wilson did an engineering apprenticeship in the mines and worked in the industry from 1977-1985. One of his first jobs was being sent to salvage any items of use from the Pennyvenie mine that had just closed. He was aware of what was happening at the time:

> There was more and more of these wee pits that closed down. I was only in the industry about eight years and in that time you were aware that local pits, small pits were closing down. Highhouse at Auchinleck you could see that it was on the verge of closing down. Other pits locally at Mauchline, Sorn pit, the Roger pit at Kelloholm

87: NUM President Arthur Scargill (in white shirt) in Cumnock during a rally during the miners' strike, August 1984. Alamy Stock Photo

and Kirkconnel these pits all closed down so you could see around about you that things were changing … It had started to dwindle and close down but that rapidly accelerated within a year or two of the strike [1984-5], pits were shutting everywhere and there wasn't much, nobody could do anything about it. You were a defeated army you had to take whatever was thrown at you.

The miners opposed pit closures in the 1970s and 1980s and Ayrshire miners were mostly solidly behind the NUM-led 1984-5 strike against closures and job losses. The strike created divisions within mining communities though. One miner who stayed out for the full year reflected on the impact:

Ma sister would come wi', 'cause she lives in Ayrshire, wi' food fer us once a month an' what you could, what you could get. [pause] So … they were tough again, times like that. But the community on the whole [coughs], they were…there was a lot of resentment at that time, when the pits closed. Er, during the strike, rather!
  I'm sorry. There's a lot o' men went back [pause] long before it! An' ma pal was one o' 'em! Now, I did nae hold a grudge agin 'im … an' the reason fer that is simple – he'd a family an' he hed tae look efter

194

his family an' hed tae go through all that, "You're a scab!" You're this, you're, you're…" [coughs] So, he had tae suffer that! [pause] But, er, I done what I felt was right an' he done what he felt was right. An' I accepted that! I didn't see any [pause], he was looking efter his family, for God Sake!

I could hae done the same tae save masel'! I was just masel', ma son was, he was working, like. But, on the whole [pause], I mean the strike was nae guid! It was bad. It was bad for the community. But as for the rest, naebody seemed tae bother!

Another couple, the Scobies, remembered the impact of the strike on their marriage, with Flora Scobie stating 'I nearly packed ma bags.' The couple also recalled the lasting resentment and discord within the community over the strike:

> JS: An' then, the likes o', there was a lot in Dalmellington started work … and the ones that what caused all the bother from Dalmellington. Waterside, at that period of time, was the head depot fer coal comin' in! Now, I forget the name o' the, the company that had all the lorries [pause] an' there was a certain crowd from Dalmellington – I knew them all – they were really bad! [pause] But you would nae turn round and say, "I'm no' doing that', but they would let, they would let the coal drivers in to dump the coal if, if the ones that was stopping it, if they would fling two or three bags off [knocking noise] for the ones that was trying to stop them frae going in!
>
> *AM: Is this during the strike?*
>
> JS: This was during the strike. Now, it caused a lot o' animosity among other members and, er, there was a bit o' harshness.
>
> FS: It was a great vil…
>
> JS: An' ba, an' badness.
>
> FS: It was a great community here.
>
> JS And, er, gradually as they started getting back t' work [pause], there was a bit o' bother. Seeing grown-up men crying like children because o' the abuse! Because maybe they'd started their work a month … before!

But there was a pervasive sense following the defeat in 1985 that resistance was futile and the end of mining was inevitable. Automation was also developing, in itself meaning less miners were needed underground. Davie Higgins, then Chief Electrician at Killoch, recalled what happened after the strike ended:

Polkemmet colliery had been lost altogether during the strike. They had had a full computerised Minos system package. I went up to Polkemmet, disconnected and dismantled the mainframe, plus all the outstations and accessories that I could muster. Lorries were dispatched to load and bring all the equipment to Killoch for installation. I drove back in my car with eight huge volumes of system instructions and the secret computer password etched in my memory. Behind me three lorry loads of equipment that no Killoch personnel had ever laid eyes on before.

There followed a daunting learning process followed by some rapid installation of infrastructure. Learning the system as we went along, within eight months we had seven underground conveyors fully unmanned, operated and monitored from the control room on the surface. Also they were working efficiently and relatively trouble free. That meant that 24 jobs could disappear.

The last pits in Ayrshire (Killoch and Barony) were closed by the end of the decade.

In November 1992, Cumnock and Doon Valley District Council

88: Miner Matt Reid of Dalmellington wearing his mining safety helmet on his last shift at Pennyvenie. By kind permission of East Ayrshire Leisure Trust/East Ayrshire Council

196

89: Pennyvenie mine manager John Kennedy, photographed on the day of the pit closure in 1978.
By kind permission of East Ayrshire Leisure Trust/East Ayrshire Council

oversaw an oral history project which included two local New Cumnock miners, James Ferguson and Richard Allan, reflecting on the impact of the end of deep mining for themselves and their community. Speaking just three years after the closure of the last deep mines in Ayrshire they recall the trauma, ruination and deep sense of loss when the pits closed. Their recollections speak volumes about the individual lives that were devastated, the impact on families and the wider deleterious effects on the community. And James and Richard, aged 65 and 33 respectively when interviewed in 1992, provided interesting perspectives on how different age groups and generations of miners were affected.

James reflected on his working days at the Beoch (1951-68) and

90: George Sturgeon (Dalmellington) at the demolition of Pennyvenie, late 1970s.
George was born and raised in Lethanhill.
By kind permission of East Ayrshire Leisure Trust/East Ayrshire Council

then at Killoch (1968-1984) and the abundance of work for miners:

> I worked nineteen years constant night shift on that type of work ...
> After the Beoch closed I was transferred to the Killoch. We did not
> all get work straight way ... we had to wait in turn until we got a job
> at the power loading. I eventually got a job [on the loading] after a
> couple of years ... At that particular time [1950s] the majority of

the miners were employed between New Cumnock, Kirkconnel and Dalmellington. The Beoch Colliery was at Dalmellington, but there was also Knockshinnoch Colliery, Bridgend, and the Bank Pit. They were all working in New Cumnock at that time and in Dalmellington there were six or seven pits in operation at that time ... there was not much other industry in New Cumnock at that time ... There was the sock factory ... Some of the men worked on the railway, some of them worked on the farms.

Recalling the mid-1970s when he started, Richard Allan commented: 'Everybody was working. There was jobs for everybody.' He continued: 'Now when there are no pits, there is no work.' Richard and James reckoned perhaps 80-90% of men in New Cumnock at that time worked in the mines and reflected on the powerful work ethic that characterised these communities. James noted: 'As far as I am concerned the best man is the one who is working every day.' As James recalled, the pit closures and long-term mass unemployment that followed was soul destroying:

> When the Killoch closed [1989] there would be approximately 500 New Cumnock miners out of work. Men like myself over fifty found it impossible to get a job. A small percentage of the men got jobs in the sock factory ... but even to this day [1992] there are a lot of men who have not been able to gain employment ... When it did close, I can assure you there were a lot of unhappy faces, because there were a lot of the miners employed at the Killoch who were over fifty, and as far as they were concerned that was them on the scrap-heap ... They did receive their redundancy money, and I think they got unemployment benefit for a year and after that they just had to dig into whatever savings they had left.

Use of the 'scrap heap' metaphor crops up often in these stories from men living the experience of being unemployed; feeling worthless; lacking identity and purpose. This was a demoralised community, disempowered twice over by the defeat of their trade union in the pivotal 1984-5 miners' strike and by the accelerated programme of pit closures in the aftermath which led to their unemployment. If laid off miners were over 50 they got concessionary coal and a weekly payment – which was something – though the latter was not generous (James got the princely sum of 75p per week from his mineworker pension). Redundancy payments ranged from £3,000 to £5,000 for those that had been working in the pits for 40-plus years, and peaked up to £16,000-£17,000 for young men with up to twenty years' work experience (though the young men would not have qualified for free coal). The wide variation in redundancy payments caused resentment, notably amongst older miners seeing the younger men with such big pay-outs. James recalled: 'Another man was very angry because he had been in the pit since he was fourteen and he was 57 when he was made redundant and he only got pennies.' James' brother got £500 after a working life as a miner for 51 years.

Alice Wallace, born 1945 in Benwhat, spoke of her brother and father's experience as the pits closed:

> [My brother] worked in the pits and he was quite happy. He was OK with that. But the pits were closing, some of them, an' a lot o' the boys were going to England and, er, he was going down there but he missed his girlfriend an' he came back up an' he got his job back in the pits! An' he got married to Carol an' they were good together, it was fine. Er, my younger brother, I mean, ten years later that was, […] he went into the pits and he took a trade and, er, just about then, the pit that he was in was closing an' some o' them did nae get other jobs, they were nae transferred. […] He did forestry work for a while after that …
>
> *YM: What about your Dad, when the pits closed? How did that affect him?*
>
> Ah, he was sixty-four, nearing the retiring age, and they wanted rid o' the older men and, er, he got the chance of redundancy an' at that time, it was very little. I think it was about two or three thousand pounds fer being all these years since he was fourteen till he was sixty-odds, two or three thousand pounds and that was it … there were younger men who had spent many less years in the pits and they got thirty-three thousand! It was just so unfair. But I think it was because they had so many years still of work, working years, and if they could nae get anything, that was gonna see them by quite a bit but it was angersome, mind you!

Others moved to find work, some within Ayrshire, trying local towns like Ayr and Kilmarnock, others further afield. May Baird, born in 1954 in the Highhouse Rows, recalled her father's itinerant experience chasing work:

> Ah [pause], ma dad, as I say, left, left the pits and went to Kilmarnock. T' the Glenfield, Glenfield and Kennedy, engineering works. An'… we went there. We got a house … an' moved there. We stayed in Kilmarnock for a year, kind of like, kind o' *gypsy-like*!! I think we

went *everywhere*! We stayed in Kilmarnock fer a year an' I would be
eighteen! Er … *sixteen*, I tell a lie! I worked in a local pharmacy here.
And [pause], we were there a year an' came back. We hed put oor
name on the list *fer* Cumnock so, we've been in Cumnock ever since!

May continued:

> I think the, kind a, downfall o' the pits was when a lot o' people went
> t' England! Um … Yorkshire … t' work. I think that … kind a … did
> the damage then. I remember some families went t' Australia! … An'
> there was some in Edinburgh … went. There was another pit there
> in Edinburgh an' I had been married t' a miner an' … that was the
> option then … But no, it's not everybody that can do that, move away
> from their family an' friends!

May's mother, Isabel Hendry, born in 1934, was set against the family
migrating to England. When her husband was laid off from the Barony, he
took work locally on poor wages instead:

> When your dad was laid out o' work, *I* was determined, I was nae
> taking you lassies away doon tae England! … An' sometimes your
> dad would say, "But it's the only times I can get *work*." *I* used t' read
> all these stories in the paper, about England, ken? But I used to say,
> "No, I'm not…" I wouldn't go to England! So, he got a job wi' the …
> *Forestry*. … But it was like … out the … fire into the frying … *out*
> the frying pan, into the fire! So … I went tae … we went there fer,
> was it *six* months? Six months. It was lovely! Lovely weather! A *lovely*
> place. But the wa, the wages was … *nothing*!!

Younger miners laid off could find themselves in a better position. James
recalled some used their redundancy to set up small businesses. Richard
Allan used his pay-off money and an NCB loan (part of the 'redundancy'
package) to invest in a shop. Another miner aged 47 when laid off
from Killoch bought a caravan with his redundancy pay, had a spell of
unemployment and then got a job at Butlins at Heads of Ayr. He recalled
fellow miners getting jobs in Forestry and many taking on casual work
and others remaining unemployed: 'Because they got two or three pound
redundancy they just went haywire, kind of style … It was bad.' James
Whiteford was 48 when he took his redundancy from Killoch in 1985. He
recalled:

I says tae ma wife, (an' she was born in a miners' row as well, up Benwhat), I said t' her, she says, "Whit are you gonna do?" I says, "I'm gonna … I'm gonna pack in, that's what I'm gonna do! I'm gonna take the money…" because that type, that sort o' money that I got, thirty thousand or summat like that … I get thirty thousand pound?! Eh? So, I ta'en it an' I never regret it! But I've never had a *full*-time job since! [pause] I've done a lot o' work! … I've, I was pretty handy! I would paper, decorate, DIY! Even outside o' houses! Me an' ma pal! So, we'd do all that! They would cut down trees an' we would go up tae that … open cast an' steal coal … when ma son had the railway pub up there in Dalmellington. Coal fire. I used tae go up there. So, I was always active! [pause] Mebbe that's … mebbe I've Margaret Thatcher t' thank fer that! I mean, because that's when I retired! … The local businesses did a *bomb*! Especially the pubs! *They* done a bomb! Every day! … I even bought a *caravan* for God Sake!! [laughing] So, but there you go! *That's* whit I done an' I *don't* regret it! I'm *proud* I was a miner! … Yeah, so I am! I always say that. *Very* proud!

'Lucky' ones got re-employment in other pits (some travelling down to England), or the local sock factory or other factories in the vicinity, like British Aerospace. Many moved out; some emigrated chasing alternative work and lives, especially younger men and those with younger families who were more mobile. New Cumnock's population declined from around 8,000 at its peak to around 2,500. Local resident and ex-miner Rab Wilson equated this to the 'Highland Clearances' and had no doubt who was culpable: 'It was booming and all that was destroyed as far as I'm concerned by Margaret Thatcher … she destroyed New Cumnock … She had virtually wiped us off the map.' The village was one of those places that celebrated the death of Thatcher in April 2013 with local parties.

Retraining for miners was limited – there was a joinery retraining centre in Irvine and Cumnock for example, but that had closed by 1992. Richard Allan was asked about retraining opportunities and replied: 'Not a lot. Nothing.' He was sceptical, saying he knew of no-one that actually got a job following any retraining or job centre schemes: 'It's just another way to keep you off the Broo', he said. Several New Cumnock miners bought a £10,000 share in the Monktonhall Colliery in Mid-Lothian when it was bought over by a workers' consortium in June 1992 (it lasted for six years before closing in 1998). James recalled: 'They are travelling up there, I think it's about 72 miles, for the sake of having a job. That is how desperate some of the men are.' This was a four-hour round-trip drive. Asked how many redundant New Cumnock miners he thought had found reemployment Richard thought 'about 20%', many moving out of New Cumnock or 'travelling great distances daily to get employment'. He concluded:

> I was going to say it's only going to get worse, but it couldn't get any worse. We are at rock bottom just now … For our dignity we have to have work. We have lost our dignity and everything now. We have no dignity, because we have to have work.

Richard's repetition of the word 'dignity' and its association with 'work' tells us a lot about what job loss meant to this generation of coal miners. He also spoke movingly about the impact this had on the mining village of New Cumnock, reflecting on the growth of crime amongst the younger generation (burglaries; car theft; vandalism) and a wider malaise: 'It's hard, very hard, and everybody has a different feeling, but the smiles and the atmosphere is not in the village … the heart has gone out of the place'. Depopulation was evident across the county. Muirkirk's population fell from around 7,000 at peak in the 1960s, to 3,000 at the mid-1980s and to 1,700 by 1998.[2]

Some of the older men, including James Ferguson, equated employment with strength and independence and saw this situation as one which challenged their masculinity, having been brought up with the idea that a man's role was to be the breadwinner and provider for the family. James commented in his interview in 1992 on the increased tendency for women to be in paid employment noting: 'Everything seems to be pointing to the fact that it is the men that are going to be the weaker sex at the end of the day'. For the men, he argued, 'they have got to get used to a different way of life'. That said, James ended his interview arguing that mining communities are resilient and rallied around to support each other in times of need: 'The community has come through all these things and I think that they will all be united right up to their final days. They have been brought up hardy and I cannot see anything to split them now'. Nicola Higgins' recalled that one of her Dad's coping strategies in hard times in the 1980s when he was in his early twenties was to steal coal:

> He was a coal stealer, so he was and we were asking what he'd done, he says, well I had to do it to get extra money for you's ken. So he was telling us a story that he used to get four bags … he paid aff the security guard to let them in [to the colliery] and when he went

---

2 *Sunday Mail*, 1 November 1998. Accessed at: https://www.thefreelibrary.com/IN+THE+VAL-LEY+OF+DEATH%3B+The+village+that+could+be+smothered+by+lust...-a060751802

in they'd get four bags of coal, two on each side and he would be peddling down [on his bike]. He said he got caught one day with the polis, and [he] says, could you drop me off at the nursery because I need to go and pick up my weans, because he was coming to get me at the nursery and he'd been caught with the polis so he had.

He used to say, whit was it he says and aw, one of his pals used to sell it to folk then go back and steal out of their coal bunkers. Aye, help them to keep it in the bags and they went back and stole out of the coal bunkers. He says it was £2.50 or £3 for a bag of coal that's what they would sell it at. I was laughing when he said, he had to ask the polis to drop him off at nursery because my mum would've killed him. And my mum she worked in a shoe factory, Shoe Fayre in at the toon, aye and that's what my dad … when I was at nursery he would go and steal the coal.

So, there's a song, I don't know if you want to look it up, it's Loretta Lynn, 'Coal Miner's Daughter', well he sings, you're a Coal Stealer's Daughter! So, he'd sit on Saturday night and sing that.

Interviewed in his home in New Cumnock in June 2023, thirty years after James and Richard shared their memories, local ex-miner (1977-1985), Scots poet and storyteller Rab Wilson provided further insights into the effects of mine closures:

You would meet folk in the pit that weren't the most top-notch scholars we might say but there was always a job for these guys, there was always work for everybody and it meant that you done a job of work, you got a wage, you felt valued, you come home you'd done a day's work, you had your dinner, you were tired you slept. You weren't unemployed sitting watching a screen all day sitting up half the night, sleeping half the day. There was a purpose and self-fulfilment and a value to life that a lot of people maybe don't have any more. And there will be families locally from Cumnock, New Cumnock, Kelloholm, Sanquhar who maybe two or three generations who have never worked, never worked. They don't know what work is and all the concomitant issues and problems that derive from that and these are the problems of mental health and drugs and deprivation.

He continued:

A lot of the guys that finished up at 50 years old they never worked again. I know people right now, they are old, old men now in their mid-80s, and they have been retired longer than they've worked for. They maybe worked in the pits for 25, 30 years but now they've not worked for 30, 35 years so half their lives has been spent retired they're not working. That was a common thing around here and these men never worked again and the pits just closed, shut down and disappeared. And now it's something you see in a museum.

To lose steady, stable, well-unionised industrial work in the collieries was traumatic and pit closures were met with shock, disbelief and a range of emotions. Reflecting on the pit closures in the 1960s and 1970s Ayrshire miner Robert Hall recalled in an interview with Ian MacDougall in 2001:

> Ye could see it coming quicker, quicker, quicker. As each pit shut down, the communities became less and less. The Doon Valley suffered tremendous damage when the pits such as ah've mentioned closed down, because it became a ghost place.

Rab Wilson recalled his last day as a miner:

> But I remember my last day at the pit ... the 1st February [1985] and I finished my shift at the pit heed at the end of the shift I took my steel toe-capped boots off and I took my old safety helmet off. I had an old fashioned safety helmet because I was a characterful person I had this old fashioned kind of black helmet that I wore. I took my boots and my helmet and I just went up the gantry ... and there was a conveyor belt that went up at a steep pitch into a Dutch hopper which was where all the rubbish went, it went into a lorry and they took it doon and dumped it. And I stood in the gantry and I had my boots and my helmet and I flung my boots onto the conveyor belt and I flung my helmet onto the conveyor belt and I just watched them go up the conveyor belt and disappear into the hopper. And I walked down to the showers in my stocking soles and had my shower and that was me. I left the pit.

Hugh Hainey started his working life in Pennyvenie as a young apprentice at the age of 16 in 1937. His family and friends from Lethanhill worked in the pit and in 1945 he carried out a survey of equipment in preparation for nationalisation in 1947. In 1978, having left the mining industry to work of the South of Scotland Electricity Board in 1948, Hugh returned to Pennyvenie to turn off the electricity. His son, Alistair Hainey recalled his father's account:

As he told the story, he said that he took responsibility for the task, signed himself out the office on his own, against protocols, and went alone to Pennyvenie and "shot the head of the mains" effectively killing the power supply to the mine. He didn't want anyone else to do it, as it had meant so much to him, his family and his friends during his life. He said that what should have been a job taking half an hour, took him almost a whole day, as he found it so difficult to bring himself to take the final step to irrevocably shut down Pennyvenie. His brother-in-law, Dan Wallace had been killed in a rockfall at Pennyvenie in March 1968, so dad's life continued to be touched by the effects of the industry long after he left the mines.

My dad seldom showed emotions outwardly, and I only remember seeing him cry around the time my mum died. He was also teary-eyed telling me this story, which says it all about how much it meant.

Muirkirk-born Davie Higgins was one of the Killoch's three Chief Electricians and the last man on site at the Killoch Colliery in Ayrshire when it closed. His working life epitomised miners' itinerant experience moving from pit to pit as he started in 1963 in Kennox colliery (Lanarkshire), then worked at Kames, Barony, Cairnhill, Killoch, Sorn and back to Killoch. He shared his story with Glenbuck-born Sam Purdie in 2021, recalling:

At the time of the Killoch closure, the suddenness of it all was to be witnessed to be believed … All the lads knew that the future was bleak. They had given up. Most had accepted that it would be better to take the redundancy payment on offer … At a meeting in Edinburgh, the closure was announced. The very next morning, we were instructed to keep as many of our men as possible on the surface for immediate redundancy interview. It had all been set up well in advance. I remember one of the interviewers boasting, "You supply the bodies, and we will supply the money." I remember the first of our lads being called. He was back in our midst within barely a few minutes. Confirm your name, this is your redundancy sum, sign here, go and get washed, the bus will be here to take you home shortly, that's it, you're finished, cheerio, you don't need to come back.

The lads were stunned by the suddenness of it all. It was no longer a laugh. They did not even have time to say farewell to old friends. We staff members felt somewhat sick. In an instant we realised that possibly the finest group of dedicated capable tradesmen were to be scattered and dismissed with utter contempt. Within a week the workforce was gone, another week and almost all staff had also gone.

On 1 Nov, it was my own hand that threw the final circuit breakers to shut off all electrical power below ground level. A long poem was written, I have it somewhere. It began:

> It was bitter cold that morning, the first day of November
> Another working day we say, but one we long remember
> Mr Mackin & Mr Higgins who chose to throw the switch.
> And the pit born proud in sixty-three has died in eighty-six.

I found myself alone on the premises, a sole employee, almost like a watchman for a few months. Until I refused the British Coal proposal for my future. On the last day of Feb 1987, I too took the payoff and walked away from an industry that had given me so much to enjoy.

It was over. The bridges were burned, and there was no road back … At the time there were also thoughts of bringing the towers down by controlled demolition. When it happened much later, it was publicised and there was even provision for the public to view the spectacle, but I was far away by then. No bad thing. It would have broken my heart. The death of an industry that had given so much to our forebears, but it took from them more than it gave. We remember with pride and regret just the same.[3]

The significance of mining work – what it meant to the men – and the profound shock of closure and subsequent redundancy seeps through David's emotional, heart-felt reminiscence. His story reveals something of the callousness, insensitivity and 'contempt' of management contrasted against the mixed emotions: the 'pride' and joy, and the 'regret', shock and sorrow, of the miners. The loss of mining work had reverberations across the community and was felt deeply by many. Auchinleck miner Joe Owens recalled sobbing at the conclusion of the 1984-5 miners' strike and again in 1992 when another wave of job losses occurred in the industry. As he stated, 'The area has been decimated.'[4]

Sometimes nostalgia creates an enduring image of mining villages as tight-knit communities where everyone knew each other and helped each other cope with the difficult circumstances of life. There is much truth in this, but such communities had their divisions, based on occupation, gender, religion and sometimes race and nationality (as with the anti-English sentiment evident during the 1980s with incoming English open cast miners 'blowing-in' to Ayrshire). Fractures were also evident during

---

3 Email, Davie Higgins to Sam Purdie, 27 Oct 2021: permission granted for authors' use.
4 Joe Owens, *Miners, 1984-1994: A Decade of Endurance* (Edinburgh: Polygon, 1994), p.4, pp.10-11.

the miners' strikes, especially 1984-5, between those who held out and the 'scabs' who did not strike or returned to work, some out of dire economic necessity unable to sustain their families over a year-long strike without wages.

Another difference was between the dominant 'ruination' narrative, which emphasised the profound loss that came with the end of mining, and other divergent voices – a minority of people who expressed their relief and welcomed the pit closures. For the latter, closures meant that sons would no longer have to work in a dangerous and unhealthy occupation and those in the pits could be liberated to escape to better jobs and more meaningful careers. Davie Higgins reflected on the toll the industry took and the importance of the mining communities in mitigating this:

> I had watched my father die at 61 years of age. A very old and broken man, not untypical of his fellows few who ever lived to collect their pension. I watched as his fellows also died, old broken men, gone before their time. Who in Westminster or anywhere else thought they wanted the pits. What the men wanted to protect was the self-respect of being an earner and not a sponger. Of looking after their own in the bonds of a community that could offer only the dole if the pits were closed. That was a major problem little understood by those who had never experienced it. In mining villages, the community looked after its own. There was always a reluctance to leave, to seek pastures new, the very culture demanded you look after your own old, the infirm and the unfortunate.

And some were lucky enough to find other jobs, for example, in social work, nursing, teaching, politics and local government. For the majority, Thatcher was the sworn enemy and reviled (with her death celebrated in many communities). But for others she was a 'saviour' whose actions saved many lives. Henry (Harry) Kennedy, born 1932 in Burnton, articulated the latter view in an interview conducted in April 2022 (when Harry was 90). He worked for almost 40 years in the Beoch mine, Pennyvenie, Barony and finally the Killoch, until being made redundant in 1985, aged 53:

> Unfortunately, there's nae [pits] left noo but as far as I'm concerned, they're quite pleased because there's naebody running aboot wi' … silicosis. Maggie Thatcher was the best woman that ever I knew. All the fellas was the same … They, they did nae like the Killoch at all! An' what folk did nae understand, there were all these silicosis, pneumoconiosis – nasty. Men that worked beside me, big, strong

men and in later years, they had nae a gasp! … As I say, there were that many o' them died wi' silicosis, pneumoconiosis an' it was *terrible* watching them, you ken, they had nae a *gasp*!! … that's, that's aboot the worst thing you can get! … I *don't* think you'd have a person in Dalmellington would be sorry when the, the pits shut. As far as Maggie Thatcher [she] was the best woman I ever ken! I'm quite sure half o' they men would nae get ony life oot it at all! When they finished up … If they'd been working, you know, a lot o' them had silicosis or … it's kind a hard, it's mebbe, you mebbe think it's kind a silly saying that but I'm quite sure they're all quite happy – at least t' get a wee bit o' life!

Some miners took their redundancy payment willingly and without regret, some anxious that they would miss out on any redundancy payment if they did not voluntarily go. Rab Wilson recalled that some in the industry relocated to other work, and those who had undergone the rigorous tradesmen's apprenticeship in the pits were particularly advantaged:

So Graham Dossie Whiteford he finished up at Kellingley [the last mine to close in England in 2015] and did a life-time of work in the industry. And there was a few others like that who went down south and worked in the pits there, the younger guys. Many of them … went into factories, local factories and things like that, retrained. I remember Tommy Thompson … became the head of the Co-operative Funeral Service in Scotland. A lot of the folk from the mining industry were very capable and able people, there were a lot of clever, able folk there that maybe wouldn't have shone if they had stayed in the pits but they left the pits and went on to do very well. Another guy who worked with me … went to British Aerospace or Caledonia Air the aviation industry in Prestwick - they took a lot especially the tradesmen. A lot of the ex-mining tradesmen they all ended up working there, got good jobs and my pal John Gibson he became a high flying, one of the sort of chief engineers in there working in the aviation industry. There were very clever, able people that maybe for some of them the closing of the pits was a saving grace for them because it gave them a new lease of life and they went on to do really well in life. Some folk … went abroad. There was a guy who went away and did really well in the mining industry in South Africa … and some folk … the tradesmen … went to the North Sea, the oil industry, jobs there. But any heavy engineering type industry there was a big railway factory at Kilmarnock … there was a heavy engineering factory in Kilmarnock that employed quite a few of the ex-mining engineers. And the electricians they would have got work in any of the factories they would have been keen to take on these.

The seismic changes in such communities from the 1970s included massive impacts on women's lives and constraints on the opportunities for the younger generation deprived now of jobs in a well-paid and well unionised industrial job. When asked by an interviewer in 1992 about the impact of mine closures on the young, James Ferguson replied: 'There are just no jobs for the young people nowadays … the situation is totally hopeless … it is just an existence.' Closure of mines was happening at the same time that factories and other industrial workplaces were closing across Ayrshire and beyond as the economy shifted from manufacturing towards the service sector. Women's stories and their lived experience of deindustrialisation have been relatively neglected compared to men's, whose stories have usually been the focus of attention, both in research and in policy-making. For women in Ayrshire this meant several things. Those women traditionally employed in industrial work – for example in textile, clothing and carpet-making factories – found themselves made redundant and seeking work, experiencing the same kind of profound impacts on their incomes, standards of living, identities, loss of status and deprivations that male miners (and others) experienced.

Nicola Higgins spoke in an interview about her experience working in a local medical supplies factory (BDF Medical Supplies; later Guardian Surgical – who made sterile surgical drapes and gowns) in her local town of Patna, where she worked in a well-paid job from 2004-2016. She described the job as 'great, all local people … It was booming... fantastic.' Over time the work became harder, with targets (and hence bonuses) more difficult to reach. Difficulties arose trying to compete with cheap Chinese imports and the Patna factory was closed in 2016, with workers relocated or made redundant. Nicola described how she felt:

> I was absolutely devastated when it shut, so I was. I loved my job … I had the best days of my life in there … It was a horrible time … there was a lot of anger.

Nicola moved on to a job at Ayr Hospital as a Kitchen Assistant and then to working with recovering drug addicts. She recalled the plethora of suicides in Patna, in part a response to the despair that accompanied the lack of jobs and opportunities in these declining ex-mining communities. This process of deteriorating job satisfaction, lost opportunities and ill-health impacts paralleled what has been remembered by others locally.

At the same time, the loss of the main male breadwinner through unemployment as pits closed put enormous pressure on families, especially sole earner households, encouraging or forcing housewives to seek paid employment to bring money in. This accelerated the post-war shift towards women entering or continuing to work in paid employment beyond marriage and childbirth, in many cases with women becoming the sole earners where men were unemployed and couldn't find work. Given the persistence of gendered norms in family and household responsibilities, this could result in women carrying a heavier 'double burden' of undertaking paid employment whilst also being still responsible for most of the 'traditional' family and household responsibilities of looking after the children, cooking and cleaning.

As deindustrialisation deepened across Ayrshire, however, and industrial employment contracted, opportunities for men and women to find good quality, skilled, decently paid, well-unionised work declined from the 1970s. In Ayrshire, as elsewhere, there emerged a 'new economy' based on less-skilled, poorly paid and more insecure and precarious work, often poorly unionised, for example in the health and care sector. Rab Wilson argued that many of the new jobs in private industry failed to match the high occupational health and safety standards of the nationalised mining industry:

> The training you got [in the mines] was the best of the best and it erred on the side of safety because it was so strong in unions and we had fought for 200 years for safety issues. It was an industry that was very highly safety conscious so that everybody was always taught to work with safety in mind and I know for a fact that in a lot of these private factories they take a lot of shortcuts with safety that would never have happened. You would have been straight oot the gate for some of the practices that go on in the local factories now around here. I'm talking, Irvine, Kilmarnock, Ayr there is practices going on in these factories that would have seen you automatically sacked and marched through the gate for safety breaches. And yet because these are private industries they take short cuts which are dangerous for workers and staff and unions don't have the power anymore to do much about it.

This shift from mining and manufacturing into the service sector and care economy has been described as facilitating the emergence of a 'new working class' – one that was less well-off, more vulnerable and more fragmented and individualised.[5] This paralleled what has been remembered locally, and somewhat nostalgically, as a disintegration of the close community ties that characterised the miners' row villages.

HEALTH AND WELL-BEING IN DEINDUSTRIALISED AYRSHIRE

There is no doubt that the collapse of coal mining, the wider process of deindustrialisation, and the virtual disappearance of manufacturing employment has had a deleterious effect on the health and well-being of Ayrshire's people. As we've noted, steady, well-paid, unionised and satisfying work gave way to mass unemployment; under-employment; more precarious and casual work; lesser paid, more disempowered (with trade unions being neutered) and less rewarding employment. The defeat of the miners' strike in 1985, followed quickly by the last Ayrshire pit closure a few years later in 1989, generated a sense of hopelessness and despair across mining communities – of middle-aged men being on the 'scrap heap' and few opportunities for the younger generation. All of this impacted adversely on people's health, both physically and mentally. In a very real sense, the past was inscribed upon people's bodies and expressed through their health – in physical and mental scars, disabilities, stress and depression, and chronic ill-health.

The prevailing situation in Ayrshire today mirrors the overall picture in coalfield communities across the UK, as indicated in a recent (2020) report:

> British coalfields lag behind national averages and are particularly affected by economic weakness, socio-economic disadvantage and ill health.
>
> According to the 2020 Scottish Index of Multiple Deprivation, the coalfield areas are still overrepresented among Scotland's more disadvantaged and deprived communities, including East Ayrshire and Doon Valley South.
>
> Unemployment levels and child poverty remain higher (by around 30%) and income persistently lower in coalfield communities (including East Ayrshire) than the Scottish average.
>
> This situation worsened over the decade or so since 2010.
>
> Former coalmining communities are affected by persistent health inequalities, and many are now in a much worse comparative position (29% of areas are now among the 20% most disadvantaged

---

5 Gabriel Winant, '"Hard Times Make for Hard Arteries and Hard Livers": Deindustrialization, Biopolitics, and the Making of a New Working Class' *Journal of Social History* 53:1 (2019), pp.107-132.

for health, up from 18% in 2012). Life expectancy for both women and men is below the Scottish average … Environmental issues persist, with 167,000 people or 36% of the total population of the coalfield areas living within 500 metres of a derelict site, compared to 28% for Scotland.[6]

This idea of deterioration and 'ruination' since the 1970s must be put in perspective and in context. Poverty and precarity were no strangers to the miners and their families throughout the history of mining communities in Ayrshire. Pit work and life in the rows before Second World War involved much risk to life and health, as we discussed in previous chapters. And health stagnated or deteriorated in the interwar Depression in Ayrshire coal mining communities. Infectious childhood diseases were still rampant and could be deadly. Before he was born in 1936, Sam Purdie lost a sister to diphtheria. Tuberculosis was also still a significant and dreaded killer (though in decline) until antibiotics and x-ray campaigns came in the decade after Second World War. Nan (Agnes) Auld (Lethanhill 1930s) described the prevalence of TB before Second World War and as we have seen respiratory disability through pneumoconiosis, silicosis, bronchitis and emphysema was rampant amongst coal miners. Those remembering this past were very aware of the fragility of life in the Depression.

The Second World War marked a significant watershed. The 1940s to the 1970s were decades of rising living and health standards for most, based on a growing economy, rising real wages, the wonderful NHS and the NCB's tighter focus on occupational health and safety standards in the mines. Strong trade unions underpinned this and fundamental to this improvement in people's lives was larger and better-quality housing. To be sure, more and more Ayrshire pits were closing well before Thatcher's election, but closures were managed and unemployment levels remained relatively low, as long as miners could tolerate the switch to alternative jobs or longer and longer journeys to the remaining viable pits. As Ayrshire poet and ex-miner Rab Wilson put it:

And this was because industry was booming and New Cumnock was booming and I wouldnae have thought as a kid I'd a thought we are a poor place here and things aren't great. But when you look at it historically now compared with what happened after Thatcher we were probably living in a 'golden age' … At the time this area

6 Coalfields Regeneration Trust, The Scottish Coalfields in 2020 (Glasgow: Social Value Lab, 2020), Accessed at: https://www.coalfields-regen.org.uk/wp-content/uploads/2020/06/SVL_-Scottish-coalfields-2020.pdf.

was booming with industry and there was no shortage of work for employment. If you left the school you were guaranteed a job, absolutely guaranteed it. You had carpet factories in Cumnock, you had Falmers jeans factory, you had a knitwear factor, you had a silk factory, Halls silk factory New Cumnock, there was a shirt factory New Cumnock. Factories everywhere and then the pits - and the pits was probably by far the biggest employer.

He continued:

Mental health was better at that time because everybody, you didn't have drug problems, there was always alcohol, but it never seemed to be a huge problem. Folk were healthy and fit, they were eating better, better food nutrition, better hygiene. A lot of great things that lead to a better society.

That said, job loss at this time of growing expectations could be devastating. Miners' Union official and Scottish Safety Officer George Montgomery recalled the impact of the closure of Barony for several years (until 1966) after the shaft collapse disaster that killed four men in 1962:

91: Barony colliery, 1950s.
Courtesy of the National Mining Museum Scotland Trust

92: Barony after reopening, 1970.
Courtesy of the National Mining Museum Scotland Trust

Anyway ah went tae the pit, and the next Tuesday ah wis handed a folder that size. There were 1,600 men's names on it - made redundant. Pit was closed. Auchinleck wis a ghost village. And a lot o' the men went away tae Cannock in Staffordshire tae work. A lot o' men were distributed through pits in Ayrshire, as a temporary measure. And then we started a campaign tae reopen the pit …. But comin' back tae ordinary people: sadder than that, there were a whole number o' men committed suicide and … But ye got told different things at different times. Somebody says, "That's [X___] namin' him. Found his body in the dump" - this is where two rivers meet in Cumnock, the Lugar and the Glaisnock - drowned. [X___], smashed tae bits on the … killed wi' a train, the Glasgow tae Dumfries express ... Another yin wis seen makin' towards the pit, and they reckoned he'd a pyjama jacket on, and he wis found suspended frae a tree. Killed. So these... when they close pits, and dae these things, these are the effects it has on people.

This situation worsened in the 1970s and 1980s as pit closures accelerated and there was declining local employment to offer alternative opportunities,

215

as Ayrshire factories also shed labour, downsized and closed. After leaving mining in 1985, Rab Wilson retrained as a nurse taking up roles working as a community nurse and a psychiatric nurse for more than two decades at Ailsa Hospital, Ayr from 1989-2012. He was well placed, therefore, to comment on the impacts of mine closures and resulting unemployment and job precarity on health and well-being. He reflected on how people lost 'purpose, self-fulfilment and a sense of value to life' leading to 'problems of mental health, drugs and deprivation':

> Some people when they got all this redundancy money, they'd never had money in all their life so a lot of them just drank it. So there was problems with drink that came fae this and the fact that you're not gonna, there's nae reason no to drink because if you've got nae work and nae prospect of work and you've got money in your pocket will go to the pub and this is what happened to a lot of them too … For a while this, you could see this local … That led to bad alcoholism as well, utter depression. So these were the kind of things that you would see and people being admitted severely depressed just couldn't get out their bed just lay about all day literally losing the will to live. And then the whole knock-on effect of that is poor health, family break-downs, divorce, domestic violence these were other issues that would come aboot because of this and families breaking up which would lead to more economic deprivation. Houses splitting up, families splitting up, problems relating because of that to poverty leading to folk … Every aspect of this had a knock-on effect which was all an ever-decreasing spiral into bad stuff - drugs, poor health, obesity, depression you name it. I wrote about it a lot in the sonnets I wrote … this kind of feeling of hopelessness and worthlessness and there was nothing for them. It was a very dark, bleak time and it's maybe only now and I'm talking almost 40 years later after the miners' strike, almost 40 years, that you can go up into New Cumnock now and see that the place is only now really, really turning a corner and things have improved.

He continued, in response to a follow-up question on domestic violence:

> Well it wouldn't be something that was openly talked aboot that much or openly visible. Some women and wives would get knocked aboot as they say if there was some kind of fall oot and usually virtually 9 times out of 10 drink would be involved. It's always been an issue. It would be something that you would hear stories about … And

marriages would breakup and I maybe it's to do with a kind of how would you explain it, my generation and the generation before me you were brought up a man had to be a man you weren't allowed to, dealing with emotions wasn't something you were taught to do. So folk would have just reacted and it would have been deemed okay to lash oot and hit somebody or use your fists.

I can remember at the pit getting grabbed by the lug [ear] ... or your arm twisted up your back and really severe, physical, it was all just seen as acceptable and the rough and tumble that it was. Nowadays you couldn't imagine that now but then it was really ken you could be really roughly treated and that went on for centuries, things are changing now. But it was seen as acceptable for men to express themselves physically and just reach out with their fists or twist somebody's arm or pulled somebody's hair that kind of thing, that did go on. If you did something or got in trouble with the law or something that was hugely embarrassing to you for whatever reason then the pit took no prisoners with folk like that and you would be mercilessly mocked or castigated for this kind of thing.

Rab was expressing here a sense of the historical modes of tough hegemonic working-class masculinity in Ayrshire mining communities that has been commented on elsewhere, from the fiction of William McIlvanney to academic studies.[7] This was premised on steady employment, facing up to dangerous work and being the breadwinner and earning enough to sustain 'macho' consumption, including alcohol and cigarettes. This was all challenged when jobs were lost. Destabilisation was unnerving: men's sense of purpose evaporated; failure to perform as culturally expected as a man was shaming, and reactions could lead to suicides, drugs and domestic violence.

Robert Hall reflected on the impact of the accelerating pace of mine closures:

But the Beoch shut in 1967, the Minnivey pit wis there and it shut in 1975, Pennvenie it closed in 1979, and as ah said, the Houldsworth was one o' the first tae go in '65 ... Ah felt maself that something serious wis wrong. The closure system started and ye could see it comin' quicker, quicker, quicker. As each pit shut down, the

---

7 See for example William McIlvanney, *The Kiln* (Edinburgh: Canongate, 2014); Ronald Johnston and Arthur McIvor, 'Dangerous work, hard men and broken bodies: Masculinity in the Clydeside heavy industries, c1930-1970s', in E. Yeo (ed), Masculinities in History, special edition of *Labour History Review*, 69:2 (2004), pp.135-52; Daniel Wight, *Workers Not Wasters* (Edinburgh: Edinburgh University Press, 1993).

communities became less and less. The Doon Valley suffered tremendous damage when the pits such as ah've mentioned closed down, because it became a ghost place.

Waterside parish priest Eddie McGhee came from an East Ayrshire mining family and worked most of his life in the community, so was a credible witness to the devastation and ruination which came with the collapse of mining. As he noted himself: 'the accident of birth meant I was a miner's boy from a mining background.' On being asked about what he saw as the issues in post-industrial Ayrshire he commented at length:

> What happened was that, for a very short space of time, the miners got all of their redundancy money, erm, and all of the local, working men's clubs had a bonanza [chuckles] and once the money was run out, that was it, they all closed! [pause] Erm, so much of that, kind of, instant prosperity was pissed up against a wall, you know! It was drunk. It was spent. 'Cause miners were not used to having THAT amount, I remember ma Dad [laughs] when he got his redundancy! He went and bought a brand-new car! You know?! Which, at that time, I don't know what it would be, let's say, ten grand! And he just paid for it! I said, "Dad, hold on a minute! That's not it how it works! You know?! You take out a loan! You take out a bank loan an' you pay a bit extra but you don't suddenly do in your capital!" Miners,

93: Pennyvenie Colliery at closure in 1978. Note the pit bing on the right.
By kind permission of East Ayrshire Leisure Trust/East Ayrshire Council

again, they were so unused to having these sums and much of it was just absolutely [pause] wasted! And then there was this sense, you know, of [pause] almost of failure, I think, maybe! I don't think that would be too strong a word. You know, there was a kind of depressive sense because there was, suddenly, all of a sudden, these places that only existed because there was coal didn't have any reason left for their existence! So, there was a kind of sense of failure, defeatism, you know, and then, again, this is just another sociological, then into all these mining villages where there had been virtually zero crime, suddenly you had drugs starting to filter in, you know, from the bigger centres of population like Ayr, Glasgow. People, people were much more mobile and then you started having [pause] pretty awful consequences an', an' I mean, I see Ayr and Auchinleck, I mean, I walk up the town an' I see the guys going down for their green juice at the chemist [methadone] and I know most of them from the jail! And this is a tiny, little village of three thousand people but with a big drugs problem and that started filtering in in the eighties. Erm, because people had lost that sense of hope. You see, even when you had this horrendous [pause] erm, poverty and awful housing and so on, there was a wage! There was a reason to get up out of bed every day and go to your work and when you take that away, erm, that begins to erode people's self-confidence and their sense of identity. Erm, and that was becoming more and more obvious even in the few years that I spent in the Doon Valley. So, if you wanted to be employed, you had to move away or find work that was easily [pause], erm, got to, you know, Ayr, erm, because there was no railway line! The bus service, as in all-rural bus services, was poor [pause] so, you had another kind of poverty creeping in! [pause] But there was no work so, then people are looking for some other kind of escape and certainly, for the younger people, erm, drugs start to move in significantly, at that time.

Kames miner Dick Boland commented that pit closures precipitated community disintegration:

Working in the pit was alright, the company was good and you knew everybody and were quite at ease. There were mornings that, when you felt that you didn't want to get up and go anywhere near it! But it was a job and gave families a standard of living. See when the pits closed, started closing all through Scotland and in Ayrshire. Community's that had been well knit, started to get troublemakers because they had no work, they had nowhere to go. You know what the saying is "The Devil finds work for idle hands" and that's when these places changed. I suppose drugs got in and that caused mayhem.[8]

As these testimonies show, the deterioration of the social fabric of the area, income and job loss for miners, as well as the identity disintegration that came with a lack of opportunities for the young, adversely impacted on physical and mental health in a variety of ways. At the extreme of these blighted lives were broken marriages, domestic violence, despair, depression, alcohol and drug-related deaths, and suicides, and all the family grief that came with witnessing and directly experiencing this. The end of deep coal mining in Ayrshire cast a long and dark shadow. This was the lived experience of Ayrshire miners and their families 'on the scrap-heap' and they remembered it, were clear about who was responsible for this carnage and relived it vividly through their storytelling, and their 'witness' oral history testimonies.

---

8 Interview with Dick Boland, 2010, Kames Colliery Disaster Audio Project. Accessed at: http://www.muirkirk.org.uk/minersvoices/dick-boland.htm.

6
'BLACK MOONSCAPE': VOICES FROM OPEN CAST MINING

Open cast (or 'surface') mining began in Ayrshire on a modest scale in the Second World War as the government sought to augment coal production, vital for the war effort. In Ayrshire, open cast sites were opened and worked between 1944 and 1946 at New Cumnock, Cronberry and Muirkirk and some open cast mining continued under the auspices of the National Coal Board (NCB). In the later 1940s Sam Purdie's father (who had been a miner pre-war) took a job as a supervisor in an open cast mine. Open cast production continued at a fairly low level in the post-war decades, never surpassing 5% of the total coal tonnage produced in the UK up to the early 1970s. The energy crisis of the 1970s changed this with output cranked up to 15million tons (UK) from open cast by 1982, around 10% of the total. East Ayrshire was a key open cast mining area. In 2008 East Ayrshire produced 3.2 million tonnes of coal - well over half of all open cast coal produced in Scotland (5.7m) and almost the same as the whole of England and Wales put together (3.8m).[1]

WORKING THE OPEN CAST MINES

During the expansion phase in the 1970s and 1980s, most open cast workers were brought into Ayrshire from England as they had prior experience of the large-scale quarrying-style operations required at this time to rip through the surface, exposing and clawing out the rich coal seams below. As Waterside parish priest Eddie McGhee recalled:

> Post miners' strike [after 1985] when the mining industry imploded and although, erm [pause] there was, er [pause] open casting, it didn't provide anything like, and most of the people who worked the open cast actually were imported because there were, they needed skills to drive these huge machines that just didn't exist in the Doon

---

1 *The Guardian*, 15 October 2022. Accessed at: https://www.coalaction.org.uk/2022/10/15/scotland-bans-coal-mining/

94: Bulldozer operating at an open cast site in East Ayrshire.
By kind permission of East Ayrshire Leisure Trust/East Ayrshire Council

Valley!

At first this created some tension between the deep miners and the open cast 'incomers', with fears in the 1980s that surface mining was responsible for taking deep miners' jobs and concerns over environmental spoilation and damage.

In an interview in 1982, reflecting on the NCB's open cast mining programme producing a 'bonanza' of profits, an ex-miner expressed his disdain:

> These open cast coal producing machines are tearing the guts out of our countryside. They are spoiling it and it doesn't matter what they say about how they can restore it … they cannot restore it to what it was … That environment is lost and that environment is never the same as it was. For years you are going to be allotted with a big bing … ugly scars. The most beautiful countryside in Ayrshire in the hills goes over that road from Dalmellington to New Cumnock. It's a scandal what they're being allowed to do. It's cheaper for them to scar the countryside and get the coal out than to develop a wee mine up there that wouldn't be seen like Clawfin.[2]

2 Mr D (anonymous), DMC-HMCDV 04MRD, Ayrshire Archives, interviewed 14 April 1982.

95: Benbain open cast site, 1987 (just north of Dalmellington) showing the digger excavating the coal and dump trucks transporting it away. This image gives a good sense of the relatively few workers that were employed, compared to deep mining.
By kind permission of East Ayrshire Leisure Trust/East Ayrshire Council

At this time in the 1980s, tensions between deep miners and open cast miners could erupt into local fights, especially after a few drinks were had. Over time, as ex-miner Rab Wilson recalled, more open cast jobs went to locals and the incomers were assimilated:

> Open-cast mining only became a thing in my memory about post-1980 and then during the miners' strike because by that time open-casts were up and running and the people … So the people when the first open-casts opened around about here the people who worked in them were all folk who had worked in that industry, had experience in that industry and they were all from the North of England. They were either Yorkshire or Durham, Newcastle area and all these guys, and it was all guys, and they came up here and stayed in local digs in local hotels and they were making quite a bit of money. And they were incomers who were foreign if you like even though they were English but they were foreign to the people here and they came here and they were making big wages and big money when folk

here were really struggling and down and oot, so it was cause a lot of resentment, there was a lot of resentment with that. And there was always a simmering us and them with these kind of folk and if you flung a match in that that was gonnae phewf, blow up and occasionally it kind of did … But then through the '90s as the pits closed the open-casts expanded and it became a big local industry. It was big on a geographical scale, it was huge on a geographical scale [and] the mark that it left on the landscape was 100 times bigger than the pits because you didnae really see the pits. The pits was a group of buildings with a shaft and it was all underground so you didnae see it but the open-casts left a huge scar in the landscape and changed the landscape around about here and eventually it's kind of like when I saw it was us and them there was a resentment and a kind of enmity went on between these groups but with anything like that they become assimilated and we become assimilated too. And eventually kind of almost an osmosis they evolve into a homogenous sort of whole of workers whether they were fae here or fae there … More and more local people were employed in the industry, and it became mostly that the workforce eventually was all mostly local, local workers that worked in the open-cast industry.

Robert Walker, born in 1952, was one of the 'locals' that was drawn into the open cast mining, attracted by the lure of good wages and the opportunity to work near his family home in Skares. Robert worked for 24 years in road haulage, so was used to driving and to long working shifts. He started in open cast mining in Ayrshire 1996 and worked in the industry for twenty years up to his retirement. He recalled:

My daughter was winching a young boy that worked in the open-cast and I happened to be talking to him one day and asking him what the kind of money was that the boys were earning, and he told me. And I was flabbergasted, and I asked him if he could get me a job and it all got sorted out and I got a job going out learning how to drive the big dump trucks on a Saturday and then a job came up and I ended up going in there full-time. Although I wasn't on the big truck to start with, I was driving a coal truck which brought the coal from down where are the seams are up to the surface. Then I went to a big truck after that that was used for shifting the overburden all the muck and rock off the top. Then I went to a bulldozer, then I was in diggers then I was in a grader then I was back to diggers and just sort of served my time in it all working in the fitting shops helping

*96: Digger at the Benbain open cast site, 1987 (just north of Dalmellington).
By kind permission of East Ayrshire Leisure Trust/East Ayrshire Council*

the fitters, driving the HIABs [loading crane], water bowsers, just became a sort of what you would call an all-rounder.

Open cast mining was akin to quarrying. The initial jobs on an open cast site would be to prepare the access roads and the site so the larger dumpers and diggers could get on. The top soil would then be removed and tipped in one designated area so it could be replaced. And the rock strata would be dug out and again placed in a different area for replacing and remediation of the site once coal extraction was completed. Once the 'overburden' was removed and the coal seams exposed coal extraction would then commence, using giant claw diggers and sometimes explosives. Patna resident Nicola Higgins, wife of an open cast worker, recalled her husband describing the machinery: 'It's like sitting on the toilet and driving your house, that's what it's like driving any of these things, aye, that's what he said.' When the coal had finished being extracted the site would then be 'remediated', draining the water from the crater(s) and using the overburden tips to fill the hole as best as possible, finishing off with the saved topsoil. Robert Walker was involved in the big Dunstonhill open cast site digging out and preparing new roads that could take what he referred to as the 'humongous' diggers and dumpers that were being transferred over from the exhausted Pennyvenie

225

open cast site. He explained:

> An open-cast can only work as a team. The hierarchy was that the guys that drove the big diggers were worshipped by the management because they were the ones that did most of the muck shifting. So the more muck that they could shift if they were good at operating these big excavators the bosses were happy but … So the next person down the line could be a dozer driver who bulldozed the roadways clear, kept them clear or pushed the muck in towards the big diggers. Then you would have your grader drivers that kept the roads smooth because the smoother the roads were the faster the dump trucks could go and dump truck drivers were seen as down the bottom end of the pile if you like but one could not work without the other. If there was no dump trucks taking the overburden away from the big diggers, the big digger would be idle. The big digger or the bulldozers couldn't work unless they were filled with fuel twice a day so you needed a guy driving the diesel lorry or the diesel bowser as they called them. So he was just as important but he was probably away down here in the hierarchy but without him the machines couldn't work. The same as the guy that sorted them when they broke down.

97: Interviewee Robert Walker, ex-open cast miner, photographed at home in Skares, 2023.

The digger driver may be up here in the hierarchy but if he broke his digger he couldn't fix it they had to call the boys from the workshops up to fix it.

The whole process at a site might typically take four or five years from start to finish. Robert provided a flavour of what the job was like:

There wasn't many [ex-] miners. There was some. There were a lot of characters, I kid you not, there were characters, the craic was usually pretty good. There were some crazy people, some of the bosses were really good; some of them were arseholes. They would roar and shout all the time and they would have their favourites and if they didnae like somebody you just wouldnae be there. It was a different world whereas nowadays it's difficult to get sacked fae a job but in those days [talking about the 1990s] if you did something wrong it was a case of get your bags son, that's you finished and you would be straight out the door there and then. And one of the reasons for that was that the machinery was so expensive that you could do a lot of damage to a machine if you abused it. So they didn't say work a week's notice because you could go out there and wreck a bulldozer or a digger or a dump truck in that time and it would be hundreds of thousands of pounds … Normally it was just a fixed hourly rate and of course it was night shift at the time and a third or whatever, weekends would be double time. So the money was there to be made if you could suffer the long hours which was just the way of life to some of us who didnae mind.

So, the draconian discipline on an open cast site was different to the nationalisation era of underground mining – and more akin to the Victorian period. The general foreman controlled everything. And this was facilitated by the fact that the industry was predominantly non-union. As Robert commented: 'No it was a rough old world but we got the work done and it was good. As I say I stuck it for 20 years … I worked at umpteen of them just chasing the dollar all the time and going where I knew the conditions weren't too bad.' This reference to 'conditions' related to occupational health and safety. As with underground mining there were significant hazards – though working in the open air did massively reduce the inhalation of dust. Robert reflected:

There were boys killed in the open-casts but very few. In my memory of it all you would be lucky if there was twelve, a dozen killed in the whole twenty odd years that I was associated with open-casts. Some of them were silly accidents brought on by the people themselves but very few, very few. You had to be aware of the dangers. There was protocol in the way you approached some machines and that was all drilled into you at health and safety meetings, toolbox talks as they called them … There was a lot of rules and you learned most of them, most of them were just common sense but you would get it drummed into you quite often. You couldn't take short-cuts. You could get killed dead easy because you're working with machines that is absolutely massive and they don't stop for skin and bone. If you get in the way then you're gone. But there was very little of that happened. I did lose some friends that were killed in the open-cast.

Robert continued, becoming more emotional, remembering colleagues and friends:

Well, I'm going to keep it brief Arthur because it's horrendous. You understand that some of these big dump trucks the wheels on them or a digger are about the same height as this roof. And they weigh 70 ton empty, loaded they are 150 ton. There were two of my pals sitting in the land rover beside one and instead of the driver following procedure he decided he would cut out from the middle of the queue, and he drove right over the top of their land rover. Anybody that worked in the open-casting hearing that will know exactly who I am talking about. But I worked with they guys. It was bad and it was a complete clown that did it … Another one … put himself in a bit of machinery. Instead of stopping it the machinery stopped him. He could have switched it off and did what he was doing. The boss had been saying don't be stopping it for too long, so he decided that he wouldn't stop it and he went in to clean it and the machine grabbed him. That was dreadful, left a young family. It's sore on you. The other one was somebody carrying on. A boy was fuelling up his truck and just connected the fuel bowser to the truck with a big rubber hose about that thick and the boy that was on the dump truck thought he would give the bowser driver a fright by edging forward a bit. But what happened was he went too far and the rubber hose caught the fuel bowser driver and pushed him … As it went tight, he got flung in below the back wheels of the dump truck and that was it … But I would say, generally speaking, considering the conditions and what we had to do it was pretty safe most of the time.

*98: Chalmerston open cast site in the early stages of development (1990).
By kind permission of East Ayrshire Leisure Trust/East Ayrshire Council*

The first tragic accident described above was at the Pennyvenie open cast site (which opened in 1987 and employed around 130 workers) in 2007, leading to the deaths of Brian French and Colin Ferguson.

For some people in Ayrshire the feeling was that the job creation outweighed the environmental deficits of open cast mining. Views were polarised. Robert reckoned the industry created around 2,000 jobs at peak. Others in local community groups, together with campaigners Greenpeace and Friends of the Earth Scotland (FES) opposed open cast mining. FES stated in 1998 that 'left unchecked, open-cast is the cancer of the countryside'. [3] South of the border the countryside appears to have been better protected as 89% of all applications for open cast sites were rejected, whereas in Scotland only 13% were rejected. [4] In 1998 Scottish Coal, ATH Resources, Ardvark TMC, Kier Mining and Hargreaves Surface Mining were amongst the main players – the latter two companies being amongst the top twenty largest private companies in East Ayrshire in the late 2000s (2007-2011). [5]

Ex-Barony and Killoch underground miner Richard Allan gave his

---

3 *Scottish Daily Record*, November 1 1988. Accessed at: https://www.thefreelibrary.com/IN-+THE+VALLEY+OF+DEATH%3B+The+village+that+could+be+smothered+by+lust...-a060751802.
4 *Ibid.*
5 East Ayrshire Council, *East Ayrshire Economic Development Strategy 2014-2025* (East Ayrshire Council: 2015). Accessed at: https://www.east-ayrshire.gov.uk/Resources/PDF/E/EconomicDevelop-mentStrategy2014-2025.pdf.

99: Chalmerston open cast site in production.
By kind permission of East Ayrshire Leisure Trust/East Ayrshire Council

view of open cast mining in an interview in 1992:

> I don't agree with the open cast because they have helped this
> community and other communities for the pits to shut and they are
> reaping all the benefits out of our community and they have never
> put anything back in. So, where is all that profit going to? … They
> bring in their own men … there should be men in the local areas to
> work in them … It's just another con.

In 1992 Richard felt strongly that the Council should have been more
rigorous in controlling the open cast companies and ensuring more local
people were employed. Interestingly, around this time (1990s) open cast
worker Robert Walker got chatting to locals walking their dogs over the
Dunstonhill area which included Lethanhill and Burnfoothill. They told
him many stories about the days of the miners' rows – the camaraderie,
culture and mutual support networks of mining communities in the past.
The physical remnants of these settlements on the hill were almost entirely
gone – ghosts of the past residing now just in the memories of these old
folk. One day he got chatting to a local old timer who had been born and
bred in the Cairntable Rows. Robert recalled:

Me being my usual flippant self said to him "I suppose that's what youse boys called the good old days". "Aye it was so son, aye they were happy days". I says "Well I'll tell you something you should all have got a gold medal for putting up with it and your father should have got it as well for the conditions they worked in". I says there was nothing good about it from what I could see and all my family, my generations before me were miners so I've got a pretty good idea of what it was like. Anyway, the tears started welling up in his eyes and he says "Ah but it was good son" … Oh and the tears were flooding out his face. He says "Ye ken something you're right son I could never go to sleep until I heard his [referring to his father] tackity boots walking up the path to the front door." I said "aye that was the good old days wasn't it."

Here we have on the one hand the brash open cast worker, extolling the virtues of winning coal more efficiently by modern methods of surface excavation and pointing out the grimmer side of working underground, with all its attendant dangers. On the other hand, the old ex-miner driven to tears nostalgically recalling the past in the now vanished mining village of his youth. There is something of a clash of cultures evident in this exchange,

100: Cairntable Row image (print from a painting, unknown artist, 1984) given to open-cast worker Robert Walker when working on the site.

231

between the modern and the past; between the materialism, individualism and consumerism of the present and the relative deprivation of the miners' rows, with its vibrant working-class culture and unrivalled mutualism in adversity. Is this nostalgia or was this a better past in many respects, one from which we today can learn much? The old miner generously followed this exchange up by gifting Robert copies of an artist's pictures of the Cairntable Row that he lived in as a souvenir of a different era of coal mining.

For some, working in the open cast mines brought a degree of job security when jobs were scarce in the county. Nicola Higgins' husband worked in the industry and she recalled the shock they experienced when they heard the news he no longer had a job in 2013:

> My husband he worked in the open cast when it shut; I remember we'd been to a One Direction concert in Manchester with my wee girl and he got the phone call and we were like, what're we going to do for money, we were like trying to rein it in, how can I take the wean here and dae that, we just went to the concert and kind of went back, because we were, we never seen it coming, we didn't know. Just travelled down to Manchester and it happens, so it was, it was a big, and you were worried about how am I going to pay my mortgage, what am I gonna dae, had to hand in the car, you were just trying to do all these wee different things, obviously to make ends meet, and I ken that, but it's, you just had to rein it right back in until you were able to work again.

Nicola commented on her husband's next job after the open cast: 'Now, [he's] out an hour and a half to get to his work in the morning and an hour and a half back, so it [in the open cast] was good because it was local'. She continued reflecting on the impact of job loss on men generally:

> You feel like a failure because you should be oot working and … because mental health's at an all-time high kind of like here tae, and it's like probably because, like it will have a big effect on it because men don't, aren't supposed to tell you their feelings and it's a, aye it would have a big effect on folk, men especially. Definitely, aye.

LANDSCAPE AND RESTORATION

Whilst open cast mining provided some jobs – somewhere between 1,000 and 2,000 at peak in East Ayrshire – and over time more local people were taken on (men like Robert Walker), the operation of digging coal from the surface created an environmental disaster, destroying much deep mining heritage and scarring the landscape for years. Researcher Huyen Le has commented:

> Despite the contributions to economic and social development, mining causes environmental degradation that can make significant and long-term impacts on ecosystems, biodiversity and human health and well-being.[6]

Nicola Higgins from Patna recalled the devastation and the danger that the remaining open cast sites posed:

> Dunston Hill isn't it? It's quite scary, [we] went a walk up there [Dunston Hill] so we did and see like what's left, it's like a big huge massive hole, ken it was actually filled up with water half of it ... I was looking over the burn and into this big huge, I would say the Grand Canyon, that's just what it looked like, but ken like it's not very, there's not a lot of security roond there, like if somebody was to run ... because it is, it's like a big quarry isn't it, it's like right down ... so it's quite somebody could droon in that ... There's a lot of like pools up there that have filled up, that is dangerous ... I think it's very unsafe.

From the 1980s to the 2000s, local communities were relatively powerless in the face of large open cast mining companies supported by a local council in East Ayrshire prioritising (quite understandably in the context of local mass unemployment) job creation. Local Waterside parish priest Eddie McGhee, from a mining family, commented on the erasure he faced walking on nearby hills:

> I am one mile from the Burnie and the Nuns' Cross. Now, as you go out further towards, erm, Commondyke farm and the Common farm, there's nothing. It's all been open-casted ... so there's nothing.

Stuart Burns, born in 1942, spent part of his childhood in the late 1940s and early 1950s in Glenbuck. He was asked what he thought of the restoration after the open cast company left the site:

---

6 Huyen Le, *Exploring the governance of post-mining restoration in Scotland in the demise of the opencast coal industry and finding the way forward* (PhD thesis, University of Dundee, 2018). Accessed at: https://discovery.dundee.ac.uk/en/studentTheses/exploring-the-governance-of-post-min-ing-restoration-in-scotland-i.

I went up to see what damage was done … Awwff terrible. There's hills there wisnae there before and there holes there that wisnae there before. Its full of big water holes. Daren't go aff the road for its just pure muck you'd go over the heid.

YM: How did that make you feel to see where you lived?

Aww. It's a damn shame what's happened up there. They were going to turn it into a big forest, they had big plans for it then … And where the fitbaw park was it's non-existent it's a big muck hole, a big swamp and I blame them.

Some of the last remaining Glenbuck residents (such as Michael Ramsey) got some financial compensation for noise and structural damage to their homes from Scottish Coal. But this didn't make allowance for the damage to the mining heritage or the landscape. In an interview in 2019, Sam Purdie recalled the shock he also felt at the desolation around Glenbuck when he returned to visit his birthplace:

I'd been abroad, as I've explained to you – the first time I went to see it, I said, I'll take a wee, sentimental trip up to see the village. No village! Not a stone! Not a vestige! That was 2002 and here are all these huge machines but, as I say, fortunately, the footprint of the village itself is preserved and can still be seen. The area where people lived and the football park, it's still there.

AM: So, the houses are still there or … not?

No, no! Everything was demolished! … For some reason, destroyed! Flattened! Gone! Eradicated from the face of the earth!

Shortly after that visit to the site of his birthplace Sam Purdie wrote a very moving six-page eulogy to Glenbuck that ended viscerally:

The unblinking eye of the predator was upon you. They decided that you were nothing. They coveted the meagre residues of black gold left in your heart so that at last even this you were forced to yield. They came like carrion crows and tore at you again and again until the desecration was total. Not a house, not a wall, not a stone nor a tree remains. All that is left are the ghosts of those who loved you, soon to be joined by the few of us who linger here. We hope to see you again but we fear that we are all consigned to the past.[7]

There is a palpable sense of loss of heritage seeping through Sam's

7 Sam Purdie, *Requiem for a Village* (2002). Unpublished essay.

101: Sam Purdie on site visit at Glenbuck, 2022.

commentary on the virtual erasure of his mining village, the place he was evidently so attached to. 'Where were all the protesters' Sam pleaded. Returning to the site of Glenbuck twenty years later, in September 2022, Sam reiterated to us his sense of bereavement over the open cast obliteration of the site: 'The open casters destroyed everything!' he recalled. 'Didn't leave a blade of grass! All o' this has been remediated. This was a black moonscape, when they left!'

It is hard to determine the extent of feeling for or against open cast mining in Ayrshire, and the degree of local organisation and protest against it. More work is needed here. In their research on open cast mining and the environment in England, *Digging Up Trouble*, Beynon, Cox and Hudson explore the accumulating nature of protest – by middle-class intellectuals as well as working-class advocates – against the 'creative destruction' of the environment by the open casters in the 1980s and 1990s, as sensitivities towards the environment changed within society. The one reference in this book to Ayrshire refers to a national lobby in London early in the Blair government in 1998 where Dr Diptish Nandy, a GP of some 24 years in Muirkirk, was reported to have been brought to tears recalling the 'persistent encroachment of three open cast sites on his local community.'[8]

8 Beynon, Huw, Cox, A and Hudson, R, *Digging up Trouble: Environment, Protest and Open Cast Mining* (Lewes: Rivers Oram, 2000).

Dr Nandy was the Chair of the Muirkirk Opencast Action Group and a year earlier spoke out unsuccessfully against granting the licence to Scottish Coal to create the open cast site at Glenbuck. Reporting on this in *The Herald* newspaper suggests that East Ayrshire Council were swayed by the job creation argument.[9] A year or so later Dr Nandy was interviewed for another Scottish newspaper and spoke of his worries over pollution:

> I have seen an increase in respiratory illness. The basic problem is dust. If it is on all cars, doors and windows – and we can see it – there's no justification to say we are not breathing it in. I've seen children with no problems come here on holiday and start wheezing.[10]

Dr Nandy's observations as an East Ayrshire practice doctor were backed up by medical research that showed a correlation between proximity to an open cast site and respiratory illness. By 1999 three UK studies had found connections between open cast sites and higher rates of respiratory disability locally. This medical evidence – as with pneumoconiosis and bronchitis before for underground miners – was contested by the companies. Scottish Coal argued that its open cast workforce were regularly monitored by the Institute of Occupational Medicine (IOM) in Edinburgh for signs of any respiratory disease. However medical researchers Munro and Crompton cast doubt on the credibility of IOM research, arguing:

> The workforce largely comprises healthy men aged 16-65 years. The community contains many outwith this age group including the elderly, and those of all ages suffering from cardiac and respiratory disease of such a severity as to prevent them from working. The latter are most at risk from an acute rise in atmospheric pollutants. The community also includes infants and young children, who might be most adversely affected by any chronic cumulative effect.[11]

After talking to local residents and the local GP Dr Nandy the *Sunday Mail* journalist provided a stinging indictment on the open cast sites around Muirkirk:

9 *The Herald*, 30 July 1997, Accessed: at https://www.heraldscotland.com/news/12313763.open-cast-mine-approved-despite-local-concerns/.

10 *Sunday Mail*, 1 November 1998, Accessed at: https://www.thefreelibrary.com/IN+THE+VAL-LEY+OF+DEATH%3B+The+village+that+could+be+smothered+by+lust...-a060751802. It is worth noting that Dr Nandy was involved several years later in a scandal over supplying methadone to drug users and an inappropriate relationship with a female heroin addict. He was struck off the medical register as a GP in 2002 by the British Medical Council.

11 J. F. Munro and G.K. Crompton, 'Health Effects of Respirable Dust from Open Cast Mining', *Journal of the Royal Society of Physicians of Edinburgh*, 29:1 (1999), p.12.

Wind, laden with dust, whistles around a Scots village. Old folk, stricken by respiratory diseases, cough sadly. In the primary school, up to half the children use inhalers for asthma. If Muirkirk, Ayrshire, is not in its death throes, then it certainly appears seriously sick. It is under siege from open-cast mining - and some believe the mines are winning. All around, huge pits bring continual noise and pollution. Plans show that mining companies - including Faldane and RJB Mining - own all the land around the village, right up to back gardens and the walls of the graveyard. One excavation leaves a sheer, 250ft drop less than 100 yards from the gardens of Muirkirk's housing scheme.

The Muirkirk Opencast Action Group represented one style of activism in the 1990s, deploying lay expertise and medical knowledge, and lobbying locally and nationally. By the early 21st century such groups had proliferated and included the Rankinston Community Opencast Action Group (RCOAG), the Mining and Environment Group: Ayrshire (formed in 1996) and the Scottish Opencast Communities Alliance (SOCA). This represented what researcher Huyen Le has called 'empowered local communities.' However, more militant direct action – what has been termed 'citizen activism' – was less in evidence in Ayrshire. The first example of an open cast site being occupied by environmental activists occurred at the Scottish Coal Mainshill site near Douglas in Lanarkshire where climate campaigners set up a camp for six months from June 2009 to January 2010, when they were forcibly evicted.[12]

Some people's relationship with the open cast sites were more positive. For some children these open cast sites could be an exhilarating, if dangerous new landscape to explore. Cheryl Hynd was born in 1978 and brought up in Glenbuck, living in one of the few remaining houses. She recalled the fun she had playing in the 'moonscape' and the good relations they had with the open cast workers:

We were never in, never in, we were playing 24/7 I think, we were in opencasts playing … As I said see they abandoned places, they buildings that was our playground so we would be, as kids we would be out first thing in the morning and then you'd to get shouted in at night. That was all before health & safety but fabulous childhood I would definitely, I wouldnae like to be in this day and age growing up because back then we had total freedom.

---

12 *The Guardian*, 25 January 2010, Accessed at: https://www.theguardian.com/environment/2010/jan/25/police-arrest-climate-camp-opencast.

YM: You said like you were like an opencast childhood what does that mean? Did you go near the opencasts?

Yeah hmm mm. So, at that point there was working opencasts and then there was the opencasts that they had moved on from but they were left great big gaping holes and machinery and stuff. So, we went in there playing, we had actual life-size machines to sit in canyon and play and your imagination and stuff, amazing. Plus to be fair in the working opencasts they allowed us in back then because a lot of the people that worked there would take us and like the Land Rovers and stuff and do site visits and things like that. So, you just grew up there …

YM: So what were the guys like that worked in the opencasts then? You were saying they were taking you about and stuff.

They were like I suppose like uncles, family friends, they would just pick you up, take you away go a good few hours, that was like your babysitter back then. So they would take us and as I say it would be like site visits you'd have all the adrenaline fae stuff going away round the opencasts and the workings and stuff but you were looked after. It was a great experience.

Cheryl's Mum, Margaret, provided a somewhat different perspective, recalling the danger and the dust:

They came down the back with the lorries and right round and the dust you couldnae get your washing oot like through the day you had to put it oot at this time. And that's when they came right next to us but it was that dusty. And then they had the water, what they called the water bowser it came down and calmed down the dust a bit. But it was dusty and it was dangerous driving on the road as well with it all you just pulled in and prayed … It was really daunting in they days and they just were so fast they didnae care they just..they didnae even turn around to see if you got oot the dust. True.

YM: How did that make you feel?

Aw I didnae mind it I don't think the opencasts didnae really bother us, bugged a lot of people but didnae bother us … They came up with like big low loaders and the next thing you knew, you would look at it and you would say "oh here it comes" your phone's away, one side to the other and it always got taken away or the electric or something. We had a lot of inconvenience, but I don't think it was something that really bothered us awful much … As well then Grasshill was still on the go then and the mine was still there. So they boys were coming doon this side and the other ones were coming around the top and you would hear them.

The family were forced to move out of Glenbuck at the final stage of the open cast operation, which demolished the remaining homes, including theirs. The Hynds were amongst the very final residents of Glenbuck. Cheryl expressed a palpable sense of loss being forcibly decanted from the remnants of Glenbuck almost fifty years after the majority of people, including Sam Purdie, were rehoused in the Muirkirk council houses. In this conversation between Cheryl and her Mum you get a sense of what this meant:

> Cheryl: It was quite an upheaval for me because I was a teenager, and I was kind of being uprooted and for all my family and friends were here they kind of came to us a lot so it was then me coming into this village. Even though this is very small it was very big to me at the time and we were going through school at the time and it was massive changes. Aw you're just taken away fae your love and you're

102: The Chalmerston open cast site signage, 1990 (note: promising 2.5m tons of coal and full landscape restoration by 1998).
By kind permission of East Ayrshire Leisure Trust/East Ayrshire Council

put somewhere else so to me it was kind of bittersweet.
Margaret: You still feel like that about it.
Cheryl: I lost a lot.
Margaret: Aye you did.
Cheryl: For all I came into a community and I was accepted.

Cheryl was overcome with emotions at that point.

Proper restoration of the landscape was a condition of open cast licences. The open cast companies were expected to deposit the sums of money necessary for this pre-production with the local council to ensure full restoration. This restoration involved infilling the sites with what were understood to be the carefully created 'tips' of rock and soil removed from the sites in the process of 'quarrying' the coal from the surface. This process of deposit and restoration was known as a 'restoration bond'. In many cases the restoration was carried out, with the companies taking their responsibilities seriously. In other cases, short-cuts left sites in a mess, particularly when companies obtained new licences from the council for extending their sites, without first ensuring the initial phases were in-filled properly. Local residents also had to put up with landscape despoliation, noise and dust pollution for as long as the site was being worked. The most significant issues, however, occurred when companies worked through and made their profits from the open cast mines, then went into liquidation before restoration had been completed or even started on many sites.

In 2013, opencast mining in East Ayrshire took a significant blow which was to have major repercussions for the community: two of the major opencast mining players, Scottish Coal and ATH Resources, went bust. 600 men lost their jobs at Scottish Coal alone. They left 22 or 23 (depending on which account you read) open cast sites in East Ayrshire unrestored. It was also discovered that there was very little in the restoration bond fund to cover the costs of remediation. The Councillor (Head of Planning) responsible resigned amidst a controversy and East Ayrshire Council was left with the task of restoring the moonscape of open cast mines over the following decade. And to foot most of the bill for costs (with some Scottish Government support). East Ayrshire Council Chief Executive Fiona Lees stated the total cost would be £161million yet there was barely £27million in the restoration bond funds – less than one-fifth of the full amount required. East Ayrshire Council's Legal Spokesman commented:

Within East Ayrshire's boundary there was the equivalent of around 4,500 football pitches worth of unrestored land … That is eye watering in itself. Then consider that this is not just a few inches of

*103: Giant dumper trucks operating at the Powharnel open cast site near
Muirkirk, photographed by Iain Brown in 2006.
By kind permission of East Ayrshire Leisure Trust/East Ayrshire Council*

unrestored land. It was like the Grand Canyon.[13]

In a report on the scandal, Jim Mackinnon, former chief planning officer
of the Scottish Government found the companies and the Council
responsible, noting this as: 'environmental dereliction which is probably
unrivalled anywhere in Scotland.'[14] A year later, little had been done, with
environmental and community groups talking of the situation as a 'national
crisis', with the derelict open cast pits filling with water creating dangerous
and polluted 'lagoons.' The RSPB also expressed concerns over the impact
of the sites on wildlife, including birds. The liquidators admitted at this
point the sites were deteriorating and over time were posing more of a risk
to the public and the environment.[15]

The massive open cast site at Chalmerston was last on the East
Ayrshire Council list for restoration and the site is currently being

---

13 *Cumnock Chronicle*, 3 November 2022. Accessed at: https://www.cumnockchronicle.com/
news/23095234.east-ayrshire-council-chalmerston-opencast-restored/
14 https://www.mining-technology.com/features/featureticking-time-bonds-scottish-open-cast-coal-
leaves-legacy-of-dereliction-4184435/. See also BBC News, 17 July 2014. Accessed at: https://www.
bbc.co.uk/news/uk-scotland-glasgow-west-28344273
15 *The Herald*, 13 July 2014. Accessed at: https://www.heraldscotland.com/news/13169742.re-
vealed-national-crisis-opencast-mine-warning/.

104: Chalmerston after Scottish Coal went into administration.
Courtesy of Lyndy Renwick

remediated as we write in 2023. It appears that what goes around comes around. In the private ownership period before coal nationalisation in 1947, as we have seen, the Ayrshire coal companies ruthlessly exploited their workers in the mines and the mining communities in their provision of sub-standard miners' row style housing, with diminished local amenities and even control over food supplies in some villages between the wars. Nationalisation brought a period of relative stability, with managed decline of the industry in an era when alternative jobs were relatively plentiful until the 1980s. With privatisation re-emerging in the 1990s under the Tories, these mining communities were kicked in the teeth a second time by rapacious open cast mining companies conspiring (with the collusion of some local council officials) to profit from surface mining, leaving an environmental disaster in their wake that took over a decade to remedy, with much of the cost shouldered by local taxpayers.

Open cast mining peaked around 2010, at which point Scotland produced almost half (6 million) of all coal tonnage (13 million) produced from surface mining in the UK. Ayrshire, as we have seen, was the largest and most productive single area in the UK for open cast coal. Kier Mining and Hargreaves Surface Mining were the major players at this final stage of open casting in Ayrshire, both amongst the 16 largest private employers in East Ayrshire in 2007-2011.[16] The last working open cast mine, run by Hargreaves at the House of Water site in Ayrshire, closed in 2020, ending all coal production in Scotland. By this point fuel policy and energy generation had moved substantively away from fossil fuels – partly in response to the global warming crisis – as evidenced by the massive wind generation energy sites that have appeared over the past two decades across Ayrshire, and elsewhere.

16 East Ayrshire Council, *East Ayrshire Economic Development Strategy 2014-2025* (East Ayrshire Council: 2015), Accessed at: https://www.east-ayrshire.gov.uk/Resources/PDF/E/ EconomicDevelopmentStrategy2014-2025.pdf.

105: Brick at the Darnconner site, May 2022.

7

'A GHOST PLACE': HERITAGE, LEGACIES AND RESIDUES OF THE PAST

The past exists in many ways in the present. In this chapter we explore the tangible and intangible traces and legacies of the past – the mark that coal mining and mining communities in Ayrshire have left on and in the present. We might refer to this as 'residues' of the past, and these take various forms in the archaeology, the physical remnants of the miners' rows, the villages and the pits – and the ways the industry has shaped the landscape. Other traces and interpretations of the past include photographs, that we have drawn extensively on in this book; maps; art; poetry, including the work of Scots poet Rab Wilson, who has written extensively on his native Ayrshire; and literary fiction, with works such William McIlvanney's Ayrshire-based novel *The Kiln* (1996), and James Robertson's *And the Land Lay Still* (2010), which explores the Knockshinnoch disaster. Ayrshire's past in coal mining has also been inscribed on people's bodies today – in physical and mental scars, disabilities and chronic ill-health – as oral testimonies in this book in particular have shown us, The harms and the damage are cumulative, with health deficits and inequalities magnified by loss of secure and identity-defining employment, lack of good job opportunities and persistent poverty and deprivation. The past exists in people's memories, anchoring the present. Indeed, the ways that this history is remembered, commemorated and memorialised is significant. Whilst these once vibrant communities have now disappeared – as pit closures, village depopulation and deindustrialisation proceeded – physical traces, people and memories endure and survive. And what comes through the oral history interviews, focus groups and memory workshops conducted for this project is a profound attachment to the 'lost' mining villages and a conscious and determined effort to keep the memory of such formative experiences alive. This is done through preserving and commemorating heritage, erecting memorials, storytelling, reunions and, where possible, revisiting the sites of people's birth and upbringing. And not just for nostalgic reasons. There is a

106: Lethanhill remains of the rear of the house among a forestry plantation, September 2021.

tangible sense that these earlier and past lives were good, were meaningful and are worthy of remembering and commemorating. The villages and mines were and remain places of meaning – theatres of memory for those who once lived there and their families. We can learn much from a very different way of life and culture in our modern age of atomisation, individualism and fragmentation and precarity in our working and non-working lives.

Visiting the lost mining villages of Ayrshire today requires a historic map and often someone with some local knowledge.[1] While in some villages, the outlines of rows or remains of buildings can be deciphered, such as the village washhouses or dry toilets, others have little distinguishing features other than the odd brick strewn about a field.

Lack of schooling in the new social housing estates often left the schoolhouses untouched as the villages disappeared. The schoolhouses at Lethanhill and Darnconner are now private residences, the only lasting symbols of the families who once inhabited these now empty landscapes.

Village war memorials to the sons, brothers and fathers lost to war

---

1 National Library of Scotland maps online: https://maps.nls.uk/. Georeferenced maps were useful for locating the exact sites of the villages

107: Darnconner Schoolhouse, May 2022.

were also left on site, now serving as reference points in the landscapes for those searching for the villages.

Next to Commondyke, stood the religious community of Birnieknowe. As the number of Roman Catholics increased in the area throughout the mid-nineteenth century, the parish of Our Lady and St Patrick's was founded with the building of the Church at Birnieknowe in 1867, followed by a school in 1878 and a convent in 1885.[2] The religious community became part of the identity of the village, with some from the area referring to themselves as coming from the 'Birnie'. The religious centre remained after the rows were gone. The Catholic children from the new

108: Benwhat war memorial.

2 Our Lady and St Patrick's, Centenary publication, 1967

109: Sister Laurienne's memorial cross is all that remains of the Birnie today. (Photo Credit: Rosser1954, CC BY-SA 4.0 <https://creativecommons.org/ licenses/by-sa/4.0>, via Wikimedia Commons

110: St Patrick's Church, Birnieknowe, Commondyke. Courtesy of New family collection

111: Miners and ironworkers row housing, now renamed Park Terrace, in Lugar. Courtesy of Margot McCuaig

housing in Auchinleck and Cumnock were bussed up to the St Patrick's school until 1966. A dwelling house now stands of the site of the religious community and a memorial cross stands alone among the grazing sheep to a well-loved nun, Sister Laurienne, who was sadly hit by a train in 1888.

Few of the miners' rows survived the tsunami of demolition or the ravages of nature. One of best preserved is at Lugar, adjacent to the site of the massive Lugar Ironworks that once operated on the hill above the village. There are miners' rows still in Ayrshire which are modernised and remain private homes in Lugar, Waterside and Dalmellington. The nearest place close to Ayrshire to see inside a miners' row is Summerlee Industrial Museum in Coatbridge. The reconstructed interiors represent decades from the nineteenth century to the 1960s. Entering these evokes something of the claustrophobic, over-crowded and sparsely furnished dwellings that dominated the isolated mining communities of Scotland up to the mid-twentieth century. They are well worth a visit.

The Ayrshire landscape, as with many former coalfields around Britain, is punctuated by mounds of bings. The wastelands of these once industrious mines now serve as locators and tangible reminders of the workers and their families. Outside Patna, the bing constantly simmers and smokes, even glowing some nights to remind the people of the surrounding areas of their heritage. The National Mining Museum of Scotland (NMMS), located at the A-listed Victoria Colliery at Newtongrange in the Lothians, is

112: The bing at Commondyke. This is where interviewee John New's grandfather was a regular fixture of the village contemplating life and whittling (carving) wood.

Scotland's only museum dedicated solely to representing and interpreting the country's coal mining past. The latter constitutes the single most comprehensive tangible heritage site, with most of the colliery buildings extant. It is a wonderful place that preserves mining history and really evokes the significance of Scotland's mining past, not least through the memories of the ex-miners (like John Kane who told us his story for our Mining Working Lives online course) who volunteer there as guides and tell their stories. However, given its geographical position in the east of the country, some distance from Ayrshire, it is perhaps not surprising that the NMMS does not feature Ayrshire significantly in its interpretation or its collections (including its images and oral history collections).

There are official memorials to the miners and the communities throughout East Ayrshire. Local communities were often instrumental in the installation of these, and in ensuring the survival and preservation of mining heritage. In Auchinleck, the Highhouse pit A frame, engine house and engine is a B listed building and is the only steam winding engine in Scotland to be preserved in situ. In 2015, the owners of the Highhouse industrial estate requested permission from East Ayrshire Council to demolish the structures on the grounds that they were beyond repair. This was rejected due to its historic status and the council were unsatisfied that it was too far gone to preserve. In the process they received forty responses

113: 19th century miners' row interior, you can see the 'swee over the stove and the rag rug on the floor here. Summerlee Industrial Museum, (Photograph: Lost Villages: 2022)

114: Exterior of the miners' rows at Summerlee, with the water pump or spout shown against the far wall. Summerlee Industrial Museum. (Photograph Lost Villages: 2022)

251

115: National Mining Museum Scotland, Newtongrange (Victoria Colliery).
Courtesy of National Mining Museum Scotland Trust

from the public, some citing its role in local identity as a connection to their mining heritage and also its industrial significance. The adjacent miners' row also remains, now repurposed as industrial units – a survivor amidst new buildings around it. The Bosewell Community Centre, also in Auchinleck, has a clock set into a sculpture of an A frame in the car park.

The most prominent example of tangible mining heritage in Ayrshire is the Barony A frame which remains as a monolith on the landscape, and can be seen for miles around as you approach Auchinleck, Cumnock and Ochitree. The story of the A frame's survival, preservation

116: Highhouse Rows, now mostly let as industrial units, May 2022.

252

117: Remains of Highhouse pit, May 2022.

and the creation of a heritage park around it reveals much about the desire of the mining community to preserve its past on its terms. Virtually all of the physical, tangible evidence of the mining industry and the miners' rows and communities in Ayrshire has been demolished. Nature reclaimed the villages, whilst colliery buildings and winding frames were almost all bulldozed, partly in the cause of public safety. The Barony A frame was saved initially as it was designated by Historic Scotland as a B-listed structure. Almost all the buildings around it were demolished a few years

118: A Frame Clock Memorial, Bosewell Centre Car Park, Auchinleck, 2022.

119: The Barony A Frame
Memorial.
Courtesy of Margot
McCuaig

after closure, by 1992. Several years later in 1997 community activists, led by
ex-Barony miner, local councillor and NUM union official Barney Menzies,
came together to form the Barony A-Frame Trust (BAFT) to restore the
rusting and derelict A-frame and construct a heritage park around it.
Support was rallied (including by the NUM, the Coalfield Regeneration
Trust and East Ayrshire Council) and funding (£1.2m) raised. What is
notable about the Barony heritage site is the grass roots initiative with the
community (through BAFT) integrally involved in the interpretation of
their own history – rather than some 'official' sanitised history imposed
from above (sometimes referred to as 'authorised heritage discourse').[3]
The exhibition panels at the open-air site feature four themes: life in the
community; friendship and cameraderie; work, health and safety; the union
and activism. What is also striking is the way that personal memories are
central to the interpretation. Memories were collected through a parallel oral
history project called 'Pitheid Patter' and these witness testimonies inform

---

3 LauraJane Smith, *Uses of Heritage* (London: Routledge, 2006).

120: The 'pitheid patter' oral history booth at the Barony A Frame site.
Courtesy of Margot McCuaig

the exhibition boards around the site and can be listened to at the specially constructed covered oral history booth positioned right underneath the A frame. The latter marks this exhibition as unusual, indeed almost unique. This makes the site a genuine sensory experience, evoking what it felt like to work in the mine and to live in the now lost miners' rows and villages – the harsh realities of overcrowding, deprivation and disease, together with the mutual support and communal spirit of these places. Social class and power are key themes which distinguish this from most museums and heritage centres. Miners and their families were exploited and were victims, and this comes through tangibly. However, a profound sense of miners and their families as active agents making their own history emerges through the interpretation at the Barony A Frame heritage site.[4]

Another notable effort to preserve, record and interpret Ayrshire's mining past was the Doon Valley Museum. This was created in 2003-4 by the local community in Dalmellington. With the aid of a National Lottery Heritage grant an eighteenth-century weavers' cottage was converted into a community museum, with local people donating photographs and artefacts. It closed in January 2017, with the house being converted into a community meeting place for Dalmellington. The museum collections were transferred

---

4 Unfortunately the sound playback in the memory booth was not functioning when the site was visited. For an insightful commentary on the Barony A Frame site see: Laurence Gourievidis, 'Safeguarding Ayrshire's Coalmining Past: Heritage, Nostalgia and Social Memory', *Revue Lisa: E-Journal,* XVII: 1 (2019). Accessed at: https://journals.openedition.org/lisa/11191?lang=en.

121: Doon Valley Museum, locally referred to as the Cathcartson.
By kind permission of East Ayrshire Leisure Trust/East Ayrshire Council

to the Baird Institute in nearby Cumnock, including a wonderful series of photographs that feature significantly in this book.

There are also several tangible physical memorials and commemorations to Ayrshire's mining past dotted around the ex-mining communities. The memorial to the miners at Muirkirk was commissioned by the Muirkirk Enterprise Group to commemorate the ninety miners who lost their lives in local mines. Unable to raise the money for a stone statue, a new resident of Glenbuck and sculptor Kirti Mandir heard this from the villagers and volunteered to sculpt the statue that now stands with only the production costs then needing to be raised. The names of those lost were collected by the Muirkirk Enterprise Group from the villagers with names added even after the memorial was unveiled. The memorial statue is placed within a heritage garden with large lump of coal nearby. It was unveiled in 2004 by Scotland's First Minister, Jack McConnell, British Defence Minister, Desmond Brown and local MP, Cathie Jemison. In 2022, a mural was added behind the statue by local artist John Andrew inspired by the local eighteenth-century poet, Tibbie Pagan.

How the industrial past is represented is a site of contest and disagreement, as Jim Phillips has argued: 'All industrial memorials are politicised and contentious.'[5] They can be sanitised and depicted in

5 Phillips, *Scottish Coal Miners*, p.271.

122: Muirkirk Miner's Memorial, with mural to local woman Tibbie and tribute to Glenbuck football legend Bill Shankly in the background.

memorials in a nostalgic way, a tool for tourism and regeneration depicting a 'lost past'. Often such commemoration omits and erases the lived realities of class conflict, dislocation, poverty, sectarianism, ill-health and other grimmer aspects of the past, as well as the process of ruination that went along with deindustrialisation. Community memorialisation such as the Barony A frame site and monuments to pit disasters and deaths like the Muirkirk memorial provide a sense of the darker past of coal mining and the toll it took on mining families and communities. They seek, as Gibbs and Clark have argued to 'educate future generations' about the communities' industrial past, and its impacts and legacies.[6] However, Jackie Clarke

6 Andy Clark and Ewan Gibbs, 'Voices of social dislocation, lost work and economic restructuring: Narratives from marginalised localities in the 'New Scotland', *Memory Studies*, 13:1 (2017), pp.39-59.

123: Knockshinnoch disaster memorial cairns. Around them there are 13 red flagstones depicting those who died and 116 for those who were rescued.
Courtesy of Margot McCuaig

has shown that memorialisation is gendered, pointing out that few if any memorials exist to working class women in industry (and the same could be said about the home, community and politics) despite the widespread employment of women in the manufacturing sector, including textiles in Ayrshire.[7]

Another example would be the memorial to the Knockshinnoch disaster. An annual memorial service still happens around about the anniversary of the disaster in 7-10 September. Survivors still attend to lay wreathes. In nearby New Cumnock there is a simple monument, depicting a miners' safety lamp and the words 'Out of the darkness, into light'. In Lugar, one of the former spouts from a miners' row has been made into a community garden where the water still runs. The project was started by three locals John Baird, Alex Baird and Andrew Blackwood and they were quickly joined by number of volunteers. The community in Logan and Lugar helped out by donating materials and money to buy items for the community garden.

While the hunt for tangible evidence in Ayrshire's landscape of these once vibrant mining communities is challenging, the villages are by no means lost as they live on in people's memories and stories. These places

---

7 Jackie Clarke, 'Afterlives of a Factory: Memory, Place and Space in Alencon', in Steven High, Lachlan MacKinnon and Andrew Perchard (eds), *The Deindustrialized World: Confronting Ruination in PostIndustrial Spaces* (University of British Columbia Press, 2018)

124: New Cumnock miners' memorial. Courtesy of Margot McCuaig

Below: 125: Water feature using the old Front Row Spout in Lugar. September 2022.

259

126: Lugar Community Garden, September 2022.

have powerful meanings and connections to nearly all those interviewed, from ex-villagers to their descendants. They were important in forming identities and sense of self both as communities and individuals. Much unofficial heritage work came to the fore through our oral history interviews for this project and through previously collected and archived personal testimonies. Lethanhill and Burnfoothill started annual 'Hill reunions in 1965. Figure 127 is an image of a memorial service in 1965.

The 1971 reunion was held in Patna school hall and included a meal followed by remarks from the reunion committee chairperson and then the infamous toast, which was given each year by a former village notable, which that year was Mr George Allen. The annual reunions were regularly reported in the Doon Valley News. The one in November 1982 attracted what was referred to as a 'capacity crowd' in the Patna Community Centre. The guest speaker was former 'Hill resident Jack Miller, son of the Lethanhill store manager. Jack spoke of schooldays, the cantatas and the school janitor Jock Park, 'the best comedian Ayrshire had ever produced.' He also spoke of the Lethanhill Home Guard during the Second World War, equating their activities to that of the popular TV show, 'Dad's Army'. Jack ended reciting a poem he was moved to write after witnessing the desolation of the former village on his first visit back to the 'Hill. The reunion ended with

127: Church service, Lethanhill, at the remains of the old school, dated 1965.
Courtesy of David Young

the showing of a film depicting Lethanhill, Benwhat and the Chalmerston colliery where many of the local men worked. The following day the customary annual Remembrance Day service took place at the Lethanhill war memorial, with a large crowd and music by the Dalmellington Silver Band.[8]

John Neil and Janis Chamber's mother, Margaret Neil (known and Pearl) and gran, Margaret McBride, (known as Daisy) attended the 'Hill reunions. Janis recalled:

> It would just be a kind of service thing. We were never, er, never at that. Um, a service and there would be a … and then they would have a prize for the oldest – well, maybe not a prize but, you know, they would say who the oldest person had been and stuff like that

128: Ticket for the seventh 'Hill Reunion in 1971. Courtesy of David Young

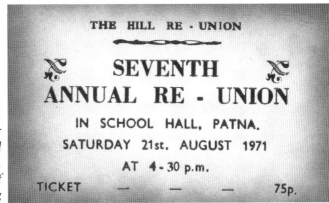

THE HILL RE - UNION

SEVENTH
ANNUAL RE - UNION

IN SCHOOL HALL, PATNA,

SATURDAY 21st. AUGUST 1971

AT 4 - 30 p.m.

TICKET   —   —   —   75p.

---

8 *Doon Valley News,* October 1982.

but ah ha, erm … an' I, I think they were every, they were every year at one point, erm, up until … they stopped. Erm, so my gran always, they always, she always wanted to go to that. She liked going up to that and obviously my mum would take her up.

YM: Would they go up the 'hill? Were they actually up the 'hill?

Uh huh, up the 'hill, yeah. Uh huh.

Born in 1897 in Benwhat (where she lived until leaving to become a housemaid in 1911 in Bearsden, Glasgow), Mrs Currie recalled in an interview in 1982 that she loved returning to the village and on one trip dug up and kept a rock fossil as a memento. She said: 'I always wanted a wee bit of Benwhat so I've got that and I've kept it. And it's a Benwhat lad that is getting it.' She recalled that reunions in the remains of the village were common: 'We went over the things we used to do and the places we went to.' John New remembered a similar family connection to place in relation to the village of Burnfoothill:

> Ma Dad went down a few times with ma Granda an', 'cause he was the oldest son, and visited the Burnie and that's why he had, kind a, fond memories of it. And ma Granda told them a lot of stories about it because they'd moved to Johnstone and were disconnected from it.

Barbara Alexander has a fountain in her garden made from the stones of the demolished Glenbuck House. John Neil and Janis Chamber's mother took them a walk up to Lethanhill and she took a brick from the remains of one of the washhouses. Clearly these place-based visits were meaningful in perpetuating the memories of the lost villages through storytelling stimulated by being situated physically on the site.

The most recent sizeable Benwhat Reunion was organised in 2011 by Councillor Drew Filson who works tirelessly to preserve the heritage of the village.[9] Benwhat is around two miles up the hill from Dalmellington. The remote location proved challenging to get the remaining now elderly villagers up to the site. Robert Walker, through his work with the opencast company, helped create a road for the coach to traverse the steep incline. On the day they had a religious service, some music from the Dalmellington Band and refreshments. Those able to walked up to the war memorial on the hill above the village. The war memorial at Benwhat has become not only a remembrance to the lives lost in the war but a way point for those searching for the lost village of Benwhat.

The parish priest at St Francis Xavier's at Waterside, Father Eddie

---

9 There is a video film of the 2011 reunion, in the possession of Councillor Drew Filson.

129: Benwhat Reunion, 2011. The villagers and their families being piped up to the site of Benwhat village. Courtesy of Drew Filson

McGhee was part of the Benwhat ceremonial delegations during his time as priest in the 1980s:

> In fact, I engaged greatly wi', with the local minister, who was married to an American. I can't even remember his name! He was married to an American lady, I remember that, an' we got on great! We did stuff together! We, we had a service [pause] for the Benwhat people. I remember walkin' a way up the, it was a great day, it was a beautiful day, erm, which was very fortunate 'cause it can be very driech, erm, you know, once you're out of the town. But we went up to Benwhat and we had a service an' it was busy! There were a lot o' people came! Now, [pause] I assume most of them would have some kind of connection wi' Benwhat but a lot o' them would just have come because, again, it was an expression of the identity of the mining communities that were nae there anymore, you know!

Eddie succinctly sums up why he thinks people are drawn to these sites. He offered more insight about his parishioners:

> I have good memories and the people were very attached to their roots, you know? The 'Hill people loved the 'Hill, you know? But at, the people frae Craigmark, they, they all loved where they had come from and never forgot it an', and tried to keep that sense of community, I think, alive even though the community, erm [pause], was actually long, long gone!

263

130: Councillor Drew Filson photographed on the site of his family home during a 'Lost Villages' project site visit to Benwhat.

The sense of attachment to the 'lost' mining villages is palpable. At Benwhat, memorial benches have been installed by families to commemorate their loved ones on the site of their old family home. A memory book allows visitors to read the stories of this community and its people.

Benwhat has also inspired poetry and music. Scots poet Rab Wilson wrote 'Ghaists' about the ruins of Benwhat:

> There's naethin left o douce, trig miner's raws,
> Whaes cobbles rang wi soun o cleek n' girr,
> Or scrape o tackets, thud o leather club,
> The flap an whirr o racin pigeons wings,
> White-peenied weemin clashin ower the dyke;
> Whaur yae road taen ye in, an taen ye oot.
> Thon aiblins wis 'The Sacred Way' fir some,
> Wha laucht an daffed alang it as they left –
> When Ne'erday cam, their friens turnt doun a gless.
> There's naethin here nou, naethin here but ghaists.[10]

Rab has recently been collaborating with Ayrshire born songwriter,

---

10 Rab Wilson, 'Ghaists', *A Map for the Blind: Poems Chiefly in the Scots Language*, (Edinburgh: Luath Press, 2011).

131: Seán Gray performing at Dalmellington Community Centre, 2022.

Seán Gray to put his poems to music.[11] The impetus to make sure these communities are not forgotten is strongly tied to the sense of place and belonging.

Former Glenbuck residents, Barbara Alexander and Sam Purdie, have worked with the local authority and Liverpool supporters club to establish a heritage centre at Glenbuck. Liverpool manager, William (Bill) Shankly, grew up in the Monkey Raw (Auchinstilloch Cottages) and for years Liverpool fans had been pilgriming to the site. Barbara lived in

132: Rab Wilson reciting his poetry at Dalmellington Community Centre, 2022.

11 To listen to these songs and find out more about their collaboration, visit Seán Gray's website: https://seangraymusic.com.

133: Interviewing on site with Glenbuck resident Barbara Alexander, 2022.

Glenbuck for thirty years until the mid-1970s. She left when she married but sadly due to her father's ill health and the remoteness of the village, her parents had to move away around that time as well. It was twenty years before Barbara returned to Glenbuck. As Bill Shankly's niece, she was asked to unveil the first plaque to Bill Shankly at the site in 1997. She remembered 'It was quite sad going up in '97 but after that and when we see what is there now, the heritage village, it's been worthwhile because it's taken all that time, from '97 until '19, 2019 for the heritage village.' As we reflected on in the last chapter, Sam Purdie returned to visit the village after working abroad and was dismayed by what he saw, expressing his shock at the razing of the village: 'destroyed, flattened, gone. Eradicated'.

It was a visit in 1997 that started the long campaign by Sam, Barbara and others to create the Glenbuck Heritage site that stands today. Barbara recalls:

I think somebody must just hae … said tae me, "Barbara, you really need to try and do something so that Glenbuck is not forgotten village, like all the other forgotten villages!"

So, that's when this … took place. An' I think mebbe at the Council, the Council, at this point, realised something had tae be done. That was in 1997 when Jack Morran walked from Liverpool to Glenbuck. It was for, erm, funds for a hospice in Liverpool. An' the plaque was instigated by Jimmy Flowers, whose sadly no longer with us, an' also, um, Liverpool Five and East Ayrshire Council an' it was a wonderful, wonderful day, the bus loads coming up! An' I kept, I still keep in touch wi' Jimmy Flowers' wife, um, and it seemed to just go on from there.

Cheryl Hynd is also a descendant of the Shankly family; on her father's side. Cheryl retains a particularly strong attachment to Glenbuck:

134: 'Cherrypickers' football team memorial at Glenbuck.

135: Bill Shankly memorial at Glenbuck.

YM: *So, what was it like, what is it like when you go back to Glenbuck?*
As I said it's like a wee bit bittersweet. At the beginning I didnae want
to go near the place because I knew it wasnae mine anymore and as
time went on and there was projects coming ahead and there was
the Glenbuck heritage and I was a wee bit hmmm I don't know if
I'm going to like this type thing. But they've done themselves really
proud, they've done us really proud. Obviously in their time and
there's our time and they've merged it together quite well and there's
aspirations fae different groups. This is Glenbuck as well and they've
got the … what was the football pitch so they're going to be caring
for that and there's some great ideas for that. So, I suppose it's like
you're seeing it through the phases, this is the next phase and this
the next part of my journey for there so I'm quite happy I'm looking
forward to it. As I say I've got the memories so it's there.

When Barbara was asked what it felt like to visit Glenbuck at the time of the
project she replied: 'Well, it's ma … spiritual home. I just feel so different. I
just love going and always I meet people! I think one o' the biggest things is
keeping the Shankly name alive.'

Cheryl and her mum Margaret also discussed why they think

people feel drawn to the village sites:

> CH: ... It's a unique place, it was a unique upbringing.
>
> MH: But people say, people I know that go up they'll say how peaceful it is you can sit, a lot of them go up in the car with a wee flask and its elderly people that goes up now and they just sit there and look at the hills and the place and see where they were born and try to imagine what it was like then. They think its peaceful and I feel it, I feel a peacefulness in Glenbuck.
>
> CH: My peer group as I say they are around the world, they are international they moved here, there and everywhere, different nationalities came and went but everybody is pulled back, everybody comes back for a visit to Glenbuck. I think at that time it was a different way of living, it was a slower paced and a safer community. And I think your memories go back to that and there is, there's a magic about the place that does just have a pull on people and you kind of gravitate back. I don't know for what reasons exactly but...
>
> MH: A bit of pulling power
>
> CH: Yep but everybody seems to have it there.
>
> MH: A lot of my ancestors were born in Glenbuck as well, so they were.
>
> CH: I think there's that as well because there's so many villagers here in Muirkirk their ancestry is there. So maybe naturally you do go back to that type of thing. You've got that feel for a place where that's your heritage so you'll go back to it.

Cheryl's gran, from the Shankly side, wanted her ashes scattered at Glenbuck:

> MH: It was Cheryl's gran. She was born there, aye, so she wanted her ashes scattered there.
>
> CH: In the Monkey Row. So that's where the Shankly memorial is at this point that were their house. So she was born and brought up in that house and that's where she wanted her ashes. But obviously as time went on it was gone the Monkey row was gone, the house was gone.
>
> MH: It was the coal yard.
>
> CH: Yep aye at the time I was growing up and the time we were there that was a coal merchant
>
> MH: So we still had the ashes because we knew it was going to get ... well the coal yard was going to go and we could maybe scatter them

but you couldnae go up when they're working away at a coal yard and scatter ashes. So we eventually got them…

CH: And it's been really nice there is actually somewhere to go and do that. It's a memorial it's not just a mine or an opencast or a void it's just, it's a nice remembrance place. Yep quite proud of that.

Barbara Alexander also expressed the wish that her ashes be scattered there. The attachment to such village communities is palpable. Similarly, in Benwhat, family members have made the pilgrimage up the hill to bring their loved one's ashes back to their 'home' as well.

Taking living family back to see the villages they grew up in was also a feature of descendant interviews. Iain Hutchison when asked about his visits to Glenbuck with his dad who lived there commented:

Yeah, I, I, I just think, what I would say about Glenbuck – it's something that had left, a village that's gone that had left a deep impression on my … father and this is because *his* father was born there, along with, er, some of his siblings, erm, and *that* was passed on to us. Er, the, the village of Glenbuck, I think it's been through various different phases since, effectively, it ceased to *be* a village! Erm, but it just left that imprint. Erm, and, any yes, it's one that passed onto *me*, erm, um, *and* I've got a brother and a sister both younger than me, *passed* it onto them as well 'cause they've both asked me to take them *up* there, er, and take a walk round what little is left and point out the, er, any landmarks that can still be seen. Er, it's just this sense, I think, of a mining community *like* other mining communities, such as Nackerty or Bothwellhaugh, erm, that are part of our *heritage* but they've almost effectively been wiped off the face of the earth but you still, kind of, have an affinity for. I don't think it will pass on to *my* kids at all but er, erm, it certainly has gone.

One of our project volunteers acted as our guide on a site visit to Commondyke. During the visit, they showed us the location of their family's row house. There was nothing visible within the boggy field to distinguish the row. We stood at the fence, looking into the field looking at the family photos and our volunteer read out a postcard sent home from a son away at war. It was a moving moment. Consolidating the 'lost' nature of the villages with the memories and mementos of the families who once lived in these once vibrant communities.

There is a tangible emotional attachment to the 'lost villages' that has transcended deindustrialisation and depopulation. Our oral history

136: Nanette McKee standing roughly at 130 Commondyke Row in May 2022 (where John Johnston sent a postcard to his mother while on training during the First World War) with her family scrapbook.

narrators have left in their recorded memories crucial intangible heritage that enables us to stand on their shoulders in these spaces and evoke something of what it was like to live the lives they lived. Some were undoubtedly nostalgic about their past lives, recalling with rose-tinted vision, the best of communal village life. Others stressed the grim conditions, recalling how tough their lives were in the past. However, taken together these eye-witness testimonies provide a much more critically nuanced picture of the past. They remembered the villages and their lives in complex, multi-layered ways. They recall the isolation, the poverty, the overcrowding and lack of amenities, including the primitive 'dry' toilet facilities. They recall the hard graft of housekeeping and rearing large families, and the dangers of the mines – the 'blood on the coal'. And they recall the blight of infectious disease and chronic coal-mining related ailments, especially breathing impairment. The divisions and fractures within these communities were also remembered, with stories about gender inequalities and unfairness, occupational hierarchies and snobbery (from supervisors, through to craftsmen, to unskilled labourers), conflict between different races, nationalities and religions – Catholic and Protestant – and competition and rivalry based around place, such as Cumnock vs Auchinleck. That said, the culture of everyday village life was also recalled in great detail and prevailing motifs were of camaraderie, of mutual support amongst families and friends and of close, enduring bonds forged in adversity in the rows and the pits. These places had profound meaning, just as being a miner or from a miners' family was an enduring source of identity and pride. As historians Gibbs and Clark have recently argued in relation to oral histories and community memorials in Scotland: 'these highlight the continued desire within industrial communities to ascribe distinct value and significance to their histories and experiences.'[12]

Jean Burns expressed this emphatically in reflecting on her life in Trabboch, weighing the poor housing and environmental conditions against the positives of living in a close knit community:

> And I'm glad those days are by. I am. I'm *proud* of what … we live! *Proud* of being a miner's *daughter – yes, I am*!! I remember an occasion with *women* and most of them were farmers' wives and there was chosen families and one said to me, "Jean, you don't say very much! Where was your…?" They thought I was farmer. I said, "Sorry to disappoint you, *my* dad was a miner!"

Eddie McGhee spoke in a similar way:

> I mean, I personally have got great memories, even though they're [pause] seventy odd years ago! There's something, erm, kinda life-giving almost about, about those kind of memories and I think that's true of, erm, people who lived in the mining villages and who still have that degree of fondness. I mean, some of it will be kind of nostalgia because the conditions were harsh! I mean, I don't think you can make any bones about it, but people rose above the actual physical conditions and [pause] I think there was a kind of spirituality if I can use that word in a secular context. There was a kind of spirituality about being a member of this community that could rise above the harshness and not only survive [pause] but flourish!

Eddie also struggled to put into words a sense of loss of identity and loss of a culture accompanied by a different and in many respects better, richer and more rewarding way of life:

---

12 Andy Clark and Ewan Gibbs, 'Voices of social dislocation, lost work and economic restructuring: Narratives from marginalised localities in the "New Scotland"', *Memory Studies*, 13:1 (2017), p.40.

There was also implicit in that a certain importance in where you came from – do not forget this! Erm, an' I, I think that has always been one o' the strengths of, of the mining communities. Erm [pause], and I think it's very much lost in post-industrial Ayrshire! … You know? I mean, I wouldn't know now where people work or how they, you know I live in this little village of Auchinleck, here, three thousand people and I wouldn't know what people do or if they've got, I mean, they've obviously got a job 'cause there is, there are little signs of prosperity [pause] but [pause] their identity, the identity in this village now is Auchinleck Talbot. You know, it's not [pause] the Common or the Burnie, or High Hoose or any of the places where miners lived, it's now, the identity of Auchinleck is very much centred round the football team, the Talbot […]
I am always first to go to a man and say, "I came from a mining community", erm, because I think it offered something almost unique.

Eddie also recognised the vital importance of capturing memories, as intangible heritage and as something which redresses a marginalised history that has suffered much neglect and erasure, and which enables a re-imagining of the vibrant and unique past of the miners' rows, working lives and mining communities.

CONCLUSION

The history of Ayrshire mining communities has been somewhat neglected in the wider literature on coal mining in Scotland and we have endeavoured here to redress this. In this book we have reconstructed the vibrant, rich and diverse social and cultural history of the miners' rows and mining communities in Ayrshire over a century of turmoil and change from the early twentieth century to the present. We have used a range of sources to reconstruct the past, with a focus on non-documentary evidence, notably spoken oral history testimonies, supplemented liberally with visual, photographic evidence. Our starting point was the miners' rows and what it meant to live in these unique village communities, and how this changed over time, with pit closures, depopulation and moving to new council housing in larger urban settlements. Personal accounts have deepened our understanding of what this was all like to live through. We explored patterns of leisure and recreation in the mining villages, emphasising the fundamentally gendered nature of such experiences, drawing on the many stories people told us. Our focus then turned to the working lives of women, as unpaid housewives and in the formal economy, and how these lives were remembered and infused with meaning. The work of the male miners was then investigated, including their embodied experience working underground and the risks and dangers they faced, as well as the changes that came with mechanisation, trade unionism and modernisation. We also explored the pit closures and the end of coalmining and what this run down of the industry meant to miners and their families. The open cast era was also examined, drawing upon open casters own lived experience and memories, as well as the perceptions of deep miners towards this very different way of extracting coal. The final chapter investigated the legacies and residues of the past in the present – the physical remains of the Ayrshire villages and pits, the ways that the industry has been memorialised, and reflects on the importance of memory in preserving the past.

In this endeavour we have stood on the shoulders of those local researchers (such as Dane Love and Donald Reid), autobiographers (such as Alice Wallace and Sam Purdie), academic scholars (such as Jim Phillips, Andy Perchard and Ewan Gibbs), poets and chroniclers (such

137: Some of the 'Lost Villages' project team. From L to R: Colin MacDonald (CCLP Co-ordinator), Yvonne McFadden, Kate Wilson, and Arthur McIvor (far right), 2022.

as Rab Wilson), novelists and photographers (such as Milton Rogovin) who have mined this seam (so to speak) before us. We hope the book is interesting, informative and readable – as those have been our aims – and that it contributes to keeping Ayrshire's mining past alive, and supports the wider work of the Coalfield Communities Landscape Partnership who commissioned it.

We have adopted an oral history approach here, privileging the voices and memories of those who lived through and witnessed these tumultuous developments. This is their story told predominantly in their words. In conclusion, what has this contributed to our understanding of the history of Ayrshire miners, their families and their ways of living? And what insights has an oral history approach delivered?

The coal mining villages of Ayrshire emerge in this account as materially poor but culturally rich, and individuals and families as tough and resilient, with dominant values based on respect and mutual support in adversity. The oral testimonies speak to the diversity of these communities, but also to their unity, the camaraderie and the spirit of these now lost places. There were tensions and divisions based on occupation, social class, gender and religion but also a profound cohesion and solidarity in the mining villages – a togetherness that is rarely seen these days. Oral history interviews enable another dimension of the past to be revealed in personal, reflective accounts and emotional stories which signify how people felt about their lives and the meanings they derived from such lived experience. Narrators being brought to tears remembering a very different past is testimony to the deep emotions reminiscence can generate. This is a participatory experience where individuals informed us about their lives in the interview encounter. They take us behind the closed doors of homes to reveal much about relationships and the actual lived experience of poverty, deprivation, ill-health and overcrowding in the traditional miners' rows, and all that meant. In essence, this gets us beyond the statistics of multiple deprivation and the 'body counts' of workplace accidents, disease and deaths to a deeper understanding of what it meant to be a miner far away from the public gaze at the coalface, or miner's wife in these cramped and insanitary dwellings. It offers insights into how people and families coped with disease, injury, disability and tragedy. But we also hear of the good times – of how folk accepted the cards they had been dealt and enjoyed life as best they could within the structural constraints of working lives and relative poverty. And, importantly, we hear of how folk were agents in their own history, transgressing gender norms and organising and campaigning – for example through their trade unions and in political campaigns – to ameliorate grim working and living conditions.

And how these experiences were remembered and narrated is important in its own right. There is nostalgia, to be sure. Sometimes narrators are guilty of exaggerating a 'golden past' of steady work and friendly, neighbourly living in the villages where nobody locked their doors; the 'good times' over the bad. But equally, they recall the insanitary living conditions and how they welcomed rehousing to better quality, larger homes. And there are hints at darker stories, of paedophiles, of sectarianism, of snobbery, of fights and of domestic violence. These are not aspects of these histories that should be air-brushed out. Clearly, memories are carefully weighed and nuanced, with narrators fully able to balance the good and the bad. Emotions were mixed and could encompass a wide range, from disappointment, sadness and dismay – a kind of bereavement – at village depopulation and disintegration, as well as relief and joy at moving on to a better life, at least in a material sense, for their families. What comes through clearly, however, is the process of ruination associated with pit closures and job losses, and the deep psychological scars left by this forced acceleration in the process of deindustrialisation. Folk also show a sharp awareness that political decisions deepened their problems, with Thatcher identified as primarily responsible and denigrated as such. Those who lived through this expressed in their witness testimonies just how traumatic this transition to a post-industrial society was, but also how they adapted

277

and coped. Again, a range of emotions seep through the oral testimonies recalling the pit and factory closures in Ayrshire, and how this affected them as individuals, as families and as communities. Ayrshire experienced wider historical developments and trends and oral histories and personal memoirs enable this history to be seen and understood through the lens of those directly experiencing it.

Marginalised voices are captured and integrated into our interpretation. We hope this book provides a somewhat re-centred history seen through the lens of women as well as men. How women experienced life in the miners' rows has been of central importance and how women's lives changed is a primary focus of attention – both in relation to family and unpaid work within the home and the shift towards paid employment as the century wore on, as well as how women and families navigated pit closures and deindustrialisation. We have also tried to locate people's experience within the landscape, reflecting on how the environment shaped people's lives, their work and their leisure time, and how coal mining affected the environment – from dust seeping into people's homes, to the dangers of the bings and the 'black moonscape' of the open cast mines.

East Ayrshire today is one of Scotland's most deindustrialised, deprived and unhealthy areas – as measured by standardised indices of deprivation.[1] The past has taken its toll on health, with the scars of industry combining with the deleterious impact of job loss and mass unemployment and all the attendant impacts on income, living standards, health and well-being, identity and sense of purpose that goes along with that. The legacies and residues of the past affect the present. Whilst mining community values persisted and survived, and continue to inform local and national politics (including the Home Rule and Scottish independence movements), as Jim Phillips has argued, self-confidence and sense of esteem is at a low ebb, as in other such deindustrialised 'left-behind' communities.[2] In this context, the process of remembering itself has a therapeutic, healing and regenerative purpose. It confirms how significant and important these lives were after pit closures, village demolition and deindustrialisation had virtually erased the material, physical remnants of their past. Oral history remembering can be healing: restoring a sense of pride and dignity; rebuilding eroded self-esteem in communities almost forgotten. This is especially important where public history has marginalised the past.

What we have tried to do in this oral history project is to involve the community in its making and to ensure that the wonderful testimonies

---

1 Coalfield Regeneration Trust, Scottish Coalfields in 2020 (Social Value Lab: 2020). Accessed at: https://www.coalfields-regen.org.uk/wp-content/uploads/2020/06/SVL_-Scottish-coalfields-2020.pdf.
2 For a fuller discussion see Phillips, *Scottish Coal Miners*, pp. 269-82

(and written transcripts) are archived and preserved (locally and at the Scottish Oral History Centre) for others to listen to or read in the future. The project interview archive, supplemented with photos and other memorabilia, is part of the legacy of this project, as is this book. The work has also reinforced to us the importance of preserving the intangible past through capturing and preserving people's memories. We would argue that this should be continued and that this is vitally important moving forward. There is a strong priority case, in our view, for an oral history curator post for Ayrshire/East Ayrshire – someone to lead on running local memory booths, reminiscence groups and the capturing, preserving and archiving of people's memories – and that this should be accorded equal importance to that attached to preserving the archaeology, buildings and material artefacts from the past. This was recognised in the late 1990s with the 'Pitheid Patter' oral history project associated with the Barony A Frame restoration. It is equally if not more important today to capture and archive such memories before this rugged and resilient generation that had experienced working underground in the pits and living in the 'raws' and the mining villages disappear forever. Waterside parish priest Eddie McGhee put this well when he said:

> When I think mining communities, I always think strong people, you know. Not all, I mean, 'cause you can go at it with a rosy tinted view, but I think strong people, committed people! And that's why, erm [pause] it's, it's so important that this memory doesn't get [pause] lost somewhere as we, you know, gallop through the 21st century!

The intangible remains, or stories, of these once vibrant coalfield communities have been the focus of this book. Arguably, these villages and workplaces are not 'lost' but live on in the memories of those still living, and in the stories of descendants of the villagers within Ayrshire and in far afield places such as Canada and Australia. Using oral history collected as part of the 'Lost Villages of East Ayrshire' project, this collection of memories of the rows and their inhabitants and what came next for these communities aims to ensure that the villages and their legacy continues as part of the story of life in Scotland in the twentieth century.

APPENDIX 1
Ayrshire Coal Mines and Closure Dates
(after Nationalisation 1947)

42 COLLIERIES IN EXISTENCE IN 1947

Afton 1, Cumnock, 1948
Auchincruive 1, 2 and 3, Prestwick, 1960
Auchincruive, Prestwick, 1973
Ayr, Annbank, 1959
Bank 2, New Cumnock, 1950
Bank, New Cumnock, 1969
Barony, Auchinleck, 1989
Beoch, Dalmellington, 1968
Blair, Dalry, 1969
Bogton, Dalmellington, 1954
Bridgend, New Cumnock, 1964
Cairnhill, Lugar, 1976
Chalmerston 6 and 7, Dalmellington, 1952
Chalmerston, 4 and 5, Dalmellington, 1959
Coalburn, New Cumnock, 1962
Cronberry Moor, New Cumnock, 1957
Dalquharran, Girvan, 1977
Enterkine 10 and 11, Annbank, 1959
Fauldhead, Kirkconnel, 1968
Greenhill, Littlemill, merged with Polquhairn, 1958, closed 1962
Highhouse, Auchinleck, 1983
Hindsward, Cumnock, 1959
Houldsworth, Patna, 1965
Kames, Muirkirk, 1968
Killoch, Ochiltree, 1987
Killochan, Girvan, 1967
Knockshinnoch, New Cumnock, 1968

Littlemill, Rankinston, 1974
Lochlea, Mauchline, 1973
Mauchline, Mauchline, 1966
Maxwell, Girvan, 1973
Minnivey, Dalmellington, 1975
Pennyvenie 4, Dalmellington, 1961
Pennyvenie, Dalmellington, 1978
Polquhairn, 1, 4, 5 and 6, Littlemill, 1962
Rig, Kirkconnel, 1966
Roger, Kirkconnel, 1980
Sorn, Mauchline, 1983
Sundrum 5 and 6, Colyton, 1961
Whitehill, Cumnock, 1965

CONSTRUCTED FROM: https://www.nmrs.org.uk/mines-map/coal-mining-in-the-british-isles/scotland/

For these mines mapped across Ayrshire see:

https://www.nmrs.org.uk/mines-map/coal-mining-in-the-british-isles/collieries-of-the-british-isles/coal-mines-scotland/

BIBLIOGRAPHY

PROJECT ORAL HISTORY INTERVIEWS

With year of birth (YOB) and villages – where known.
These are people who kindly contributed to the project by sharing their memories.
Archived at the Scottish Oral History Centre, University of Strathclyde and at East Ayrshire Leisure Trust Archives

Agnes (Nan) Auld	1932 Lethanhill/Patna/Pennyvennie
Barbara Alexander	YOB unknown, Glenbuck
Mary Baird	1954 Catrine/Highhouse
Grace Bradford	YOB unknown, Auchinleck
Jean Burns	1936 Trabboch/Drongnan
Stewart Burns	1942 Glenbuck
Janis Chambers	1951 Lethanhill/Patna
Sheila Crosswaite	1942 Lethanhill/Patna
Margaret Fleming	1957 Catrine/Highhouse
Robert Gray (Snr)	1936 Darnconner
Hugh Gunning	1955 Lugar
Tam Hazel	1927 Glenbuck
Isobel Hendry	1934 Glenbuck
Nicola Higgins	1989 Patna
Iain Hutchison	1949 Glenbuck
Margaret Hynd	1947 Glenbuck
Cheryl Hynd	1978 Glenbuck
Henry (Harry) Kennedy	1932 Burnton
Alex Kirk	1941 Lethanhill then moved to Burnfoothill
Eddie McGhee	1947 Muirkirk/Waterside/Auchinleck
Nanette McKee	1949 Auchinleck/Commondyke/ Darnconner/Benwhat
Jean McMurdo	1926 New Cumnock / Lugar
Frances McNulty	1948 Logan

Margaret McQue	1947 Logan
David Murray	1930 Lugar
John Neil	1953 Lethanhill/Patna
John New	1957 Commondyke
*Sam Purdie	1936 Glenbuck
Ella Reynolds	1930 Glenbuck
Flora Scobie	1941 Benwhat
John Scobie	1938 Dalmellington
Eddie Smith	1944 Darnconner/Auchinleck
Robert Walker	1952 Skares
Alice Wallace	1945 Benwhat
Jean Wilson	1932 Benwhat
Rab Wilson	1960 New Cumnock
Tom Wilson	1926 Benwhat
James Whiteford	1938 Connel Park
Marion Wylie	YOB unknown, Lugar

Several additional interviewees chose to be anonymous.
Interviewers: Yvonne McFadden (lead); Arthur McIvor; Kate Wilson; Billy Cassidy; Rosanna Brown; Bethany Bell; Bob F. Gray
*Sam Purdie was interviewed twice for the project, once in 2019 (by Arthur McIvor) and later in 2021 (by project volunteer Bob Gray).

RECORDED STORYTELLING WORKSHOPS

The Dalmellington Recovery Group (7 attendees). Session 1 May 2023; Session 2 June 2023
The Chat-teas, Auchinleck (13 attendees). Session 1 May 2023; Session 2 June 2023

ARCHIVED ORAL HISTORY COLLECTIONS / ARCHIVED INTERVIEWS

Cumnock and Doon Valley interviews (Burns Monument Collection / HMCDV - 1982)
Archived at Burns Monument Centre, Kilmarnock
 Mr McKean (Cronberry)
 Mr Twist and Mr Frew (Highhouse Rows)
 Mr Hutson (Cumnock)
 Mr D (anonymous)
 Mrs McCombe (Lethanhill)
 Mrs Nancy Murphy (Dalmellington)

Mrs E. Ballantyne (Patna)
Mrs Currie (Benwhat)
Mrs Currie (Craigmark)
Mr and Mrs W. Tyson (Dalmellington)
Mr McPhail (Benwhat)

Cumnock and Doon Valley District Council interviews (1992), Burns Monument Centre, Kilmarnock.
Richard Allan (New Cumnock)
James Ferguson (New Cumnock)

Scottish Working People's History Trust (Ian MacDougall interviews, 2000-01) Archived at the School of Scottish Studies, Edinburgh University
Robert Hall
George Montgomery
John Rodie
Felix Todd
Tom Wilson (Benwhat)

Margaret Sim – Lethanhill (1998: private collection)

Scottish Oral History Centre (University of Strathclyde) coal miners' collection (Archive ref 017), interviews with Ayrshire miners conducted in 2000 (Ronald Johnston and Arthur McIvor)
Billy Affleck (017/C2)
William Dunsmore (017/C16)
Dick Easterbrook (017/C17)
Andrew Lyndsay (017/C4)
Davy McCulloch (017/C18)
Thomas McMurdo (017/C20)
Alec McNeish (017/C13)
Alec Mills (017/C1)
John Orr (017/C3)
Bobby Strachan (017/C11)

Nicky Wilson, NUM President (SOHC Witness Seminar, 28 April 2014).

PERSONAL TESTIMONIES, MEMOIRS AND AUTOBIOGRAPHICAL ACCOUNTS

Hugh Hainey, no title, transcribed by Alistair Hainey, c. 1990s
Jim McVey, 'Memories of Lethanhill', n/d
Sam Purdie, 'Requiem for a Village' (unpublished paper, 2002)
Sam Purdie, 'Glenbuck' (2004)
Sam Purdie, 'The Scottish Miner' (unpublished paper, 2015)
Alice Wallace, *Benquhat – Then What* (self-published autobiography, n/d)
Andrew Sim, 'Autobiography and some other interesting Sim family

stories', n/d

ARCHIVAL MATERIAL

Ayrshire County Council, Housing Committee Minutes 1919-1960, Ayrshire Archives.

SELECTED PUBLICATIONS / RECOMMENDED READING

Campbell, Alan, *The Scottish Miners, 1874-1939: Vol 1, Industry, Work and Community* (Aldershot: Ashgate, 2000).
Clark, Andy and Ewan Gibbs, 'Voices of social dislocation, lost work and economic restructuring: Narratives from marginalised localities in the "New Scotland"', *Memory Studies,* 13:1 (2017), 39-59.
Duncan, Rob, *The Mineworkers* (Edinburgh: Birlinn, 2005).
Beynon, Huw and Ray Hudson, *The Shadow of the Mine* (London: Verso, 2021).
Beynon, Huw, Cox, A and Hudson, R, *Digging up Trouble: Environment, Protest and Open Cast Mining* (Lewes: Rivers Oram, 2000).
Farrell, Robert, *Benwhat and Corbie Craigs: A brief history,* (Lugar: Cumnock and Doon Valley District Council, 1983).
Gibbs, Ewan, *Coal Country: The Meaning and Memory of Deindustrialisation in Postwar Scotland* (London: University of London Press, 2021).
Gourievidis, Laurence, 'Safeguarding Ayrshire's Coalmining Past: Heritage, Nostalgia and Social Memory', *LISA E-Journal,* XVII:1 (2019), https://journals.openedition.org/lisa/11191?lang=en.
High, Steven, Lachlan Mackinnon and Andrew Perchard (eds), *The Deindustrialized World: Confronting Ruination in Post-Industrial Spaces* (Vancouver: University of British Columbia Press, 2017).
Hutton, Guthrie, *Mining: Ayrshire's Lost History* (Catrine: Stenlake, 1996).
Love, Dane, *Ayrshire's Lost Villages* (Auchinleck: Carn Publishing, 2016).
Mackenzie, Mhairi, Chik Collins, John Connolly, Mick Doyle and Gerry McCartney. 'Working-class discourses of politics, policy and health: "I don't smoke; I don't drink. The only thing wrong with me is my health." *Policy & Politics,* 45:2 (2015), 231-249.
McIvor, Arthur and Ronald Johnston. *Miners' Lung: A History of Dust Disease in British Coal Mining* (Aldershot: Ashgate, 2007).
McKerrell, Thomas and James Brown, 'Ayrshire Miners' Rows, 1913: Evidence Submitted to the Royal Commission on Housing

Scotland for the Ayrshire Miners' Union', *Ayrshire Collections*, 3:1 (Ayr: Ayrshire Archeological and Natural History Society, 1979).

McMurdo, Ian, *Knockshinnoch: The Greatest Mine Rescue in History* (Auchinleck: Carn Publishing, 2017).

McQuillan, Thomas Courtney, *The 'Hill: It's People and It's Pits. A History of the Village of Burnfoothill/Lethanhill* (Lugar: Cumnock and Doon Valley District Council, 1988).

Moore, John (ed), *Among thy green braes: a Guide to Cumnock and Doon Valley District* (Lugar: Cumnock and Doon Valley District Council, 1977).

Moore, John, *Doon Valley Diary: The Critical Decade, 1963-72* (Lugar: Cumnock and Doon Valley District Council, 1980).

Owens, Joe, *Miners, 1984-1994: A Decade of Endurance* (Edinburgh: Polygon, 1994).

Perchard, Andrew, '"Broken Men" and "Thatcher's Children": Memory and Legacy in Scotland's Coalfields', *International Labour and Working-Class History*, 84 (2013), 78-98.

Sam Purdie, 'The Kames Pit Disaster, 1957', *Scottish Labour History*, 56 (2021), 46-53.

Orange, Hilary, *Reanimating Industrial Spaces: Conducting Memory Work in Post-industrial Societies* (London: Routledge, 2015).

Jim Phillips, *Scottish Coal Miners in the Twentieth Century* (Edinburgh: Edinburgh University Press, 2019).

Reid, Donald, *The Last Miners of Ayrshire's Doon Valley* (Irvine: Kestrel Press, 2016)

Reid, Donald, *The Lost Mining Villages of Doon Valley: Voices and Images of Ayrshire* (Dalmellington: Donald L. Reid, 2012)

Shevlin, Marie, *The Dalry Raws* (Auchinleck: Carn Publishing, 2023).

Turner, Angela and Arthur McIvor, '"Bottom Dog Men": Disability, Social Welfare and Advocacy in the Scottish Coalfields, 1897-1939', *Scottish Historical Review*, XCVI (96), 2:243 (2017), 187–213.

Wark, Gavin, T*he Rise and Fall of Mining Communities in Central Ayrshire in the 19th and 20th Centuries*, Ayrshire Monographs No. 22, (Ayr: Ayrshire Archaeological and Natural History Society, 1999)

Wight, Daniel, *Workers not Wasters* (Edinburgh: Edinburgh University Press, 1993).

REPORTS

Hume, John, *Report on the Industrial History of the Cumnock and Doon*

Valley Area (Unpublished Report, May 2017).
Coalfield Regeneration Trust, *Scottish Coalfields in 2020* (Glasgow: Social Value Lab: 2020), https://www.coalfields-regen.org.uk/wp-content/uploads/2020/06/SVL_-Scottish-coalfields-2020.pdf.

PHD THESES

Cronin, Jenny, *The origins and development of Scottish convalescent homes, 1860-1939* (PhD thesis, University of Glasgow, 2003). https://theses.gla.ac.uk/2316/
Henry, Marion 'Every village would have a band': Building Community with Music. A Social and Cultural History of Brass Bands in the British Coalfields, 1947-1984 (PhD thesis, Sciences Po, University Paris / University of Strathclyde, 2021)
Le, Huyen, *Exploring the governance of post-mining restoration in Scotland in the demise of the opencast coal industry and finding the way forward* (PhD thesis, University of Dundee, 2018) https://discovery.dundee.ac.uk/en/studentTheses/exploring-the-governance-of-post-mining-restoration-in-scotland-i.

WEBSITES AND OTHER SOURCES

Email, Davie Higgins to Sam Purdie, 27 Oct 2021 (on the closure of Killoch): permission granted for authors use.
Email, Davie Higgins to Arthur McIvor, 'My Time Amongst the Miners', 14 November 2021.
Seán Gray, Ayrshire Songwriter: https://seangraymusic.com
Rab Wilson, Ayrshire Scots poet: https://www.luath.co.uk/rab-wilson
https://cumnockhistorygroup.org/places-miners-rows/
https://newcumnockhistory.com/mining-minerals/coal-mining/knockshinnoch-disaster-1950/knockshinnoch-memorial/
Place names CCLP project:
http://www.snsbi.org.uk/pdf/SNSBI_2021-04-11_Williamson_and_Taylor_Place-names_of_the_coalfield_communities.pdf
Johnny Templeton: http://www.muirkirk.org.uk/minersvoices/index.htm.
And see our Lost Villages website at www.thelostvillages.co.uk

INDEX